ANATOMY OF THE CUBAN MISSILE CRISIS

ANATOMY OF THE CUBAN MISSILE CRISIS

James A. Nathan

Greenwood Press Guides to
Historic Events of the Twentieth Century
Randall M. Miller, Series Editor

Greenwood Press
Westport, Connecticut • London

Library of Congress Cataloging-in-Publication Data

Nathan, James A.
    Anatomy of the Cuban Missile Crisis / James A. Nathan.
        p.   cm.—(Greenwood Press guides to historic events of the twentieth century,
    ISSN 1092–117X)
    Includes bibliographical references and index.
    ISBN 0–313–29973–0 (alk. paper)
    1. Cuban Missile Crisis, 1962.   I. Title.   II. Series.
E841.N37   2001
973.922—dc21   00–025115

British Library Cataloguing in Publication Data is available.

Library of Congress Catalog Card Number: 00–025115
ISBN: 0–313–29973–0
ISSN: 1092–177X

First published in 2001

Greenwood Press, 88 Post Road West, Westport, CT 06881
An imprint of Greenwood Publishing Group, Inc.
www.greenwood.com

Printed in the United States of America

The paper used in this book complies with the
Permanent Paper Standard issued by the National
Information Standards Organization (Z39.48–1984).

10 9 8 7 6 5 4 3 2 1

Contents

A photo essay follows p. 70

Series Foreword

As the twenty-first century opens, it is time to take stock of the political, social, economic, intellectual, and cultural forces and factors that made the twentieth century the most dramatic period of change in history. To that end, the Greenwood Press Guides to Historic Events of the Twentieth Century presents interpretive histories of the most significant events of the century. Each book in the series combines narrative history and analysis with primary documents and biographical sketches, with an eye to providing both a reference guide to the principal persons, ideas, and experiences defining each historic event, and a reliable, readable overview of that event. Each book provides analyses and discussions, grounded in both primary and secondary sources, of the causes and consequences, in thought and action, that give meaning to the historic event under review. By assuming a historical perspective, drawing on the latest and best writing on each subject, and offering fresh insights, each book promises to explain how and why a particular event defined the twentieth century. No consensus about the meaning of the twentieth century emerges from the series, but, collectively, the books identify the most salient concerns of the century. In so doing, the series reminds us of the many ways those historic events continue to affect our lives.

Each book follows a similar format designed to encourage readers to consult it both as a reference and a history in its own right. Each volume opens with a chronology of the historic event, followed by a narrative overview, which also serves to introduce and examine briefly the main themes and issues related to that event. The next set of chapters is composed of topical essays, each analyzing closely an issue or problem of interpretation introduced in the opening chapter. A concluding chapter suggesting the long-term implications and meanings of the historic event brings the strands of the preceding chapters together while placing the event in the larger historical context. Each book also includes a section of short biographies of the principal persons related to the event, followed by a section introducing and reprinting key historical documents illustrative of and pertinent to the event. An annotated bibliography—of significant books, films, and CD-ROMs—and an index conclude each volume.

The editors made no attempt to impose any theoretical model or historical perspective on the individual authors. Rather, in developing the series, an advisory board of noted historians and informed high school history teachers and public and school librarians identified the topics needful of exploration and the scholars eminently qualified to examine those events with intelligence and sensitivity. The common commitment throughout the series is to provide accurate, informative, and readable books, free of jargon and up to date in evidence and analysis.

Each book stands as a complete historical analysis and reference guide to a particular historic event. Each book also has many uses, from understanding contemporary perspectives on critical historical issues, to providing biographical treatments of key figures related to each event, to offering excerpts and complete texts of essential documents about the event, to suggesting and describing books and media materials for further study and presentation of the event, and more. The combination of historical narrative and individual topical chapters addressing significant issues and problems encourages students and teachers to approach each historic event from multiple perspectives and with a critical eye. The arrangement and content of each book thus invite students and teachers, through classroom discussions and position papers, to debate the character and significance of great historic events and to discover for themselves how and why history matters.

The series emphasizes the main currents that have shaped the modern world. Much of that focus necessarily looks at the West, especially Europe and the United States. The political, commercial, and cultural expansion of the West wrought largely, though not wholly, the most fundamental changes of the century. Taken together, however, books in the series reveal the interaction, between Western and non-Western peoples and society, and also the tensions between modern and traditional cultures. They also point to the ways in which nonwestern peoples have adapted Western ideas and technology and, in turn, influenced Western life and thought. Several books examine such increasingly powerful global forces as the rise of Islamic fundamentalism, the emergence of modern Japan, the Communist revolution in China, and the collapse of communism in eastern Europe and the former Soviet Union. American interests and experiences receive special attention in the series, not only in deference to the primary readership of the books but also in recognition that the United States emerged as the dominant political, economic, social, and cultural force during the twentieth century. By looking at the century through the lens of American events and experiences, it is possible to see why the age has come to be known as "The American Century."

Assessing the history of the twentieth century is a formidable prospect. It has been a period of remarkable transformation. The world broadened and narrowed at the same time. Frontiers shifted from the interiors of Africa and Latin America to the moon and beyond; communication spread from mass circulation newspapers and magazines to radio, television, and now the Internet; skyscrapers reached upward and suburbs stretched outward; energy switched from steam, to electric, to atomic power. Many changes did not lead to a complete abandonment of established patterns and practices so much as a synthesis of old and new, as, for example, the increased use of (even reliance on) the telephone in the age of the computer. The automobile and the truck, the airplane, and telecommunications closed distances, and people in unprecedented numbers migrated from rural to urban, industrial, and ever more ethnically diverse areas. Tractors and chemical fertilizers made it possible for fewer people to grow more, but the environmental and demographic costs of an exploding global population threatened to outstrip natural resources and human innovation. Disparities in wealth increased, with developed nations prospering and underdeveloped nations starving. Amid the crumbling of former European colonial empires, Western technology, goods, and culture increasingly enveloped the globe, seeping into, and undermining, non-Western cultures—a process that contributed to a surge of religious fundamentalism and ethno-nationalism in the Middle East, Asia, and Africa. As people became more alike, they also became more aware of their differences. Ethnic and religious rivalries grew in intensity everywhere as the century closed.

The political changes during the twentieth century were no less profound than the social, economic, and cultural ones. Many of the books in the series focus on political events, broadly defined but no books are confined to politics alone. Political ideas and events have social effects, just as they spring from a complex interplay of non-political forces in culture, society, and economy. Thus, for example, the modern civil rights and women's rights movements were at once social and political events in cause and consequence. Likewise, the Cold War created the geopolitical framework for dealing with competing ideologies and nations abroad and served as the touchstone for political and cultural identities at home. The books treating political events do so within their social, cultural, and economic contexts.

Several books in the series examine particular wars in depth. Wars are defining moments for people and eras. During the twentieth century war became more widespread and terrible than ever before, encouraging new efforts to end war through strategies and organizations of international cooperation and disarmament while also fueling new ideologies and instruments of mass persuasion that fostered distrust and festered old national rivalries. Two world wars during the century redrew the political map, slaughtered or uprooted two generations of people, and introduced and hastened the development of new technologies and weapons of mass destruction. The First World War spelled the end of the old European order and spurred communist revolution in Russia and fascism in Italy, Germany, and elsewhere. The Second World War killed fascism and inspired the final push for freedom from European colonial rule in Asia and Africa. It also led to the Cold War that suffocated much of the world for almost half a century. Large wars begat small ones, and brutal totalitarian regimes cropped up across the globe. After (and in some ways because of) the fall of communism in eastern Europe and the former Soviet Union, wars of competing cultures, national interests, and political systems persisted in the struggle to make a new world order. Continuing, too, has been the belief that military technology can achieve political ends, whether in the superior American firepower that failed to "win" in Vietnam or in the American "smart bombs" and other military wizardry that "won" in the Persian Gulf.

Another theme evident in the series is that throughout the century nationalism continued to drive events. Whether in the Balkans in 1914 triggering World War I or in the Balkans in the 1990s threatening the post–Cold War peace—or in many other places—nationalist ambitions and forces would not die. The persistence of nationalism is yet another reminder of the many ways that the past becomes prologue.

We thus offer the series as a modern guide to and interpretation of the historic events of the twentieth century and as an invitation to consider how and why those events defined not only the past and present but also charted the political, social, intellectual, cultural, and economic routes into this century.

Randall M. Miller
Saint Joseph's University, Philadelphia

Preface

This book is an effort to summarize what is now known about the Cuban Missile Crisis and, more important, to place the crisis in its proper historical setting. The approach is narrative, chronological, and comprehensive yet readable and concise. The resource book is directed at students and interested lay audiences.

The book begins with an overview of the Cuban Missile Crisis and its historical meaning. It proceeds with a discussion of the American problem in sustaining a policy of containment of Soviet power in the nuclear age, especially in the face of a wave of revolutions against the old order in the developing world. Finally, the text reflects on the meaning of the Cuban Missile Crisis in terms of the conduct of American foreign policy throughout much of the rest of the Cold War.

Of foremost concern to American policymakers was the Cuban revolution. Few in the U.S. government had anticipated that Fidel Castro's followers, numbering less than a thousand, would topple the dictatorship of Fulgencio Batista. Thus President Dwight Eisenhower was surprised at Castro's successes, and in the month before Batista's downfall the U.S. government searched for alternatives. But Castro made swift headway in gaining followers. And when, in January 1958, Castro's new regime came to power, it was accorded almost immediate diplomatic recognition by the Eisenhower administration.

The U.S. government made some efforts to court Castro in his first role as leader of the Cuban government, but Castro was convinced that the United

States would be hostile. Soon he was seeking Soviet assistance while spurning most American offers of aid.

A series of raids by Cuban exiles in 1959 confirmed to Castro his own forecast of an inevitable American ill will toward Cuba. But despite Castro's confiscation of foreign assets, the American policy toward Cuba was largely to "wait and see" how the regime would conduct itself.

The still unexplained explosion of an arms cargo carried on board a Belgian freighter in Havana harbor in March 1960 was a turning point. The explosion of the *Coubre* seemed to convince Castro that the time for a more open, sustained relationship with the Soviets was at hand. Scholars have discovered records confirming that at about the same time, the Eisenhower administration began to approve a series of covert measures to overthrow Castro's revolutionary regime.

An invasion of Cuba, carried out by Cuban exiles, was planned during the Eisenhower administration but was not officially approved until the first days of the administration of President John F. Kennedy. By April 1961, when the American-trained force landed at the Bay of Pigs, the operation had become common knowledge throughout the Americas. It was disaster. After a gallant fight, most of the invading exiles were captured by Castro's waiting forces. Kennedy, fearful that an obvious set of American fingerprints on the operation would taint the United States in world opinion, refused to approve air cover that might have given the invading force a better chance of survival—at least on the beach.

The resulting fiasco permeated U.S. policy. The Kennedy administration spent enormous intellectual and material resources trying to undo the impact, both domestic and foreign, of the Bay of Pigs disaster.

Meanwhile, Soviet policy under Premier Nikita Khrushchev had gone on a multiple-track offensive in Berlin, in the developing world, and in trying to force a settlement of the Berlin issue. Kennedy had campaigned against a "do nothing" Eisenhower administration, yet he too was short of options in dealing with the Berlin issue and Cuba. The Western position on Berlin was tough, if not impossible, to defend without nuclear weapons. But if the Soviets decided to settle the problem of a divided Berlin by extending their occupation from East to West, it meant war.

In the Cuban crisis, the Kennedy administration quietly strove for a diplomatic solution, Meanwhile, plans were begun to recoup, by covert means if possible and by overt means if necessary, American interest in Cuba.

It was unclear whether President Kennedy favored covert or overt measures. Robert Kennedy, his brother and the U.S. Attorney General, oversaw "Operation Mongoose," a Central Intelligence Agency (CIA) plan that called for a massive U.S. operation against Castro and covert measures to

destabilize the Communist regime in Cuba. But the president never authorized another over-the-beach invasion.

National Security Advisor McGeorge Bundy later argued that Mongoose
was a self-administered "psychological salve" on the wounded ego of the
Kennedy administration. Whatever the psychological motivation for such
planning, the president played a double hand with Cuba. He sent some parts
of his administration to plan military actions and sabotage against Cuba
while a tiny coterie of Kennedy intimates plotted a rapprochement instead.

After President Kennedy met Premier Khrushchev in Vienna in June
1961, two months after the Bay of Pigs fiasco, Khrushchev became convinced that the United States would not opposed Cuba moving squarely into
the Soviet camp. But Khrushchev was mercurial. Later he began to doubt
American forbearance of the Soviet position in Cuba. At the same time, he
was forced by American disclosures of the dramatic lag in Soviet missile
production to somehow rectify Russia's embarrassing inferiority in missile
capability. Both goals were to be met by secretly placing forty-two missiles
in Cuba in the summer of 1962.

When President Kennedy made the American discovery of Soviet missiles in Cuba public on October 22, 1962, he informed the Russians that
Cuba would be blockaded and attacked if the missiles were not removed.
Khrushchev ultimately removed the missiles after a series of exchanges
with the United States.

What was publicly acknowledged at the outset was that American forces
would not invade Cuba if the soviet missiles were withdrawn. However,
what went unacknowledged for nearly two decades were elements in the negotiations between Kennedy and Khrushchev indicating that the resolution
of the Cuban Missile Crisis was a trade: the United States would withdraw
its missiles located in Turkey across the Black Sea from Russia some
months after the Soviets withdrew their missiles from Cuba.

The secret element of the negotiations was grist for subsequent misunderstandings, in that Americans misinterpreted the limits of their own reach
and influence. A heady optimism characterized American policy after the
Cuban Missile Crisis. It was based in a sense that the United States had gotten unequivocally "on top of" the Cold War. Confrontation, crisis, and challenges were thenceforth thought to be manageable.

The sheer hubris among American policymakers contributed to
disjunction between themselves and the American people. The general
population remained shaken by the prospect of nuclear war, whereas
policymakers such as McGeorge Bundy were privately convinced that the
prospects of nuclear was had not been all that serious during the crisis and,

however real they might have been in October 1962, had radically diminished thereafter.

But for the American people, the Cuban Missile Crisis was unsettling, even traumatic, in the short run. Subsequent psychological studies detailed the effect of parents' preparations for nuclear was on the psyche of their children. The bomb shelters and schoolroom "duck and cover" exercises, which were to prepare children for a nuclear explosion by having them cower under a desk, were also frightening and real reminders of American vulnerability. The Cuban Missile Crisis had brought to Americans a unique sense of being part of large events they could not control. Paradoxically, the way the Kennedy administration seemed to have resolved the crisis, with the Soviets backing down, created the illusion of security as long as Americans remained resolute in standing against Communist threats and presidents stood as profiles in courage.

Increasing Soviet competence in missile development kept the public sense of unease alive; indeed, public alarm was stoked from the mid-1970s by an influential American lobby called the Committee on Present Danger. Although nuclear fear abated somewhat after the Cuban Missile Crisis, public dread surfaced again in the early 1980s. Public unease about the blithe comments of many early Reagan-era officials that "with enough shovels" everyone can make it through a nuclear war may well have contributed to Ronald Reagan's aboutface in dealing with the Russians in 1984–85.

Acknowledgments

The resources, time, and generous support for this book were made possible by the administration of Auburn University at Montgomery, especially the kindness of Dean Robert Elliot and the consistent help of Dahdee Bullen and General Charles Cleveland (Lt. Gen. Ret.) of the Alabama world Affairs Council.

This book also was abetted by the editorial efforts of Randall Miller, series editor, and Barbara Rader and her staff at Greenwood Press.

I also would like to acknowledge the contributions of Sheldon M. Stern, of the JFK Library, and Peter Kornbluh, of the National Security Archive, to the development of the Chronology of Events.

I was abroad during most of the writing of this work. In 1999 I was a visiting professor at Bilkent University, which has the oldest and best English language library in Turkey. I am indebted to the Bilkent faculty, staff, and students.

The polishing and refinement of this book have not been easy. Working in China as the recipient of a Senior Distinguished Fulbright award, I have had access to no real library or scholarly resources—such was the toll of the Cultural Revolution and the price of continuing Chinese censorship.

The book is dedicated to my family—sons Michael and Alex and especially my wife, Lisa, who was forced to exit from the warmth of our dime-sized Beijing apartment, with young son in hand, so that Dad had time and quiet to write. Lisa's patience and love were indispensable.

Chronology of Events

1941–45   During World War II the United States and Great Britain join with the Soviet Union to defeat Germany. The alliance begins to crumble after the Nazi surrender.

1947–48   The Soviet Union consolidates its position in Eastern and Central Europe. The United States embraces a policy of containment.

1948   The Western Allies use an airlift to overcome a Soviet blockade of Berlin

1949   The United States joins NATO. Mao Zedong (Mao Tse Tung) establishes Communism in China. The Soviets test their first atomic bomb.

1950   The Korean War begins. Senator Joseph McCarthy [R, Wis.] accuses the U.S. State Department of harboring "known" Communists.

1952   The United States develops the hydrogen bomb (H-bomb). General Dwight D. Eisenhower defeats former Illinois governor Adlai Stevenson in the presidential election. Fulgencio Batista comes to power through a military coup in Cuba.

1953   Soviet leader Joseph Stalin dies. The Korean War ends. The United States sponsors a coup in Iran. Fidel Castro attacks a Cuban military barracks on July 26. Castro is captured and sent to prison.

1954 The United States sponsors a coup in Guatemala. The French are defeated in Indochina by a Nationalist Communist insurgency led by Ho Chi Minh.

1955 Soviet and Western Allies heads of state meet in Geneva. The Soviets withdraw from Austria. Fidel Castro is freed from prison under a general amnesty and goes to Mexico to found the 26th of July Movement to promote revolution in Cuba.

1956 Eisenhower defeats Stevenson a second time in a landslide. The Soviets crush a Hungarian uprising. Soviet leader Nikita Khrushchev gives a "secret speech" denouncing Stalin. Castro returns to Cuba and begins guerrilla operations.

1957 The Soviets launch *Sputnik*, the first man-made object to be sent into space.

1958 Khrushchev announces a deadline to settle the Berlin issue. Batista flees to sanctuary in the Dominican Republic in December. The U.S. government suspends arms shipments to the Batista government.

1959

January Fidel Castro assumes power in Cuba. Mass trials and mass executions of former Batista regime officials begin.

May Under the new Cuban Agrarian Reform Law, farmlands of over 1,000 acres are expropriated and foreign land ownership is forbidden. Diplomatic relations between Cuba and the Soviet Union resume.

October Turkey and the United States sign an agreement to deploy fifteen nuclear-tipped Jupiter missiles in Turkey.

1960

February Soviet first deputy prime minister Anastas Mikoyan attends the opening of a Soviet trade exhibit in Havana and negotiates economic agreements with Cuba.

March 4 The *Coubre*, a Belgian freighter laden with arms, explodes in Havana harbor, killing a hundred or more at dockside and beyond.

March 17 President Eisenhower authorizes a program to fund Cuban exiles in training to invade Cuba. The Central Intelligence Agency (CIA) program is to be run from Guatemala.

May	The Soviet Union and Cuba establish diplomatic relations
May 17	The CIA-sponsored anti-Castro broadcasts called Radio Swan is begun from an island off the coast of Panama.
June	The first shipment of Soviet oil arrives in Cuba. American refiners there refuse to process the oil.
July	The United States suspends the Cuban sugar import quota. The Soviet Union agrees to buy sugar previously destined for the United States. Khrushchev says that Soviet "artillerymen" can defend Cuba with "rocket fire."
August	The CIA turns to organized crime in its first steps to try to assassinate Castro.
September	The first large arms shipment from the Soviet Bloc arrives in Cuba. Castro and Khrushchev embrace and support each other at the UN.
October	Cuba nationalizes U.S. private investments on the island worth approximately $1 billion. Some 200 small U.S.-based companies remain in the hands of American owners. The U.S. ambassador is recalled to Washington by the Department of State.
December	Cuba professes solidarity with the Sino-Soviet Bloc. The Soviet Bloc buys the Cuban sugar crop two years in advance.

1961

January	Khrushchev states that Soviet rockets protect Cuba and that there are "no Soviet military bases in Cuba."
January 3	The United States and Cuba sever diplomatic and consular relations.
January 6	Khrushchev gives "sacred wars of national liberation" speech.
January 10	The *New York Times* reports on Cuban exile training in Guatemala for an invasion of Cuba.
January 20	At his inaugural, President John F. Kennedy vows that the United States will "pay any price" to preserve Western interests and declares it an "hour of maximum danger" for the United States.
Late January	The CIA delivers to would-be assassins a box of poisoned cigars to be given to Castro.

April 7   The *New York Times* reports that plans to invade Cuba with exiles trained "by experts" in Louisiana, Florida, and Guatemala are an "open secret."

April 12   President Kennedy declares that U.S. armed forces will not take part in any invasion of Cuba.

April 14   B-26 bombers piloted by Cuban exiles attack Cuban air bases. President Kennedy cancels an additional set of air strikes.

April 17–18   Fourteen hundred Cuban exiles attempt an invasion of Cuba at the Bay of Pigs; 114 are killed and 1,189 are captured. Castro orders the arrest of some two hundred thousand suspected dissidents. The CIA authorizes a last-minute bombing effort with six U.S. airmen. Four are brought down by anti-aircraft fire.

April 19   In a memo to the president, Attorney General Robert Kennedy concludes that "something forceful and determined must be done. . . . The time has come for a showdown" with Cuba.

                 Khrushchev assures Kennedy that the Soviet Union "does not seek any advantages or privileges" in Cuba. Khrushchev warns the United States against arming Cuban émigrés for future attacks.

April 27–28   Secretary of State Dean Rusk privately raises with the Turkish foreign minister the possibility of withdrawing U.S. Jupiter missiles from Turkey. The United States accedes and delays its request to withdraw the Jupiters.

June 3–4   President Kennedy meets with Premier Khrushchev in Vienna. Khrushchev delivers an ultimatum on Berlin to settle the issue or the USSR will hand over control of the East Berlin Zone to East Germany. Kennedy says prospects for war are "very real."

July   Kennedy doubles U.S. military reserves, increases the draft, and pushes civil defense. U.S. officials and other Americans close to the Kennedy administration hint at a physical division of Berlin as an acceptable solution to the Berlin crisis.

August 13   Soviet forces aid the East Germans in erecting the Berlin Wall.

August 28   The USSR explodes a massive 58 megaton H-bomb.

September 1   A tank-to-tank standoff at the Berlin Wall begins. Soviet and American troops are poised for war.

September 21   A National Intelligence Estimate shows that the Soviet ICBM (intercontinental ballistic missile) program is far behind previous U.S. estimates. Only some ten to twenty-five Soviet ICBMs are believed to exist. In reality, the Soviets have around four working ICBMs.

October 21   Deputy Secretary of Defense Roswell Gilpatric publicly deflates the "missile gap" as untrue.

November 29   CIA director (DCI) Allen Dulles and Bay of Pigs invasion director Richard Bissell are fired. John McCone is made the new DCI.

November 30   President Kennedy authorizes Operation Mongoose to destabilize Castro. The program is placed under the guidance of Attorney General Robert Kennedy.

December 1   Castro declares, "I am a Marxist Leninist and will be one until the last day of my life."

1962

January 1   The New Year's Day parade in Cuba demonstrates the extent of Soviet Bloc arms deliveries to Cuba.

January 19   Robert Kennedy chairs Mongoose meetings, concluding: "solution to the Cuban problem today [a]... top priority.... No time, money, effort—or manpower is to be spared."

January 22–30   At the close of the Organization of American States conference, the foreign ministers from the twenty-one American republics vote to exclude Cuba "from participation in the inter-American system."

February   The Joint Chiefs of Staff give a "first priority basis" to the completion of all contingency plans for military action against Cuba.

April   U.S. Jupiter missiles in Turkey, manned by American personnel, become fully operational. In late April, Khrushchev decides to deploy Soviet missiles to Cuba.

U.S. troops begin a military exercise designed to test contingency planning for an invasion of Cuba.

Mid-July	The first Soviet cargo ships head from the Black Sea for Cuba with false declarations and false shipping weights. U.S. intelligence spots the buildup but not its extent: 40 medium range and intermediate range ballistic missiles; 24 surface-to-air missile batteries; 84 MIG-21 jet fighters; IL-28 nuclear bombers; missile boats; submarines; mobile tactical nuclear weapons; and 40,000 elite troops.
July–August	Raúl Castro visits Moscow and agrees to missile deployment.
August–September	Republican attacks take place on the Kennedy administration over the Soviet buildup.
August 10	CIA director John McCone tells President Kennedy, over subordinates' protests, that Soviet MRBMs (medium range ballistic missiles) are on the way to Cuba.
August 23	President Kennedy calls a meeting of the National Security Council to address McCone's concerns about Soviet missiles. Secretary of State Dean Rusk and Secretary of Defense Robert McNamara argue against McCone's interpretation.
August 31	President Kennedy is informed that a U-2 mission confirms the presence of surface-to-air missiles (SAMs) in Cuba. Senator Kenneth Keating [R, N.Y.] says on the Senate floor that there is evidence of Soviet "rocket installations in Cuba."
September 4	Kennedy, Rusk, and McNamara review the evidence regarding SAM sites. Robert Kennedy meets USSR ambassador Anatoly Dobrynin, who delivers Khrushchev's assurances that no surface-to-surface missiles or offensive weapons have been placed in Cuba. President Kennedy then authorizes a statement to the effect that the United States will not tolerate *offensive* missiles in Cuba.
September 19	The United States Intelligence Board reports that "the establishment on Cuban soil of Soviet nuclear striking forces which could be used against the U.S. would be incompatible with Soviet policy."
October 1	McNamara meets with the Joint Chiefs of Staff and indicates that a MRBM deployment is possible. The U.S. Atlantic Command is directed to plan "to be prepared to institute a blockade against Cuba."
October 2	A partial U.S. embargo of Cuba is declared. The transport of U.S. goods to Cuba is banned.

October 4   Robert Kennedy meets the "Special Group of Advisors" on Cuba informing them that President Kennedy believes that "massive activity" against Cuba should be undertaken, including the mining of Cuban harbors.

October 6   The U.S. Atlantic Command reports increased readiness so that it can mount a full-scale invasion. These plans are known as Oplan 314 and Oplan 316.

October 8   Cuban president Osvaldo Dorticós, addressing the UN, declares: "we have sufficient means with which to defend ourselves; we have indeed our inevitable weapons, the weapons which we would have preferred not to acquire and which we do not wish to employ."

October 13   U.S. State Department ambassador-at-large Chester Bowles, in a long conversation with Soviet ambassador Dobrynin, says that the United States has "some evidence" that Soviet nuclear missiles are in Cuba.

October 14   Major Richard Heyser, flying a U-2 reconnaissance plane, obtains the first photographic evidence of Soviet MRBM sites in Cuba.

October 15   A two-week-long exercise named PHIBRIGLEX-62 begins, with 20,000 U.S. Navy personnel and 4,000 Marines scheduled to practice overthrowing the tyrant Ortsac—*Castro* spelled backwards.

October 16   President Kennedy convenes his Executive Committee (ExCom), an informal group of advisors. The ExCom is told that the Soviet missiles will be operational in two weeks.

October 17   ExCom considers options. Kennedy leaves for a political campaign trip.

October 18   Kennedy meets with Soviet foreign minister Andrei Gromyko in the Oval Office. Gromyko denies that the Soviet Union has placed offensive nuclear weapons in Cuba. The president restates his September warning. Photos of missile sites are on Kennedy's desk. Meanwhile ExCom, under presidential prodding, moves away from an air strike option to that of a blockade.

October 19   Kennedy meets with the Joint Chiefs of Staff (JCS). Air Force chief of staff General Curtis LeMay argues that if the United

States fails to use force, it is as "bad as the appeasement at Munich." Kennedy orders a blockade and leaves on a scheduled campaign trip.

October 20   Kennedy feigns an upper respiratory infection and returns to Washington, D.C., from the campaign trail. The JCS reportedly suggest the use of nuclear weapons. Kennedy directs the ExCom to consider the blockade option.

October 21   Kennedy argues the merits of diplomatic solution to the ExCom.

October 22   U.S. military goes to DEFCON 3, a state of high nuclear alert. The alert is sounded in clear, open communications, and all U.S. bomber aircraft are armed with nuclear weapons for the only time in Strategic Air Command (SAC) history. Kennedy gives a speech informing the American people of the missile threat. Castro mobilizes his military.

October 23   Robert Kennedy (RFK) meets secretly with Soviet ambassador Dobrynin. (Later, in retirement, Dobrynin says that RFK suggested the Jupiter trade at this meeting.) The Organization of American States unanimously supports a U.S. quarantine of Cuba.

October 24   Soviet ships reach the quarantine line and stop dead in the water. President Kennedy receives a letter from Khrushchev calling the quarantine "an act of aggression" Kennedy delays boarding Soviet ships and orders Russian-speaking U.S. personnel on U.S. ships at the quarantine line.

October 25   U.S. ambassador to the UN Adlai Stevenson presents photographic evidence of the missiles at the UN. American military are placed at DEFCON 2, the highest alert ever. Kennedy tells Khrushchev, "you still do not appear to understand what it is that has moved us in this matter."

October 26   A letter from Khrushchev states that the Soviets will remove their missiles if President Kennedy publicly guarantees the United States will not invade Cuba. Robert Kennedy meets with Soviet ambassador Dobrynin and tells him that the removal of U.S. missiles from Turkey is possible.

October 27   A U.S. U-2 spy plane accidentally flies into Russian airspace via Alaska. Another U-2 is shot down over Cuba. The United States gets a Russian letter: the United States must promise not to invade Cuba and must remove missiles from Turkey. Robert

Kennedy meets with Dobrynin. A private agreement is reached that includes the swap of Jupiters in Turkey for Russian missiles in Cuba and a U.S. assurance that it will not invade Cuba. The quid pro quo element of this arrangement is to be kept confidential. President Kennedy and Dean Rusk prepare a contingency plan for the public acceptance of the trade.

October 28   Khrushchev announces on Radio Moscow the dismantling of Soviet missiles in Cuba and does not refer to U.S. missiles from Turkey. The crisis is over. Castro is furious that the decision was made "over his head."

October 30   Mongoose activities are shut down temporarily. Premier Khrushchev sends President Kennedy a message regarding the settlement of outstanding USSR–U.S. issues, including the nuclear test ban treaty and the Berlin question.

November 8   The last Mongoose sabotage effort is reported.

November 21   President Kennedy terminates the quarantine measures against Cuba.

1963
April 25   McNamara tells Kennedy that the last Jupiter missile has been removed from Turkey.

August 5   The United States signs the Limited Test Ban Treaty with Russia.

November   The United States considers rapprochement with Cuba.

November 22   President Kennedy is assassinated.

December 23   President Lyndon Johnson decides not to pursue any rapprochement with Cuba until after the 1964 presidential election.

1964
October   Khrushchev is replaced in a bloodless coup and is sent into retirement.

1978
November 30   President Jimmy Carter discounts reports of MIG 23 planes based in Cuba and notes that the Soviet government has given him assurances that no shipments of arms would violate the terms of the 1962 agreement.

1979

January 17   The United States concludes that the MIG is not configured to carry nuclear weapons and is not in violation of the understanding of 1962.

1981

April 22   Cuban newspapers announce that anyone who wants to leave Cuba may depart from Mariel harbor. A large number of "economic" refugees are accepted in the United States.

October   The United States announces military maneuvers to influence Castro into diminishing support for Central American revolutionaries. Castro asks the Soviets to protect Cuba from U.S. attack and are reminded by Soviet leader Leonid Brezhnev that they are "11,000 kilometers away"; Brezhnev also tells Castro that Russia "will not stick [its] neck out for Cuba."

1982

April   Under President Ronald Reagan, the White House issues a National Security Directive ordering new measures to increase anti-Castro sentiment in the United States and the Americas because the new administration believes that Cuba is the source of insurgencies in Central America.

1983

September 14   President Reagan said of the 1962 Kennedy-Khrushchev understanding: "As far as I'm concerned, that agreement has been abrogated many times by the Soviet Union and Cuba in the bringing in of what can only be considered offensive weapons."

1987   At a Florida meeting of American ExCom veterans of the Cuban Missile Crisis, Dean Rusk reveals President Kennedy's authorization to Rusk to make the swap of U.S. Jupiters for Russian missiles public via the UN if the Soviets did not accept a private understanding.

1991

September   Soviet president Mikhail Gorbachev states that he will withdraw all Soviet troops from Cuba. Cuba struggles to liberalize and retain state supervision and state security apparatus.

1992

September   In the United States, the Cuban Democracy Act extending the reach of U.S. sanctions on Cuba passes with the support of Arkansas governor Bill Clinton, a presidential candidate.

November   The Cuban and Russian governments sign an accord to keep a Russian intelligence station in Cuba. Rent is reportedly $200 million per year.

1996

May   The U.S. Congress passes the "Helms-Burton" law, which penalizes foreign businesses trading with Cuba and bars their executives from entering the United States. The law is passed after the Cuban government orders the shootdown of two aircraft piloted by Cuban exiles. Havana says the planes were violating Cuban airspace.

THE CUBAN MISSILE
CRISIS EXPLAINED

I

Introduction

Two generations have passed since the actions of the United States, the Soviet Union, and Cuba brought the world to the brink of the unthinkable—nuclear war—in October 1962. In consequence, the Cuban Missile Crisis has become one of the most studied international confrontations of the twentieth century. The attention is merited, as President John F. Kennedy's speechwriter, Theodore Sorensen, put it, by the fact that the world caught its most intimate view of "the gun barrel of nuclear war"[1] and faced death of the proportions prophesied by the biblical description of Armageddon.

The continued vast body of academic and policy literature produced over a subject seemingly as narrow as the events in Cuba in 1962 is clearly related to what was at stake. Moreover, an epic catastrophe so narrowly avoided provides an opportunity to learn something. As Kennedy-era advisor McGeorge Bundy observed, "[H]aving come so close to the edge, we must make it our business not to pass this way again."[2]

The Cuban Missile Crisis seemed the ultimate test of the United States in dealing with nuclear weapons. Indeed, managing the threat of nuclear weapons was the great preoccupation of the Cold War. When Russia achieved a nominal strategic nuclear parity with the United States, American strategy hit a wall. Massive retaliation was no longer a credible option. But diplomacy allowed little room for negotiations, especially in the atmosphere left by the depredations of Senator Joseph McCarthy [R, Wis.].[3] Diplomacy fell into disrepute.

President Kennedy came to office as a former partisan of McCarthy, even if he was uncomfortable with McCarthy's worst excesses. Kennedy was also a critic of the Eisenhower administration as not being aggressive enough in the Cold War.

Yet Kennedy was no war-lover. He himself had experienced war in the Pacific theater and had lost his much-loved and promising brother Joseph in World War II. Privately Kennedy tried to work out an understanding with the Soviets from the onset of his administration. He was successful in the case of Laos, which was quietly liquidated by negotiations with the Russians. But in most areas of contention, Kennedy was confronted with an increasingly assertive Soviet Union led by a bombastic Nikita Khrushchev.

The Russians felt compelled to argue that if war was no longer "inevitable" (as Khrushchev contended), they were still at the forefront of history, leading the Socialist camp and competing in the Communist world with China and in the world at large with the United States. In this competition the Soviets were handed a new ally in the Caribbean when Fidel Castro, his brother Raúl, and Ernesto "Che" Guevara—the revolutionary vanguard of Cuba—overthrew the dictatorship of Fulgencio Batista.

The success of Castro against Batista was secured with only incidental help on the part of the Soviets. Cuba was the only country up until then to join the Soviet Bloc voluntarily, with no Soviet troops and precious little Soviet encouragement. In fact, the Soviet courtship of Cuba was slow, hesitant, and surreptitious. But it soon became an intimate alliance directed against the United States.

For the Soviets, Cuba was a model of what could happen in the developing world and a foretaste of the promise of increasing competition with the capitalist world. Castro had his own aims in Latin America and was intent on spreading revolution.

Both the administrations of Presidents Dwight D. Eisenhower and John F. Kennedy were intent on breaking Castro's totalitarian and Sovietized grip on Cuba. Eisenhower started a huge CIA operation that culminated, in the earliest days of the Kennedy administration, with the use of Cuban exiles to invade Cuba. The invasion was to have U.S. air cover, but Kennedy, worried that the presence of U.S. troops would taint the successor government in Cuba and the effort itself, decided two days before the invasion to sharply limit America's visibility in the effort. When the invasion took place in mid-April 1961 at the Bay of Pigs, the invaders were met by massive and overwhelming firepower personally directed by Fidel Castro. The invasion was an unmitigated disaster that haunted the Kennedy administration thereafter.

Compounding the Bay of Pigs disaster was a Spring 1961 meeting between Kennedy and Khrushchev. Kennedy hoped to privately work for an understanding with Khrushchev, especially on the issues of the control of Berlin[4] and arms control. Perhaps buoyed by Kennedy's embarrassing failure at the Bay of Pigs, Khrushchev bullied the young president and threatened war over the issue of control of the divided city of Berlin.

After a huge military buildup on both sides culminating in the tests of a number of Soviet nuclear weapons, the Berlin crisis was settled. The Soviets may have believed they were acting from a position of strength, but in truth the outlines of a settlement acceptable to both sides were tactfully suggested by the Kennedy administration itself.

When Khrushchev confirmed the American suggestion in practice—by physically dividing the city—it proved a propaganda victory for the West. In the long run, the division of Berlin provided the Cold War an element of stability. In the short run, it posed dangers. Most notable, in September 1961 there was a standoff between Soviet and American tanks that almost led to war. The standoff, in large part, was precipitated by an American commander in Berlin who slipped from the grasp of White House control by asking Khrushchev to pull back the Russian tanks a few meters. The Americans reciprocated, and the crisis faded shortly thereafter.

The Berlin crisis was critical in the management of the Cuban crisis. From the first days of the Kennedy administration, the White House viewed the American military with concern, if not suspicion. Kennedy and his closest advisors worried that U.S. military commanders were nothing less than reckless in their advice and plans. The Bay of Pigs fiasco was one indication. The Berlin crisis was another. Kennedy had learned that the military needed to be watched and managed. He also knew that if he as president appeared "soft" in times of crisis, there was a twofold risk. First, the Soviets might take advantage of a perception of weakness. Second, being a newly elected president who had criticized the previous administration of not being strong and bold enough, he could not appear soft and overly eager to accommodate Soviet power. Hence the successful resolution of face-offs could involve negotiations as long as the American administration did not seem to give anything substantial to the Soviets for a return to the status quo.

A similar pattern of events characterized the Cuban Missile Crisis. The "last chapter," the Kennedy administration was convinced, had not been written on Cuba. From the Bay of Pigs to the Cuban Missile Crisis, considerable covert planning and resources were deployed to seek Castro's downfall—with no success whatsoever. Indeed, American plans may have contributed to the Soviet decision to "protect" Cuba with nuclear missiles.

The Soviet missiles that were surreptitiously and hurriedly placed in Cuba were not considered to be highly strategically important by many of Kennedy's top White House advisors, but their political symbolism was immense. Moreover, because the missiles were placed in Cuba in contravention of abundant Soviet promises and assurances, it seemed (at least to the advisors who counseled the president, and to the president himself) as if the Kennedy administration was not paying the price of appearing weak and ir-resolute at the Bay of Pigs. Kennedy was convinced he would have to do something or, as he confirmed to his brother, be "impeached" by Congress and American opinion.

The president employed two tracks of negotiation in the Cuban Missile Crisis. With his own advisors as with the public, Kennedy strove to create a record of toughness and resolution in dealing with the Russians. He de-manded that they withdraw their missiles. He also claimed that this demand, enforced by a blockade of Cuba and the mobilization of nearly all Amer-ica's military resources, would not be conditioned by any American concessions.

But on a more subtle level Kennedy tried to steer his advisors' sugges-tions and discussions toward a moderate, controlled, and proportionate re-sponse that would not evoke war. Most private and secret of all with his most trusted intimates, Kennedy proposed a behind-the-scenes negotiation that involved a quid pro quo exchange with the Russians. The United States would give up its medium range missiles in Turkey; the Russians would give up their nuclear missiles in Cuba.

In the end, Kennedy publicly acknowledged that all he hoped to give (and, in fact, was successful in achieving) was a pledge not to sponsor or en-gage in another effort like the ill-fated Bay of Pigs invasion. The promise was significant, and it did lead to a stand-down of most of the CIA's ques-tionable anti-Castro activities such as the eight documented plots to assassi-nate Castro.

The Cuban Missile Crisis led to a radical re-evaluation of the prospects for war and negotiation with the Russians. From then on, both Khrushchev and Kennedy actively attempted to establish a détente; within a year this led to a hot line (a direct and immediate telephone linkup) between Washington and Moscow so the Cold War leadership could communicate easily if there ever were another nuclear crisis. The United States and the Soviets also reached an atmospheric test ban agreement, a significant environmental and arms control measure.

The nascent easing of tensions with the Soviets did not survive the Ken-nedy administration. Under Lyndon Johnson the Vietnam War widened, with the same leadership that had counseled President Kennedy during the Cuban Missile Crisis. Toughness had been a confirmed "lesson" of the de-cade. Another lesson was that crisis and confrontation could be managed and that in the end superior American will and power would prevail. All these lessons were tested and found wanting in Vietnam. But the Cuban Missile Crisis stands as a testimony to the need for historical investigation of perceived truths. A contemporary understanding of the crisis confirms that diplomacy, even with the most wily and dangerous adversaries, is an essential component of power and policy. The disavowal of diplomacy, even when it was essential to reach a settlement in the Cuban crisis, not only tainted the truth but handicapped American policy for decades thereafter.

The conclusion of the crisis had profound consequences, not the least of which was establishing the mindset for a series of steps that led the way to the disaster in Vietnam. The end of the Cuban crisis seemed to be an archetypal effort of the successful and determinedly civilian orchestration of a great American panoply of persuasive instruments. Diplomacy in this era changed. Indeed, coercion and diplomacy began to become synonymous. As former State Department official and Harvard economist Thomas Schelling explained, "[t]he power to hurt is bargaining power.... To exploit it, is diplomacy—vicious diplomacy, but diplomacy."[5]

The way in which American power affected the Soviets in the Caribbean seemed to herald an era wherein a vastly expanded American armory was to become the relevant, useful, and rational instrument of American policy. The apparent triumph of the United States in the Cuban crisis reinforced the venerable American hope that a stable international order could be sustained if it were underwritten by America's readiness to employ effective force. What was novel was the new "science" adduced from events: "crisis management." "There is no such thing as strategy," exclaimed the exultant secretary of defense, Robert McNamara, in the aftermath. From then on, the business of international politics was "only crisis management."[6]

The belief that force could be managed for discrete diplomatic ends was exhilarating, for it resolved a dilemma that had been building for nearly 200 years: on the one hand, force seemed to have expanded beyond any meaningful purpose; on the other, diplomacy had declined as a meaningful exercise in moderating the conduct of states.

In the heady aftermath of the Cuban Missile Crisis, American policymakers came to believe that if international relations were "managed" correctly and backed by deep wellsprings of American power, nuclear war could be avoided. The immediate lesson of the Cuban Missile Crisis for a soon-to-be-disillusioned generation of American policy officials (once they faced the test of Vietnam) was that force—given the proper application of intellect and guidance—could be made both proportionate and effective. The Cuban Missile Crisis thus seemed to offer the promise that the sterile and fruitless actions of diplomacy, replete with archaic conference halls and interminable discussion, could be replaced by the management center, the telex, and rapid-fire "signals" divined by those savvy minds who were alert to war's horrors yet not inured to them.

For the Russians, there were other lessons. Khrushchev had boasted he would soon "bury" the West in an avalanche of consumer goods and missiles. The offer of an entrée to Latin America was a welcome vindication that he had done better than his predecessor, Joseph Stalin. But Khrushchev's bluster and bluff had been called and impeached at home as much as abroad. In 1964 a fellow Bolshevik hierarch member, Dmitri Polyanski, would use the post-crisis flirtation of Castro with Chairman Mao Tse Tung's China as evidence that Khrushchev was unfit: the Soviet premier had leapt before he had looked, expanding Russian interests. Khrushchev's critics claimed there should be some correspondence between Soviet ambitions and Soviet arms:

Comrade Khrushchev was pleased to announce that Stalin had not succeeded in penetrating Latin America whereas he had. First, the policy of penetrating Latin America had not been our policy, and second, this meant that our country had to commit itself to providing military supplies an ocean away.[7]

Under Khrushchev's successors, a vast "blue water" navy and an immense arsenal were acquired to match growing ambitions with material means. The race, under Khrushchev, proved insupportable in the face of superior fire-power and under the threat of atomic annihilation. A better-armed Russia had little better luck in sustaining far-flung positions amassed a decade later—in cooperation, this time, with Castro. Indeed, the extent of the new commitments were one cause of the ultimate disintegration of the Soviet Union.

NOTES

1. Theodore Sorensen, interview, CNN, March 1997. Internet transcript on CNN's Cold War Web site, The Cold War, 1998 Cable News Network <www.cnn.com/specials/cold.war/episodes/10/interviews/sorensen>.

2. McGeorge Bundy, *Danger and Survival: Choices about the Bomb in the First Fifty Years* (New York: Random House, 1988), p. 462.

3. Senator Joseph Raymond McCarthy from Wisconsin presided over the permanent subcommittee on investigations. He held public hearings accusing army officials, members of the media, and public figures of being Communists. His charges were never proven, and he was censured by the Senate in 1954.

4. Berlin was divided at the end of World War II between the Soviet Union, who controlled the eastern half, and the Western Allies, who controlled the western half. East Germany became a feeble state because its most talented citizens fled to a better life and freedom in the West. The Soviet solution was to hand over control of Berlin to East Germany, but the West reminded the Russians that they were in Berlin by treaty right. The West did not recognize the East German re-

gime, so any claims they made would be illegitimate. However, the West decided that what the Russians did in their sector, including controlling the outflow of refugees, was not a matter the West would contest.

5. Thomas C. Schelling, *Arms and Influence* (New Haven, CT: Yale University Press, 1966), p. 2.

6. Coral Bell, *The Conventions of Crisis: A Study in Diplomatic Management* (London: Oxford University Press, 1971), p. 2.

7. Alexander Fursenko and Timothy Naftali, *One Hell of a Gamble: Khrushchev, Castro, Kennedy and the Cuban Missile Crisis, 1958–1964* (New York: W. W. Norton, 1997), p. 25.

2

Kennedy, Apocalyptic Power, and the Cold War Backdrop

It had snowed the night before, but inauguration day 1961 was unusually cold and clear. A hatless and coatless president declared to a shivering crowd his generation's unique fitness for office: "temperated by war, disciplined by a hard and bitter peace."

President John F. Kennedy promised a great new exertion to sustain American interests everywhere:

Let every nation know, whether it wishes us well or ill, that we shall pay any price, bear any burden, meet any hardship, support any friend, oppose any foe to assure the survival and success of liberty. We will do all this and more.[1]

THE TRUMAN DOCTRINE AND THE NEW FRONTIER

Kennedy's inaugural address—indeed, all his campaign speeches—conveyed a new tone. But in substance he was reaffirming the Cold War dictum first given to the American people in the form of the Truman Doctrine, a pledge made by President Harry Truman to the Congress in March 1947 to oppose Communism anywhere, no matter what the challenge, and to

help free peoples to maintain their free institutions and their national integrity against aggressive movements that seek to impose upon them totalitarian regimes. This is no more than a frank recognition that totalitarian regimes imposed upon free peoples, by direct or indirect aggression, undermine the foundations of international peace and hence the security of the United States.[2]

The security of the United States, declared Truman, could only be found in the context of "international peace." American security was therefore interdependent with that of states far from American shores, such as Greece and Turkey. But the specific threat of the early Cold War was not given any limit. As Truman put it,

Collapse of free institutions and loss of independence would be disastrous not only for them but for the world. Discouragement and possibly failure would quickly be the lot of neighboring peoples striving to maintain their freedom and independence.[3]

President Kennedy's message in early 1961 was hardly different from Truman's in 1947. In fact, events at the end of the 1940s and early 1950s had largely confirmed containment as American policy in practice, even though it all but disappeared from the official rhetoric of the Eisenhower years. Kennedy's elaboration of containment was new in that it expressed an exuberant, self-aware tinge of youth. The language of the "New Frontier" was vivid but vague, novel only in its majestic cadence and forceful delivery.

The broad goals of the inaugural were given definition soon enough. From the first minutes of his tenure in office, Kennedy fixed on Russia and Cuba. As he declaimed in his first address to Congress, "Communist domination in this hemisphere can never be negotiated. We pledge to work with our sister republics to free the Americas of all such foreign domination and tyranny."[4]

There is no record of any member of either the departing Eisenhower administration or the incoming Kennedy administration who wanted to compromise or coexist with Castro. Even the barest hint of compromise in the Caribbean would have disastrous electoral consequences for an administration that had just come to power on the thinnest electoral mandate in modern history.

As the Soviet leadership became more involved in strengthening Castro's Cuba, there was an inevitable risk of confrontation. However, what made the Cuban Missile Crisis unique was not a mere conflict of interest but the size of the wager both powers placed on a favorable outcome. Above all, there were unparalleled risks. Never before had confrontation been made so much a matter of personal prestige of the leadership of both sides. Never before had declamatory policy left so little room for compromise. Never before had nuclear weapons been so publicly and tangibly committed to the outcome by both sides. And never before had so many American cities been so vulnerable to so much—and such immediate—destruction. To Secretary of Defense Robert McNamara, recalling the crisis four decades later, it was clear that the "world came within a hair breadth of nuclear war. . . . We came so close—both Kennedy and Khrushchev felt events were slipping outside their control. . . . We lucked out."[5]

ARMS, ARMAGEDDON, AND DIPLOMACY

The Cuban Missile Crisis occurred at a time when the use of nuclear weapons seemed much more real than it does now, after the end of the Cold War. It was a time when there seemed to be no other choice. At least to many in the American policy community, if American vital interests—or even interests that were symbolic of vital interests—were threatened, then the United States would have no choice but to defend them with vigor. This was the essence of the promise of Kennedy's New Frontier. When he came to office it was on the winds of a promise of asserting and protecting American interests wherever and however they might be threatened.

The classic statecraft, both before and after the Cold War, requires an admixture of force and diplomacy. But diplomacy was not a long suit of the new Kennedy administration. Indeed, the administration came to Washington believing it faced a challenge in areas where diplomacy was not relevant: from missiles to subversion, the challenge of Soviet power hardly seemed congenial to the traditional forms of elaborately scripted conferences and private discussions. Rather, the menace of Soviet power and propaganda would be met and exceeded on its own terms.

The problem of atomic power bedeviled American policymakers from the onset of the nuclear age. But by the mid-1950s, during the Eisenhower administration, atomic weapons assumed a kind of policy hegemony, dominating all other instruments of statecraft. From highway programs to urban planning, American policymakers rationalized their programs in terms of nuclear war. Both the federal highway program and urban building designs, for example, were required to meet the needs of a potential nuclear emergency. Federally funded buildings had to be provisioned with bomb shelters, and federal highway bridges had to be able to carry loads equal to a mobilizing nuclear force or urgent mass evacuations.

Overseas, small encroachments and alliance politics were configured to support the nuclear threat. The worries of alliance partners that the United States would not come to Europe's aid early and with the full deterrent power of the American atomic arsenal were assuaged by the installation of short range missiles around the periphery of the Soviet Union.

Yet nuclear weapons were challenged, even by those who depended on them, as excessive. President Dwight D. Eisenhower, assailed by suggestions that he develop nuclear weapons that were more "useful," explained to

his close aids, some of whom were counseling a preemptive blow against
Russia:

No matter . . . how certain that within 24 hours we could destroy Kuibyshev and
Moscow and Leningrad and Baku and all the other places . . . I want you to carry this
question home with you. Gain such a victory, and what do you do with it? Here
would be a great area from the Elbe to Vladivostok and down through South East
Asia torn up and destroyed and without government. . . . I ask you what would the
civilized world do about it? I repeat, there is no victory in any war except . . . through
our dedication . . . to avoid it.[6]

Eisenhower knew that the concept of atomic victory annulled most clas-
sical aims of diplomacy and war. It implied neither the bending of an enemy
to one's will nor even the defeating of his army. The reality—and futility—
of nuclear war captured what Karl Von Clausewitz, the great nine-
teenth-century military theorist, had insisted: war's purpose needs to be the
extension of "politics by other means." Nuclear war, in contrast, more approached what the Nuremberg lawyers spoke of when they wrote the laws
of genocide.

Once the Soviets achieved a kind of nominal strategic nuclear retaliatory
capacity, atomic war seemed too fearful in consequence to be redeemed.
Yet, while nuclear weapons paralyzed one side, there was an emerging
American community of "defense intellectuals" who feared that these same
weapons would embolden the Soviets. As the doyen of defense theorists,
Henry Kissinger, then a Harvard professor, explained:

It can be argued that fear of all-out war is bound to be mutual . . . but . . . [i]f the Soviet bloc can present its challenges in less than all out form, it may gain a crucial advantage. Every move on its part will then pose the appalling dilemma of whether we
are willing to commit suicide to prevent encroachments, no one of which seems to
threaten our existence directly, but which may be a step on the road to our ultimate
destruction.[7]

The Mid-1950s: Nuclear Containment at
Home and Abroad

In the mid-1950s, as soon as the Soviets acquired deliverable strategic
weapons, Eisenhower began to indicate that he was willing to move toward
a settlement. As he told the Soviets at Geneva in 1955, "[Once] it was that
wars began where diplomacy fails, [now] diplomacy must begin because
war has failed."[8] But diplomacy was not the Eisenhower administration's
long suit. Eisenhower's pick for Secretary of State, John Foster Dulles, cooperated with right-wing Republican demands to "clean out" the State De-

partment. Neither a friend of the professional American diplomatic service nor a practitioner of classic diplomatic skills, Dulles was, as Eisenhower noted, "a sort of international prosecuting attorney."[9]

Dulles came to office convinced that the policy of containment—the bedrock of the Truman years—conceded the initiative to the Communists. Containment, Dulles believed, implied the use of conventional forces and the constant possibility of using them in "brush-fire" wars. "Limited wars" like those in Korea and the one the French were fighting in Indochina were expensive and debilitating. Limited wars had limited and unsatisfactory conclusions that gave weight to the Republican right's charge that the consequence of policy was a compromise with nothing less than a worldwide conspiracy aimed at the elimination of American freedoms and prosperity. Dulles, instead, threatened "massive retaliation" at "times and places" of the administration's choosing. But the Dullesian alternative proved hollow as the United States stood aside when most of Indochina was conceded to the Communists in 1954 and when the Hungarians rebelled in 1956. The real implication of a profoundly nuclearized foreign policy was that it was frustrated by reality abroad—foremost by the Soviet acquisition of nuclear weapons—even though it served to "contain" some of the most disruptive fulminations of the radical right at home.

The Long Depreciation of Diplomacy: Munich's Shadow

The haunting memory of the 1938 Munich Conference, at which the profoundly pacifist leadership of Britain, along with France, hastened to Germany in order to stave off war, became the West's most vivid nightmare of foreign policy failure. A British policy self-labeled as "appeasement" led Britain and France to concede to Hitler's Germany a part of Czechoslovakia. Within a year, the Germans took all of Czechoslovakia and soon were pressing in on Poland.

Henceforth the "lesson of Munich" became a kind of policy imperative. As one important Cold War–era policy planner, William P. Bundy, observed, Munich became the "basic datum" of American foreign policy. Appeasing dictators would cause "vast miscalculation." And it was likely, in any case, to beget even more terrible forms of violence:

The rejection of armed action contribute[d] to the most ghastly human phenomena [World War II]. To Kennedy, Johnson, Rusk [McGeorge Bundy], . . . McNamara, . . . [war] could prevent vast evil and open the way to progress. War was viewed . . . not as *Catch-22* or *M.A.S.H.* or even *Patton* . . . but as the only way to deal with world order.[10]

As Munich suffused the memory of American policymakers, compromise with the Soviets assumed a mantle of taint, if not treason, to many in American politics. Even as late as the mid-1980s, a prominent congressman, Jack Kemp, would claim that nuclear agreements with Russia were nothing short of "nuclear Munichs."[11]

In the context of the Cold War, diplomacy had fallen into low repute. President Franklin D. Roosevelt's February 1945 conference at Yalta with the Soviet leader, Generalissimo Joseph Stalin, and British prime minister Winston Churchill was tied to the ghost of Munich. The Republican Party platform of 1952, drafted by Dulles, denounced the Yalta accords as "secret understandings" that "aided communist enslavements." According to the Republicans, the negotiators of Yalta had put the capstone on "twenty years of treason."[12]

By the 1950s, international conferences were still staged. Diplomats met. Communiqués were issued. But most meetings were eyed with suspicion. At a conference in 1954, Secretary of State John Foster Dulles asked one of his aides whether he might not be satisfied if the Soviet foreign secretary would accept free elections and the renunciation of Germany. "Why, yes," his aide responded. "Well, that's where you and I part company," Dulles retorted. "[B]ecause I wouldn't. There'd be a catch in it."[13]

KENNEDY ACTIVISM

The ringing declamation of seemingly unlimited burdens was the most memorable part of Kennedy's famed January 1961 inaugural address—featuring the exhortation that Americans would "pay any price, bear any burden, meet any hardship, support any friend, oppose any foe to assure the survival and success of liberty." But at the same time the president asked Americans to "began anew—remembering on both sides that civility is not a sign of weakness. . . . Let the U.S. never negotiate out of fear. But let the U.S. never fear to negotiate."[14]

Yet the Kennedy team was activist, schooled in the excitement of the New Deal and World War II and the bitter contest with the radical right. The new administration almost immediately faced the sting of domestic critics who charged it with weakness in Cuba and Laos, as well as gullibility in agreeing to meet Nikita Khrushchev, the Soviet premier, in Vienna in the late spring of 1961. Kennedy may have not begun office with a "fear of negotiations," but the domestic political climate was hardly congenial to an early settlement of the toughest immediate international challenges: Berlin and Cuba.

Negotiations on the New Frontier

It was hard to see what kind of deal could be made in Berlin. Both the Soviets and the Americans effectively gave up on a compromise even before the failed Paris summit in May 1960. Ostensibly the failure occurred because of the ruckus that ensued after an American spy plane was shot down over Soviet airspace in the hours before the conference convened. Discussions with the Russians came nearly to a halt in the wake of Khrushchev's angry departure from Paris.

Diplomacy was at low ebb, and few on Kennedy's incoming senior national security team held much regard for the diplomatic enterprise. Nor was diplomacy's nominal embodiment, Secretary of State Dean Rusk, well regarded by the other members of Kennedy's new national security team. To the Kennedy courtiers, Rusk could not win for losing. His irrelevance or inconsequence, said Kennedy intimates, was due to the gentle Georgian's "almost too amiable" nature.[15] Rusk was labeled as a man "unembarrassed" by "banality." He was said to be "[i]nscrutable," "[c]ompulsively colorless," and "Buddha like." But even as his cruelest detractors noted that Rusk was "splendid" in negotiations, his talent seemed hardly relevant to the cause of waging the Cold War with renewed vigor.[16]

To the bright and assertive Kennedy team, the State Department led by Rusk seemed to have been denatured. The professional Foreign Service was criticized as an insipid swamp of diplomatic gobbledy-gook. The Foreign Service personnel system was said to engender only bromides instead of action-filled recommendations. Though Kennedy relied on Rusk, he was not beyond demeaning the secretary's management of the State Department. As the new president ocmplained to *Time* magazine's Hugh Sidey, "all those people over there . . . are constantly smiling. I think we need to smile less and be tougher."[17]

Kennedy took matters into his own hands, creating ad hoc alternatives to the professionals and using advisors to distill wisdom from deep within the opaque interior of the national machinery. He organized foreign policy at the top. The president appointed and received ambassadors at his own initiative and encouraged American ambassadors to report directly to him. Kennedy was his own secretary of state. Some people even speculated that was why he kept the secretary of state on, even as the painful burlesques of Rusk rode the cocktail circuit.

Force and Politics

Even though Rusk had expertise in negotiation, no other members of the new Kennedy team were disposed to bother with crafting minute and delicately drawn agreements that might take the hard edge off the Cold War. Rather, diplomacy was an action tool, partly defensive and partly intended "to get the country moving." Just because the country had "gone communist, didn't mean it couldn't be gotten back," Kennedy had once said. But due care had to be taken. "Domestic policy," he cautioned, can "only defeat us[;] foreign policy could kill us."[18]

Kennedy was no war-lover, but the lethal element of international relations was the Kennedy team's over-arching preoccupation. Kennedy and, especially, Secretary of Defense Robert McNamara grappled with the problem of central deterrence at a time when it was clear that the use of strategic weapons could be suicidal. Yet many in the policy community seemed almost frivolous about the use of nuclear weapons. When Kennedy, urged on by Eisenhower, focused on the small nation of Laos in 1961, the new president was startled to discover that the Joint Chiefs of Staff suggested employing nuclear weapons as well as sending in at least 60,000 (and perhaps 160,000) U.S. troops, armed with tactical nuclear weapons, to prevent Communist domination of the tiny land-locked nation.[19]

President Kennedy and his brother, Attorney General Robert Kennedy, were appalled at the military's near insouciance about nuclear weapons. The resultant methodology that Kennedy developed in Laos, early on, can now be seen as an indication of how he was to deal with the Cuban Missile Crisis. The president sought to make it appear as if an armed solution might be necessary at the same time that he strove to engineer, through quiet—indeed, almost invisible—diplomacy, a well-veiled exit from an insupportable position. A Geneva Conference on Laos was initiated in May 1961. In June 1962 the conferees agreed to a neutral government. All sides covertly and liberally violated the agreement, but the Laotian issue essentially disappeared from the headlines. Kennedy had finessed the matter by pure dint of distance. After all, Laos was far from the concerns of most Americans. And with the help of court scribes, the outcome in Laos was depicted not as a standard diplomatic settlement but as something bright and new. Arthur Schlesinger rhapsodized, "[t]his . . . first experiment in Kennedy diplomacy under pressure . . . [was] marked by restraint of manner, toughness of intention, and care to leave his adversary a way of escape without loss of face."[20]

In truth, however, Kennedy backed off from an untenable commitment and redefined the American stake in Laos so that the tiny mountain and jungle locale became all but inconsequential, not only in the headlines but also in terms of U.S. policy resources.

NOTES

1. *Public Papers of the President, 1961* (Washington, DC: U.S. Government Printing Office, 1962), pp. 23–24.

2. The Truman Doctrine: Special Message to the Congress on Greece and Turkey," *Public Papers of the President: Harry S Truman, 1947* (Washington, DC: U.S. Government Printing Office, 1963), pp. 176–80.

3. Ibid.

4. John F. Kennedy, "Annual Message to the Congress on the State of the Union, January 30, 1961," *Public Papers of the President, 1961*, pp. 21–23.

5. Interview, *For the Record*, CNN, 18 June 1998.

6. Robert H. Ferrell, *The Diary of James C. Hagerty* (Bloomington: Indiana University Press, 1983), p. 69.

7. Henry Kissinger, *Nuclear Weapons and Foreign Policy* (New York: W. W. Norton, 1969), p. 11.

8. Blanche Wiesen Cook, *The Declassified Eisenhower* (Garden City, NY: Doubleday, 1981), p. 154.

9. Robert H. Ferrel, *The Eisenhower Diaries* (New York: Norton, 1981), p. 237.

10. William P. Bundy, "Remarks" (University of Delaware, 16 October 1973, transcript).

11. James A. Nathan and James K. Oliver, *U.S. Foreign Policy and World Order*, 4th ed. (Nerw York: HarperCollins, 1989), p. 431ff.

12. Stephen Ambrose, *Eisenhower*, Vol. 11 (New York: Simon & Schuster, 1983), p. 543.

13. Richard Goold-Adams, *The Time of Power: A Reappraisal of John Foster Dulles* (London: Weidenfeld & Nicolson, 1963), p. 293.

14. John F. Kennedy, "Inaugural Address, January 20, 1961," *Public Papers of the President, 1961*, pp. 23–24.

15. Theodore Sorensen, *Kennedy* (New York: Bantam Books, 1969), p. 303; Arthur M. Schlesinger Jr., *Robert Kennedy and His Times* (New York: Ballantine, 1978), p. 559.

16. Arthur M. Schlesinger Jr., *A Thousand Days: John F. Kennedy in the White House* (New York: Fawcett Crest, 1967), p. 402.

17. Ibid., p. 376.

18. Ibid., p. 395.

19. Robert F. Kennedy, *Thirteen Days* (New York: New American Library, 1969), pp. 117–18.

20. Schlesinger, *A Thousand Days*, p. 317.

3

Enter Cuba

Throughout the fall of 1960, Senator John F. Kennedy pummeled his opponent in the presidential race, Richard Nixon (President Dwight D. Eisenhower's vice president), for being older but hardly wiser in the ways of the Soviets. Indeed, according to the campaigning Democratic senator from Massachusetts, the Eisenhower administration's conduct of foreign policy was an exhibition of sleep-walking. President Eisenhower and Richard Nixon, Kennedy charged, had presided over a "missile gap" and a declining American world position in everything from science to economic growth to global prestige. In October 1960 Kennedy began to blast the Eisenhower-Nixon administration for failing to support those Cubans who "offer . . . hope of overthrowing Castro."

Kennedy may well have known that many of his charges were far from the truth. As the Democratic Party candidate, he had been briefed by then CIA director Alan Dulles that a policy of bringing down Castro with CIA-sponsored proxies had been under way for nearly a year. And, in fact, Richard Nixon claimed in a 1962 memoir that before the campaign season had begun, he had taken it upon himself to inform Kennedy that the United States had been working with Cuban exiles to undo the regime of Fidel Castro. There was a consensus. Castro had to go. The ancient stricture of President James Monroe (1828) that other powers should refrain from taking a new position in the Americas had been impeached. The only question, by the time of the 1960 presidential campaign, was how to regain Cuba for the West.

The Democratic nominee for president focused much of his campaign on the relationship between world affairs and the American mission. The American people, declared Kennedy, stood "at a turning point in history" and had to choose "between the public interest and private comfort, between national greatness and national decline."[1] There were no limits to Kennedy's vision. Americans were challenged to reach "for mastery of the sky and the oceans and the tides, the far side of space and the inside of men's minds."[2]

CASTRO ASSUMES POWER AND MOVES TOWARD RUSSIA

The issue of Cuba was hard to avoid, especially when the implications of nuclear weapons came home to roost there. Fidel Castro had been sympathetic to the Soviets and in many ways antisympathetic to the United States from the onset. U.S. efforts to abort Castro's revolution, undoing it with Cuban émigré proxies, had failed disastrously at the Bay of Pigs. As much as the United States tried to undermine Castro and his move to embrace socialism in Cuba, the U.S. efforts only managed to strengthen his grip and increase the pace of his search for Soviet material assistance.

The Cuban revolution officially began on July 26, 1953, when 150 young revolutionaries, led by Fidel Castro, attacked a Cuban government outpost—the Moncada barracks—located in Cuba's Oriente Province. (The revolutionary effort thereafter was known as the 26th of July Movement.) The attackers were stopped, and most were either captured or shot. Fidel Castro was captured. After a heroic and well-published defense carrying the theme "history will absolve me," Castro was sentenced to fifteen years in prison. However, after three years he was released. In Mexico City, Castro soon made common cause with a young Argentine doctor, Ernesto "Che" Guevara, and about eighty others. Castro's tiny band of revolutionaries returned to Cuba in 1956. Paddling frantically to push ahead their wind-deprived sailboat, Castro and his group made it to a thick swamp just shy of Cuba's Sierra Mountains.

In only three months Castro's derring-do and reputation among peasants attracted international attention. In a three-part article Herbert Mathews, an American foreign correspondent for the *New York Times*, detailed Castro's "overpowering" personality and the rationale of his cause. The 29-year-old Castro was depicted like a budding matinee idol—a "powerful six footer, olive-skinner . . . and dressed in a gray fatigue uniform," Mathews wrote. The reassuring news for American readers was that Castro was a reincarnate Thomas Jefferson in fatigues—a "radical, democratic . . . anti-Communist," "with no animosity toward the United States." Retrospectively, Mathew's assessment of Castro as a man of destiny was accurate, but his portraits of Castro's views of the United States went wide of the mark. For a letter dated June 5, 1958, on display at the Museum of the Revolution in Havana, Castro told his secretary and confidant, Celia Sanche, that after the revolution there would be another armed effort—against the United States: "I feel," he confided, "that is my destiny."[3]

By the end of 1958 Castro's forces prospered and their numbers grew. The Cuban government's forces overreacted. The atrocities attendant to the efforts of Cuban dictator Fulgencio Batista at flushing out guerrillas produced new recruits for Castro. In short order, the redoubt of the 26th of July Movement grew quite large. With the support of a hospital, cigar factory, grocery store, and even a butcher and a baker, peasant-soldiers found not just promises but the structure of mutual aid that fortifies successful revolution. Meanwhile the long-time Cuban ruler, Fulgencio Batista, turned to air drops of napalm on suspected rebel emplacements as a counterinsurgent tactic. The results, as often as not, were even more recruits for Castro's cause. As his forces gained ground, there were significant costs exacted from American interests. Believing U.S. claims of evenhandedness to be a ruse, Raúl Castro, Fidel's younger brother and lieutenant, ordered the abduction of some fifty U.S. nationals, mostly Navy personnel and Marines. The capture of U.S. naval personnel incensed U.S. naval chief of staff Arleigh Burke, who requested that President Eisenhower authorize the roundup of Castro sympathizers at the U.S. naval base in Guantánamo, the apprehension of known rebel sympathizers in the United States, the release of U.S. turbojets suitable for close-in ground support, and the landing of a large number of Marines at Guantánamo.

Secretary of State John Foster Dulles and President Eisenhower, however, decided to negotiate with the rebels. As the secretary told a press conference on July 1, 1958, the United States was "willing to use any proper method to get the [hostages] out." The next day, the State Department suspended the sale of T-28 training turbo-prop planes indefinitely to the Cuban government. Batista and the U.S. embassy in Havana were outraged. But reports of Batista's unpopularity seemed to hold great weight with the Eisenhower administration.

Along with the increasing fragility of Cuba's governance, the Eisenhower administration was growing concerned about Cuba's shaky economy. The United States retained an immense financial stake in Cuba's sugar crop, oil refineries, electric power, and tourism. The rebels exacted "taxes" from all American sectors they could touch. And if the Americans hesitated, the rebels took U.S. nationals hostage in order to make their case more persuasive. Alarmed policymakers held meetings at the highest levels of the U.S. government to puzzle over a strategy. Yet in the end there was no recourse but to pay. Only as Castro's forces mobilized for a final assault did the Eisenhower administration seriously consider efforts for a "third way"—an alternative to both Castro and Batista.

In late November 1958, as Castro's noose started to tighten on Havana's railroads, water routes, and surrounding highway, long-time Eisenhower friend and former U.S. ambassador William Pawley appealed to the 58-year-old dictator:

I offered him [Batista] an opportunity to live at Daytona Beach, with his family and friends . . . [we] would make every effort to stop Fidel Castro from coming into power . . . but . . . the caretaker government would be men who were enemies.[4]

Meanwhile John McCone, deputy director of the CIA, informed Eisenhower that Castro now had the support of 95 percent of the Cuban population. A surprised Eisenhower wondered how a "rebel force gained strength so rapidly . . . a prospect [that he had] never heard before."[5] Perhaps reflecting how out of touch the president was becoming, Eisenhower said he would speak to Secretary of State John Foster Dulles, who lay mortally ill with cancer, to seek "better coordination" as to what the U.S. government might do.

Finally, Acting Secretary of State Christian Herter was asked to take charge. He instructed the reluctant U.S. ambassador to use all the means at the embassy's disposal to get Batista to abdicate. Batista fled in the last hours of 1958 with a huge quantity of Cuba's monetary reserves and his immediate family. Some 400,000 troops he once commanded were left to face Castro's ragtag thousands, who easily commandeered abandoned jeeps, trucks, and tanks in their final sweep toward Havana. There was no bloodbath, as the embassy feared. Four last-minute attempts by the CIA to find alternatives to Castro failed. By the second week of January 1959, Fidel Castro and his followers were firmly in charge.

Fulgencio Batista, personally a "nice man" in Eisenhower's view, was denied a visa to the United States. Regardless of his private view of Batista, Eisenhower was not about to sully the United States as a sanctuary for dictators. The president would try to get along with Castro.

FIDELISM: FIRST SHADOWS

Although many Americans believed Castro to be a genuine, heroic nationalist liberator, U.S. officials kept their fingers crossed as Havana approached chaos. Prisoners of all kinds were freed. Cuban workers walked off the job. American tourists were stranded as rebels took the hotels for their own use. A U.S.-flagged cruise ship directed to pick up Americans was refused a berth. From his sickbed, John Foster Dulles signed a message that accepting "statement[s] of intention of the new government" of Cuba were "made in good faith and that it is our national interest to recognize the Provisional government of Cuba without delay."[6] Thereafter the way for U.S. nationals to leave Havana started to open up.

But Castro's initial remarks hardly gave heart to U.S. officials who hoped for a normal relationship with Cuba. In his first conversation with Cuban and American business leaders, Castro announced that the U.S. military missions should pack up and leave. More troubling was word of hundreds of executions. Finally, there was Castro's view of elections and revolutionary government: "[T]here is no danger of a dictatorship since a government becomes a dictatorship only when it lacks the support of the people, and this government has the support of all Cubans."[7]

At first, Fidel Castro was without any formal position in the 26th of July revolutionary government. Soon, however, reports surfaced in the American press that he was soliciting arms assistance from the Soviet Bloc. The U.S. State Department's assessment was disturbing. Castro, U.S. analysts concluded, was prone to "violence" and freely allowed "his top leaders . . . [to pursue] contacts with Communists-front groups." But the State Department held out the hope that there was no real evidence "that Castro is a Communist sympathizer."[8]

Whether or not Castro was a "Communist sympathizer," it was soon clear to most observers that he was intent on making a complete rupture with Cuba's recent past by pinning all the evils of the old order on the work of the United States. One Havana joke of the day summed up the thinking of the new regime:

A revolutionary, named Arturo, unexpectedly dies. Pallbearer X speaks to pallbearer Y on the other side of the coffin.

Pallbearer X: Ah yes, it was imperialism that did him in.

Pallbearer Y: What do you mean?! Arturo was hit by car!

Pallbearer X: Yes exactly! It was a Ford!

Cuban capital, both human and financial, now flooded Miami as production, exports, and tourism plummeted. Castro predicted an imminent American armed attempt to overthrow, with the result that there would be "200,000 dead gringos in the streets" and that the U.S. intervention force would have to "kill 6 million Cubans" before it would see any success. To the U.S. officials, however, Castro's first remarks were viewed as merely "rhetorical."[9]

Given the Americans' inclination to discount the worst, there was nothing naïve in the mandate of a Cuban delegation that arrived in the United States at the end of March 1959 to request a $100 million aid package. The U.S. government, in fact, exceeded Cuban expectations, approving up to $800 million.[10]

But at the same time that his representatives were petitioning the United States for aid, Castro was chipping away at its predominate position. First, he overtly sought additional sources of aid from other governments in the hemisphere; second, his representatives covertly wooed emissaries from the Soviet Bloc; third, he sent some of his more enthusiastic acolytes to Latin America in order to widen his revolutionary base. U.S. naval intelligence soon got wind of these efforts and predicted invasion of Haiti, Santo Domingo, Paraguay, and Nicaragua, all manned by "exiles from all over the Caribbean" who reportedly "flocked into Havana" for instruction and succor.[11]

Castro, at the age of 32, decided to assume the formal role of prime minister in early March 1959. Reportedly he was working twenty-two hours a day dictating policy. One might think he would have concerns other than worrying about the fate of neighboring countries. But Castro—like the French Revolutionaries, like Lenin, and even like Jefferson—believed if others emulated Cuba's revolutionary example, then Cuba would obtain new allies who would give it a margin of safety from the anticipated onslaught of a larger power (in this case, the United States). For Castro was convinced that an invasion would take place, no matter what the initial indications of good will from the United States might seem to portend.

On March 3, 1959, forty-four airmen who had served in Batista's air force were found innocent of various crimes against the Cuban people by a judicial court. Castro immediately went on television and, in an angry sermon on revolutionary justice, ordered a new trial. Another trial was immediately held—and the airmen were found guilty and sentenced to prison terms ranging from two to thirty-three years. Privately, the American embassy discovered that more than three hundred associates of the Batista regime had already been executed. In fact, the numbers were even larger.

U.S. congressman Adam Clayton Powell, an early supporter of Castro, also offered the administration additional and damning information. Powell, a powerful and flamboyant Democratic Party member of Congress from Harlem, reported that Castro had "gone haywire." The secret of Castro's legendary work habits, said Powell, was "Dexedrine," a powerful amphetamine; but the result was "incoherent" speeches and conversations so confused that Castro's closest associates were often reduced to tears. Confusion at the top only made Havana's pervasive "sense of fear" and resentment worse. Midnight tribunals, draconian wage reduction, rent cuts, and skyrocketing unemployment struck Powell as equal parts farce, travesty, and wickedness.[12]

A respected patriarch of Latin America, José Figuieres, the president of Costa Rica, echoed Powell's report. Figuieres sent word to Washington that Castro was "off his rocker." The effect of barbiturates, overwork, sleep deprivation, and the influence of out-and-out Communists like Che Guevara and Raúl Castro were bringing Cuba to the edge of disaster, claimed Figuieres.[13]

But to the U.S. embassy staff in Havana, Castro was not showing any signs of a breakdown nor was there any reason to fear the emergence of a Communist government. The only question that preoccupied the embassy staff was how U.S. officials should deal with Castro after he accepted an invitation to speak before the American Society of Newspaper Editors in Washington, D.C., in April.

Indeed, Acting Secretary of State Christian Herter was more perturbed over Castro's "singularly bad behavior" in accepting the American Society of Newspaper Editors invitation "without even informing the State Department."[14] Eisenhower's own predilection was to see if a visa could be denied Castro. But to CIA chief Allen Dulles, a policy of not letting Castro into the United States would "backfire" and actually give unnecessary legitimacy to Castro's anti-Americanism.[15] Not that the CIA was partial to Castro. The Communists, Dulles reported, had well penetrated the Cuban government and were pursuing plans to unseat the "remaining dictators in Latin America." Dulles hoped that Congress might soon taken the initiative and cut off Cuba's ability to export sugar to the United States at favorable prices. The president responded to Dulles with remarkable prescience, predicting that then the Soviets would pick up the slack and America, not Cuba, would be "in the soup."[16]

Castro knew that most Cubans were not ready to embrace the Soviets or break with the United States. Cuba seriously needed whatever aid and stabilization funds Washington could offer. The funds had been promised, but they had not yet been delivered. Castro's immediate purpose was to placate the American public in order to secure the promised financing. Touching every major bastion of American ruling elite—including Washington, Princeton, New York City, Boston, and Houston and a stopover in Canada—during his April visit Castro presented the revolution's best face. Behind the curtain of speechifying and flim-flam in the United States lay an ongoing and covert courtship of the Soviet Union. Castro seemed to calculate that if the Russians saw him on the edge of a rapprochement with the American imperialists, perhaps the Soviet Bloc would be more responsive to his private requests for arms and aid.

By and large, Castro's effort was amazingly successful. In every American forum—television interviews; private audiences; appearances before thousands of students at Princeton, Yale, and Harvard; to a televised assemblage of the UN—Castro denied that he entertained any affection for a Communist doctrine that would rob Cubans of their newly won independence.

The U.S. government, in fact, was reassured by Castro's visit. Herter reported to Eisenhower that he now regretted the president had not met with Castro personally, because Castro turned out to be a "most interesting individual, very much like a child . . . puzzled and confused by the practical difficulties."[17] Vice President Richard Nixon confided to Eisenhower a similar impression, stating that Castro was "either incredibly naïve about communism or under communist domination—my guess is the former. . . . [H]is ideas . . . are less developed than those of almost any world figure I have met in fifty countries." The State Department's typically neutral comment was that Castro was "enigma."[18] Eisenhower wrote of this observation, "We'll see in a year."[19]

CUBA, THE COMMUNIST WORLD, AND THE SINO-SOVIET SPLIT

Che Guevara had been a young Argentine doctor living Guatemala when the CIA helped engineer the overthrow of an elected Marxist government there led by Jacobo Arbenz. Che and his closest associate, Raúl Castro, understood that any future revolution would need what Arbenz lacked: a loyal gendarmerie. Hence the logic of Raúl Castro's petition to the Soviet Union for security assistance once Fidel Castro had assumed power in Havana. The younger Castro's overture for covert assistance in building Cuba's security forces, in the spring of 1960, was soon made good.

Cuba's leftward movement was accelerating. The new land reform package was given over to the administration of Osvaldo Dorticós, well known as an important member of the Cuban Communist Party. This was meant as a public gesture to the leader of the Soviet Bloc, Nikita Khrushchev.

At the time the Castros were placing Cuban security out for tenders, the Soviets were in need of allies. More concrete was the Soviet fear that the Chinese might seduce Castro and other emergent nationalist governments and substitute China for the Soviet Union at the forefront of revolution.

Mao Tse Tung's spectacular and risky economic one-upsmanship, the Great Leap Forward, had aimed at reducing Chinese dependence on Moscow. And China was wholly unsympathetic to change in Russia regarding the unflattering reassessment of Joseph Stalin and the search for a more moderate international atmosphere. As the Chinese demanded ever more military and economic aid from the Soviets, the Russian hierarchs began to rethink their nuclear and missile programs in China. Khrushchev made three visits in an eighteen-month period at the end of the 1950s to smooth relations between Mao Tse Tung and Moscow. Mao considered Khrushchev a lightweight and was deliberately provocative. Dr. Li Zhisui, Mao's physician, subsequently remembered "the Chairman . . . deliberately playing the role of emperor, treating Khrushchev like the barbarian come to pay tribute." As Mao put it more crudely to Dr. Li, he enjoyed toying with the Soviet dictator and "sticking a needle up his ass."[20]

In September 1958, China did inform Moscow of an offensive against Taiwan that could have pulled Russia and China into a war with the United States. But Khrushchev dutifully supported Mao's initiative—a vast bombardment of a Chinese Nationalist position on two islands close to the mainland. For weeks, Chinese gunners shot some 41,000 shells a day. Notwithstanding a vast Soviet resupply effort, the U.S. Navy and Air Force helped Taiwan regain local superiority. Mao was forced to back down, for the time being. But he told a closed gathering of Chinese officials, "If we must fight, we will fight. If half the people die, there is still nothing to fear."[21]

Mao's apparent indifference to war shocked the Russians. What they found especially astonishing were Mao's suggestions that American troops be tempted to invade China: U.S. soldiers would be allowed to penetrate the country deeply; once ensnared in China's heartland, they could be wiped out by a Soviet nuclear strike. Mao's insouciance toward the possibility of nuclear war chilled the Kremlin. And his tendency to regard Khrushchev's reluctance to take further risk irked the Soviet leader. Mao, he remembered, "obviously regarded me as a coward."[22]

In Khrushchev's third and last trip to Beijing, Mao refused to allow him to offer Eisenhower the release of two American pilots who had parachuted into northern China around the time of the Korean War. In the context of the burgeoning Berlin crisis the gesture would have been useful; at the same time it would have conveyed the impression of Soviet Bloc solidarity and hence burnished the Western impression of Russian power. But the Chinese refused.

Fed up, the Russians suddenly pulled out of China. Nuclear cooperation between the two powers fizzled in 1959. By the fall of 1960, all other military and economic cooperation ended. Soviet advisors withdrew. Rolled-up blueprints were put in briefcases and carried back to Russia. A total of 1,390 experts went home. Over 350 contracted projects were aborted.[23]

Facing critics who claimed Khrushchev had been duped into believing he could have a rapprochement with Eisenhower, and abandoned by the Chinese, the Soviet premier strove to give a new definition to the concept of "socialist unity." In public in 1961, Khrushchev began to promise vigorous Soviet-led Communist competition for those areas still under, or emerging from, Western tutelage.

NOTES

1. Theodore C. Sorensen, *Kennedy* (New York: Bantam, 1969), p. 256.

2. Theodore H. White, *The Making of the President: 1960* (New York: New American Library, Signet Edition, 1967), pp. 204–5.

3. Ernesto F. Betancourt, "Kennedy, Khrushchev, and Castro," *Society* 35, no. 5 (1998): p. 77ff.

4. *Foreign Relations of the United States* (FRUS), Vol. VI (Washington, DC: U.S. Government Printing Office, 1991), Doc. 173, p. 281.

5. *The Declassified Documents Quarterly* (Woodbridge, CT: Research Publications, 1983), p. 1342.

6. FRUS, Vol. VI, Doc. 217.

7. Cited by the U.S. ambassador in Cuba, 9 January 1959. FRUS, Vol. VI, p. 394ff.

8. Ibid., p. 356.

9. Ibid., p. 402.

10. Ibid., p. 408.

11. Ibid., p. 396.

12. Ibid., p. 425ff.

13. FRUS, Vol. VI, Doc. 267, pp. 442–44.

14. FRUS, Vol. VI, Doc. 266.

15. FRUS, Vol. VI, p. 442.

16. Ibid.

17. Ibid., p. 475.

18. FRUS, Vol. VI, Doc. 287, p. 476.

19. FRUS, Vol. VI, Doc. 292, fn., p. 382.

20. Li Zhisui, *The Private Life of Chairman Mao* (New York: Random House, 1994), p. 261.

21. Mark Kramer, *The Soviet Foreign Ministry Appraisal of Sino-Soviet Relations on the Eve of the Split*, Bulletin 6–7 (Washington, DC: Woodrow Wilson International Center for Scholars, n.d.) <cwihp.si.edu>.

22. William Taubman, *Khrushchev vs. Mao: A Preliminary Sketch of the Role of Personality in the Sino–Soviet Split*, Bulletin 8–9 (Washington, DC: Woodrow Wilson International Center for Scholars, n.d.) <cwihp.si.edu>.

23. John Gittings, ed., *Survey of the Sino-Soviet Dispute* (London: Oxford University Press, 1968), p. 139.

4

Cuba: Cold War Competition and Containment by Stealth

In the Eisenhower-Dulles years, competition with the Russians had already moved out of Europe. Even President Eisenhower, ever sensitive to allied interests, was hardly sympathetic to the classic colonial interests of Britain and France. But American access to a market closed by European colonialism was one thing; the adoption of socialism and the supporting of the Soviets in the UN by a country emerging from colonialism was quite another—and, to U.S. officials, a much more serious matter.

PRELUDES AND OVERTURES ...
TO THE BAY OF PIGS

Eisenhower had a real horror of war and the costs associated with preparing for conflict with a great adversary like Russia. The logic of covert intervention in the third world was more consonant with the foreign affairs stewardship of his administration. It avoided direct confrontation with Russia, limited risks to American servicemen, and was, like the nuclear deterrent, part of the administration's preference for getting "more bang for the buck."

The price of using troops in Korea from 1950 to 1953 had been enormous: some $70 billion a year had been spent in that "limited" effort, and over 47,000 U.S. servicemen had died. The presidency itself could be counted as a casualty of the Korean War, for it was Harry Truman who left office with the lowest levels of public support in the history of American polling.

One alternative to using troops in the third world—covert intervention—seemed a ferry that would carry all loads. Eisenhower apparently thought that covert action might sustain containment, advance American interests, and avoid costly confrontations.

Coup in Iran

In March 1953, Eisenhower reached an agreement with British prime minister Anthony Eden that it was time to seek a new leadership in Iran. Mohammed Mossadegh, Iran's elected premier and a nationalist, threatened to leave Britain with virtually no petroleum source.

When Mohammed Mossadegh became prime minister of Iran in 1951, he soon entered into a competition with the young "shah," 31-year-old Mohammed Reza Pahlavi, for power. The young shah had courted the United States during World War II in the hope that the United States would favor an independent postwar Iran. In the spring and early summer of 1953, the CIA, working with the British, sponsored an uprising against Mossadegh and his nationalists. First the shah fled, making his way to Rome where he was soothed and reassured by no other than CIA chief Allen Dulles. Then, twelve days later, Mossadegh departed under pressure but was captured before he could make his way out of Tehran. He was sentenced to three years in prison and put under house arrest on his country estate. On August 22, twelve days after he had fled, the shah returned to Tehran and became the new premier. But Mossadegh remained a potent symbol of secular nationalism. Released from confinement on grounds of old age, an elderly Mossadegh would still be able to command a throng of 80,000 cheering well-wishers even in Iran, a country already famous for repression.[1]

The British never did regain their old dominance because 40 percent of the new Anglo-Iranian Oil Company was now owned by the Americans. The rest was shared between Iran and a number of other international partners.[2]

In succeeding years the United States regarded the shah as a key ally in the Middle East and provided Iran with billions of dollars in aid and arms. Growing protest from exiled Iranians and from within Iran against the shah's rule were heeded by the Carter administration. Gradually, U.S. policy evolved from asking the shah to share power, to asking him to relinquish power, to, finally, asking him to leave the country. On January 16, 1979, the shah, faced with mobs of excited Iranians, left Iran as he had in 1953; this time, it was for good.

But for Eisenhower, the example of Iran had become the template for the most successful elements of the strategy of containment. Containment by coup seemed cheap and effective. It appeared to serve every interest from economic expansion to geo-strategically out-maneuvering the Soviets. It was irresistible.[3]

Coup in Guatemala

Unlike Iran, Eisenhower soon confronted a nationalist challenge that was significantly dependent on domestic Communists for support. There was a succession of dictators who serviced and promoted a vast concentration of private American political and economic power in Guatemala. Of primary influence in Guatemala was the United Fruit Company. Since the late nineteenth century, it had controlled vast tracts of banana-producing and nonproducing acreage and owned banks, towns, and even the nation's railroad. When in 1944, General Jorge Ubico, an avowed admirer of Hitler, was overthrown, he was replaced by a military junta that included Jacobo Arbenz Guzman. Arbenz was subsequently elected president in 1951, and a number of Communists were taken into the government. Anticommunist labor and political leaders were suppressed.

In March 1953, matters came to a head as Arbenz expropriated more than 230,000 acres of uncultivated land for which United Fruit was compensated $600,000 in long-term interest-bearing bonds—the low valuation previously placed on the land by United Fruit to escape Guatemalan taxes. The president of United Fruit argued, "It's not a matter of the people of Guatemala against the United Fruit Company; the question is . . . communism against the right of property, the life and security of the Western Hemisphere."[4]

Washington came to see matters in a similar light. U.S. Ambassador to Guatemala John E. Puerifoy described Arbenz as a man who "thought like a Communist and talked like a Communist, and if not actually one, would do until one came along." Puerifoy reported his impressions to Secretary Dulles, who informed the President that "Guatemala would within six months fall completely under Communist control."[5]

Eisenhower authorized a covert action that resulted in a coup. The CIA employed Carlos Castillo Armas, a graduate of the U.S. Army Command and General Staff School, to lead a band of mercenaries from a base camp in Honduras with air support flown by American CIA pilots. Within a week, Arbenz was forced out. Armas arrived in Puerifoy's private plane and assumed power.

About 70 percent of the population was immediately taken off the elections role. In the March 1955 election, Castillo Armas received 99.9 percent of the votes cast. There was no opposition. Eisenhower noted in his memoirs that "Castillo Armas was . . . confirmed . . . by a thundering majority, as President. He proved to be far more than a mere rebel; he was a farseeing and able statesman . . . he enjoyed the devotion of his people."[6]

The President was, in the words of one White House operative in PB success, "pleased as punch."

The United Fruit Company lands previously parceled out to peasants were reassigned to the United Fruit Company. Labor organizations lost all rights. In short order, Castillo Armas established a committee that could secretly name anyone a Communist. Guatemalans so labeled were subject to immediate detention and execution. Tens of thousands were arrested and shot within months. The killing went on for years.

It would be easy to dismiss Eisenhower as merely a disingenuous and hypocritical captain of American imperialism—a label that, in fact, found resonance in leftist political circles for years. But the context of these interventions must be understood. Eisenhower and Dulles found it difficult to believe that revolutionary change in the non-Western world might be the product of indigenous forces. After all, from the standpoint of the imperatives of American policy of the day—containment—Washington generally viewed revolutionary leftist political activity as a product of external Sino-Soviet penetration. Moreover, even if U.S. policymakers had regarded such revolutionary change as legitimate (and there is no evidence whatsoever that they did), U.S. domestic politics precluded admitting such a thing.

Hence despite the initial press in the United States of the private circumspection of U.S. embassy staff in Havana, it was unlikely that the Eisenhower administration would embrace Castro or his regime. The means to confront a Communist-leaning Cuba were well honed, deniable, cheap, and, it was believed, effective. The CIA had become instrumental in keeping dominos from falling in South Vietnam, Iran, and Guatemala. Why should it not be used only 90 miles from Key West, Florida? This was a question the CIA itself raised soon enough.

CASTRO COURTS THE SOVIETS

In the summer of 1959, a high-level Cuban defector brought word of Soviet plans to send covert Spanish Civil War–era trainers to Cuba and, even more disturbing, news of Cuba's request for top-of-the-line, Soviet-designed Czech MIG fighter-bombers, too. If Khrushchev and some of his closer associates thought they could brighten the prospects for rapprochement in Europe with Eisenhower or Kennedy while striving to penetrate the Western Hemisphere, it was a misapprehension.

Alarm in the Eisenhower administration was palpable. Emblematic of the rising U.S. concern over Cuba was a Cabinet meeting chaired by Eisenhower, who suggested that "evidence Castro himself was tilting toward the Communists in Cuba or the Soviets" was one thing, but if and when the Cubans joined the Soviet Bloc, the president "would have to go to Congress to start a war with Cuba."[7]

Castro—perhaps more than the Russians—understood American hemispheric sensitivities, geopolitical interests, and the sway that American investors held in the Eisenhower administration. Although Castro's closest lieutenants spent months imploring the Soviets to take the first step to accustom the Cuban public to a new Soviet-Cuban relationship, Castro remained cautious. When, at last, a traveling Russian cultural exhibit was scheduled to visit Cuba, Castro had second thoughts. Mercurial as ever, he fretted about the likely U.S. reaction. Anastas Mikoyan, one of the Russian regime's old Bolsheviks, exploded in exasperation: "How could the opening of a cultural exhibit bother the enemy?"[8] But dance troupes, ping-pong, soccer, art, and even traveling professors were as much the stuff of real diplomacy as official delegations and treaties. And Castro understood how they would play to American audiences, even vicariously.

Khrushchev strove to give new life to Russian leadership and had picked the third world in which to demonstrate his mastery of world communism at a time when Castro and his closest lieutenants were trolling for support in the socialist bloc. Meanwhile, the Eisenhower administration had promoted the CIA to meet the challenge of revolution in the developing world. For the Eisenhower administration, the distance from Guatemala to Cuba was short in every sense. Having succeeded in orchestrating a remarkably successful coup in Guatemala, it seemed only logical for the United States, once Castro and the Soviets openly embraced, to consider what Castro had so long predicted: some kind of undertaking to remove, or at least discourage, socialism's newest apprentice.

PLANNING FOR CASTRO'S DOWNFALL

Castro's initial visit to the United States—Operation Truth, as he dubbed it—succeeded in allaying a growing conviction that Castro had to be undone. Both Vice President Richard Nixon and the new U.S. ambassador to Cuba, Philip Bosnal, thought Castro "could be handled."[9] But within days of returning from his American tour, Castro started to present a different and disturbing face to the United States.

An even more draconian agrarian reform law was suddenly presented to the large landowners of Cuba; modeled on the Stalinist example, it was drafted by Che Guevara and dated May 17, 1959. Indeed, Cuba was in desperate need of reform. As John Kennedy noted on the Senate floor in 1959, American firms essentially controlled Cuba in a way that was hardly congruent with an independent nation:

United States companies owned 40 percent of all sugar lands, almost all the cattle ranches, 90 percent of the mines and the mineral concessions, 80 percent of the utilities, practically all the oil industry and supplied two-thirds of Cuba's imports.[10]

Notwithstanding some public U.S. sympathy to Cuba's land policies, Castro expected the worst from the Americans. Perhaps the first reports of "plots" were nothing more than a fictive warrant for the Cuban premier to authorize more arrests, more confiscations, and further controls over Cuban society. But the United States, in turn, developed an antipathy to the Soviet police-state style of Castro and his entourage. The initial agnosticism about the character of Castro's regime and rather fatuous assumption that he could be "managed" faded. In its stead, the Eisenhower administration in the summer of 1959 heard alarm bells.

CIA Plans Accelerate

By June 1959, CIA director Allen Dulles lobbied Eisenhower to take action against Cuba along the Guatemalan-Iranian model. By mid-summer 1959, Eisenhower was on record expressing doubt that Castro would ever allow room for alternative domestic challenges to his rule. The CIA was thereupon instructed to discuss the creation of a paramilitary capability to be used in a number of "Latin American crisis situations . . . of which Cuba . . . was only one of a number of possible targets."[11] Most of the CIA's work immediately gravitated toward Cuba.

Intelligence planning to destabilize Castro accelerated. It is an open question whether the CIA had a hand in provoking the go-ahead for the very measures it was contemplating, but the coincident rise of anti-Castro activity among Cuban exiles convinced the Castro regime that the United States was upping the pressure. For instance, on October 11, 1959, an unidentified airplane dropped incendiaries on a Cuban sugar mill. Without any evidence, the Cubans assumed that the airplane was part of a U.S. conspiracy and launched a series of protests. Most members of the U.S. government, however, seemed equally puzzled at how these events had transpired and were angered by Castro's charges. Indeed, there were U.S. Cabinet–level discussions on how U.S. Coast Guard, Federal Aviation Authority, FBI, and local police could coordinate to prevent Cuban exiles from using U.S. territory as a springboard for any kind of invasion or sabotage.

From the summer of 1959 on—and perhaps even earlier—the CIA discussed undoing Castro. But the record does not reveal exactly when such activity was authorized by the president. The White House's National Security Council (NSC) records, for instance, are nearly barren of any mention of CIA operations; indeed, the president told Allen Dulles not to "offer the specifics of covert operations"[12] to the NSC at the end of the Batista regime in December 1958. No doubt the same caution was exercised by Eisenhower as he contemplated thwarting Castro starting in mid-1959.

What is known is that in November 1959 a formal interagency decision was taken to work with anti-Castro groups to "check" or replace Castro.[13] It is unclear what the first fruits of this effort were. On March 4, 1960, a Belgian freighter, the *Coubre*, carrying arms to the Castro government, exploded unaccountably close to shore in Havana harbor, killing more than 100 civilians. Eisenhower's aides denied U.S. complicity in the incident, and no documents or evidence exist to indicate that the United States had a hand in the tragedy. Yet the United States had tried to dissuade the Europeans in general and the Belgians in particular from sending arms to Castro. And exile-based sabotage against the Castro regime was growing, it seemed, by the day.

Castro, long convinced that the CIA was bent on undoing the 26th of July Movement at any cost, declared the *Coubre* explosion an American plot against Cuba. He thundered that Cuba "would never be intimidated." Then he pounded on with what would be the war cry for years: "*Patria O Muerte!*" (Victory or Death!).

From the French Revolution to the present, the battle cry "the Revolution is in danger" has been used to secure greater governmental power. Castro's anger was no doubt real and unfeigned, but the *Coubre* event energized his embrace of the example and assistance of Soviet security forces in order to guarantee his revolution. Days after the explosion of the *Coubre*, Castro quietly informed the Soviets that he planned to accelerate domestic control in Cuba. "Counter-revolutionaries" would be ruthlessly hunted. Cuba would be purged of "worms" who would destroy the revolution from within or endanger it from without by abetting the coming Yankee invasion. The revolution would be defended to the "last drop of blood."[14]

Two weeks after the *Coubre* explosion, on March 16, 1960, the CIA unveiled a formal program to senior Eisenhower administration foreign policy officials to overthrow Castro by means of invasion. Preparations for an invasion had been in the works for some time. The March 16 planning document, for instance, contains a section stating that work was "already in progress in the creation of a covert intelligence and action organization within Cuba which will be responsible to an 'exile' opposition.' "[15] The

CIA expected that the group with which it had contact would be "ready" within sixty days. But ready for what? A coup? Sabotage? The staging of some sort of provocation? If an invasion were in the works, planning would have begun in earnest and at least parts of it would have been cleared by certain elements of the elaborate American foreign affairs machinery months earlier.

CIA plans to unseat Castro could not have proceeded without the sanction of the president. Part of the March 1960 invasion contingencies seem to be linked, therefore, at the highest level of the U.S. government to a winter 1959 CIA go-ahead to its Special Services Division. An assortment of gadgets, such as silenced guns, knives, poisoned cigars, and poisoned scuba gear, were released and others devised to kill Fidel Castro. Presidential involvement seems certain, as it was congruent both with Eisenhower's style and with his close relationship with Allen Dulles. Eisenhower's vice president, Richard Nixon, also seems to have been intimately involved with the administration's clandestine maneuvers against Castro, which further suggests that Eisenhower would have known of, and approved, the CIA plans.[16]

Cuba: Trade and Imperial Practice at Mid-Century

Undoubtedly the planning for the invasion of Cuba gathered a powerful warrant from the remarkable visit, in early February 1960, by Anastas Mikoyan, deputy premier of the Soviet Union. A man with the dour Soviet-era mien of an Armenian waiter, Mikoyan was a man whom the West considered a kind of *bazzari*, a sort of wily rug merchant. True to his billing, the Soviets offered Castro a rather lopsided deal. The Russians would assume a large part of the Cuban sugar crop—a commodity the Soviets had no need of because they generally used beet sugar, not cane sugar, for their confections and tea. In giving up its sugar that could not otherwise be sold, Cuba received oil, which had formerly been provided by the West at world market prices. Soviet oil was of poorer quality and came at a somewhat higher nominal price, at least at first. Military aid and technical economic assistance were also thrown in, as one type of imperialism was substituted for another.

At this time "Big Oil" was at its apogee in the councils of the U.S. government. Eisenhower had helped to position U.S.-based Esso in Iran even while domestic oil production was at 90 percent of American consumption. Eisenhower was a logistician. Oil, he knew, was the choke point of the capitalist world economy; and Eisenhower, the Soviets, and the Cubans understood the special sensitivity and strategic nature of petroleum. When American refiners refused to process Soviet oil shipped to Cuba, it was not just a confirmation of implacable American hostility. It seemed an invitation to Castro to proceed with the complete nationalization of foreign-owned oil processing and storage. The American foreign policy community was as angered as it was convinced that Castro had irretrievably left the camp of the West. The whole interaction of Castro and the United States was a kind of textbook proof of modern social science wisdom that "things defined as real become real in their consequences."

Meanwhile the American public was repulsed by Castro's excesses. Some 8,000 political prisoners were said to have been jailed in the first year and half of his rule. Many were condemned to be in prisons for decades. Firing squads eliminated hundreds, with the bloody work largely overseen by Castro's brother Raúl. "[T]here's always a priest on hand to hear the last confession," Raúl flintily commented to those who claimed the regime lacked compassion.

But what exhausted Eisenhower's patience the most, apparently, was what Castro had done to U.S. business interests in Cuba. The American secretary of defense, Charles Wilson, the former chief executive officer of General Motors, had gained certain fame when explaining his philosophy of government: "What's good for General Motors would be good for" the United States. The sentiment was real. And it looked to the administration in Washington as if the whole of a sixty-year political investment and close to $1 billion in private investment had come to nothing.

Eliminating Castro

By the time Soviet trade with Cuba began to supplant the former American contribution to the Cuban economy, the United States considered ever more energetic measures to deal with Fidel Castro. A grand array of options was pondered, ranging from the comic to the malign. An example of the former was a plan to dust thallium powder into Castro's shoes as they were put out at night to be shined at a hotel. Thallium salts are a depilatory. If *El Jefe Supremo* were to lose all his hair—including, of course, his famous beard—then, the CIA suggested, his revolutionary credentials would also vanish! Neither Castro nor his shoes were secured, and Castro was left with his follicles unmolested.

The CIA also rigged up exploding seashells that, when brought to the surface by a scuba-diving Castro, would be set off by a radio signal from a nearby U.S.-manned ship. Even more disturbing was the use of Chicago- and Miami-based mobsters. The criminals who had lost their gambling franchise in Cuba would be "the ultimate cover," in the words of CIA planner Richard Bissell. Lucky Luciano and other notorious gangsters, the CIA ascertained, were more than willing to murder Fidel. There is abundant testimony that Sam Gianacana and John Rosselli, two Chicago mobsters, were singled out for their alleged skill in the arts of eliminating inconvenient persons. Rifles were dropped to Mafia-contracted assassins. The Mafia also retained several women of uncertain virtue who were tasked to seduce and poison Castro.[17]

That the United States was proving hostile and aggressive was no surprise to Castro, although the Soviets seem to have been taken aback by the ferocity of America's determination to regain control over the island. But the fact that Soviet influence was even greater than had been supposed can be attributed, in no small way, to the sheer extent of American efforts to redirect Cuba.

NOTES

1. Andrew Tully, *The CIA* (New York: William Morrow & Co., 1962), p. 98. Tully puts Mossadegh's age at 79, but Mossadegh reportedly was born in 1880, making him 81 in 1961. See Jonathan Kwitny, *Endless Enemies: The Making of an Unfriendly World* (New York: Congdon & Weed, 1984), p. 168.

2. Daniel Yergin, *The Prize: The Epic Quest for Oil, Money, and Power* (New York: Simon & Schuster, 1991); and Daniel Yergin, *Shattered Peace: The Origins of the Cold War and the National Security State* (Boston: Houghton Mifflin, 1978), pp. 180ff.

3. Dwight D. Eisenhower, *The White House Years: Mandate for Change, 1953–1956* (Garden City, N.Y.: Doubleday & Co., 1963), pp. 163ff.

4. Peter Lyon, *Eisenhower: Portrait of the Hero* (Boston: Little, Brown, 1974), p. 590.

5. Testimony before U.S. Congress, House Select Committee on Communist Aggression, *Hearings Before the Subcommittee on Latin America*, 83rd Cong., 2nd sess., 1954, pp. 24–26.

6. Eisenhower, *The White House Years*, p. 426.

7. Michael R. Bechloss, *The Crisis Years: Kennedy and Khrushchev, 1960–1963* (New York: HarperCollins, 1991), p. 97.

8. Alexander Fursenko and Timothy Naftali, *One Hell of a Gamble* (New York: Norton, 1997), p. 34.

9. Robert Smith Thompson, *The Missiles of October: The Declassified Story of John F. Kennedy and the Cuban Missile Crisis* (New York: Simon & Schuster, 1992), p. 86.

10. Fursenko and Naftali, *One Hell of a Gamble*, p. 65.

11. Central Intelligence Agency, *Inspector General Report: Inspector General's Survey of the Cuban Operation—October 1961* <http://www.seas.gwu.edu/nsarchive/latin_america/cuba/ig_report/index.html>.

12. *Foreign Relations of the United States* (FRUS), Vol. VI (Washington, DC: U.S. Government Printing Office, 1991), Doc. 191.

13. FRUS, Vol. V, Doc. 387.

14. Fursenko and Naftali, *One Hell of a Gamble*, p. 41.

15. http://www.seas.gwu.edu/nsarchive/latin_america/cuba/ig_report/index.html>.

16. Bechloss, *The Crisis Years*, pp. 134–36.

17. U.S. Senate, *Alleged Assassination Plots Involving Foreign Leaders: An Interim Report of the Select Committee to Study Government Operations with Respect to Intelligence Activities*, 94th Cong., 1st sess., Report no. 94–465 (Washington, DC: U.S. Government Printing Office, 1975), pp. 72–109.

5

The Politics of a "Perfect Failure": The Bay of Pigs Invasion

In June 1960, the Soviets treated Raúl Castro to a triumphal public trip to Moscow. After a lavish reception, Fidel Castro's younger brother was surprised and delighted with the Kremlin's offer of thirty top-of-the-line-tanks and 100,000 first-quality rifles, ten times the amount Fidel had hoped for. The price, the Soviets said, would be nominal—or, as Deputy Premier Anastas Mikoyan put it, purely symbolic—because the Soviets were now committed to socialist fraternity with Cuba.

The expansion of Communism propelled the Eisenhower administration to look for new ways of reversing the Cuban revolution. By mid-1960, ridding Cuba of Castro would not work in the absence of other efforts. The Communist Party of Cuba had grown from some 10,000 members at the time of revolution to 130,000 in the spring of 1960. But it was the conjunction of motivations that drove the Eisenhower administration to mount the largest covert campaign in the history of the CIA. First, there was the fate of American interests on the island. Second, there was the tightening of internal control alongside of Castro's increasingly inflammatory rhetoric after the *Coubre* incident. Third, there were the military ties between Castro and the Communist Bloc. All were sufficient to compel Eisenhower to authorize a program that included the invasion of Cuba.

As the government mobilized to prepare for an invasion, CIA director Allen Dulles was instructed by the president "to make sure that all participants were 'prepared to swear that they never heard of it.' "[1] But Eisenhower's calculation that the only "two or three people" in the U.S. government should be "directly connected" with the invasion planning in "any way" was unrealistic.

How was the United States to mobilize the resources for what was called at first Operation Trinidad without alerting the bureaucracy and, for that matter, the U.S. press and the Cubans as well? It could not be done. A covert invasion was thus doomed to fail on two scores. First, if it were to be a secret, it had to be small and hence too underfunded in terms of men and materiel to dislodge Castro and his hundreds of thousands of troops and militia. Second, if it were to be a brigade-size operation, it would be too large to be kept secret from anyone who followed current affairs in Latin America and, especially, Cuban and Soviet intelligence.

Inevitably, the requirements of the operation grew. The Guatemalan training redoubt chosen by the CIA was immense, occupying the entire side of a large mountain. As the scale of operation increased, the American imprimatur became clear. Senior State Department planners privy to the operation became concerned that the operation was attaining such a size that even if it were successful in regaining the island for American interests, it would nonetheless be regarded in the rest of the world much like the Soviet invasion of Hungary in 1956.[2]

KHRUSHCHEV AND CASTRO

The Soviets, knowing something of U.S. plans, extended the Soviet nuclear deterrent to Cuba. In July 1960, Nikita Khrushchev issued a public pledge. To a group of Russian teachers he proclaimed:

it should be borne in mind that the United States is not now at such an unattainable distance from the Soviet Union as formerly. Figuratively speaking, if need be, Soviet artillerymen can support the Cuban people with their rocket fire. . . . And the Pentagon could be well advised not to forget that . . . we have rockets which can land precisely in a present square targeted 13,000 kilometers away. This, if you want, is a warning to those who would like to solve international problems by force and not by reason.[3]

Eisenhower was not so much alarmed as he was irritated by the Soviets' indifference to traditional U.S. claims of an exclusive U.S. sphere of interest in Latin America. And although his administration was not fundamentally worried about what seemed familiar bluster, it felt it had to respond. Thus the import of Cuban sugar into the United States was virtually banned. The Soviets, as Eisenhower himself had predicted, then offered to purchase the entire Cuban sugar crop for the next two years—in advance.

In September 1960, Castro and Khrushchev both made a second journey to the United States. Castro's purpose was to counter American efforts to isolate him in the Organization of American States and the United Nations. Khrushchev's agenda was more complex, but he placed a personal meeting with Castro as a first priority because Castro had come to symbolize to the Bolshevik hierarchy a real vindication of the Soviet example. Musing in retrospect about the 1962 Cuban Missile Crisis, Deputy Premier Anastas Mikoyan explained:

You Americans must understand what Cuba means to us old Bolsheviks. We have been waiting all our lives for a country to go Communist without the Red Army, and it happened in Cuba. It makes us feel like boys again.[4]

The opening of the fifteenth session of the United Nations General Assembly was one of the strangest shows that New Yorkers had ever witnessed. Arriving at New York's Idlewild Airfield in the early fall of 1960, humping their own rucksacks and hammocks, a fifty-man Cuban delegation found itself detained until sidearms and rifles were checked with U.S. Customs agents. The unruly Cuban entourage soon made itself unwelcome at its assigned hotel and found alternative accommodations in a run-down area of Harlem. The Cubans paid twice the going rate and threw one party after another. It was a great propaganda coup. Fidel was making himself at home in the bosom of America's underclass and in the shadow of Wall Street.

Soon, Nikita Khrushchev made a well-publicized visit to Castro's hotel. Although he was taken aback at Castro's unusual appearance and messy accommodations, a picture of Castro's enthusiastic bear hug of the old Bolshevik was the stuff of headlines worldwide.

A few days later, at the UN, Khrushchev beat the table at which he sat with a shoe in order to make his displeasure known about U.S. policy, while Castro for the most part slouched in green combat fatigues, evidently stupefied with boredom. But when Khrushchev arose and began to speak about Cuba, Castro jumped up to cheer. When it came to be his turn, Castro declared that "[t]he Prime Minister of the Soviet Union [had spoken] clearly and sincerely . . . [and] I say this objectively." In contrast, "[t]he United States Government cannot [be said to] be for the integrity and sovereignty of nations."

Castro then listed a volley of complaints that consumed hours. He alleged that Cuba had been victimized by one sinister historical and current machination after another. Most important, Castro said, the United States was sponsoring "military training . . . in order to promote subversion and the landing of armed forces in our country." But "let us suppose for just a moment [that American planners are] mistaken . . . playing with the fate of the world. . . . [For W]e are living in the atomic age."

In a remarkable show of diplomatic boorishness, Castro denounced the American politicians. Senator John Kennedy, he said, was "an illiterate and ignorant millionaire" and an "imbecile." And as for "the other one, Mr. Nixon . . . [he also] lack[ed] political brains."[5]

The American political reaction to an insulting Bolshevik on its doorstep was predictable. Former president Harry Truman, commenting in Independence, Missouri, told the U.S. press that by letting Cuba fall into Communist hands Eisenhower and Nixon had "surrendered . . . the basic foundation of American foreign policy—the Monroe Doctrine" and had "exposed" the Panama Canal to mortal peril. Truman's conclusion was that the Eisenhower administration was riddled with "bums" who lacked the "guts" to rid America of a Communist bacillus.[6] Somewhat more temperate, John Kennedy suggested that the United States "strengthen . . . democratic anti Castro forces in exile." Thus far, Kennedy proclaimed (though he well knew otherwise), "these fighters for freedom have had virtually no support from the [Eisenhower] government."[7]

Stewing that Kennedy had unfairly alluded to intelligence briefings regarding CIA plans to invade Cuba, Vice President Richard Nixon faced the problematic task of defending President Eisenhower without revealing ongoing covert operations. In private, Nixon complained that the CIA—perhaps, he believed, riddled with liberal Democrats—was deliberately dawdling until the American presidential elections were over. Were they "falling dead over there?" he brooded.[8]

In fact, the Eisenhower administration was hardly sleeping. Indeed, CIA activities against Cuba and the preparations for an invasion had been so large in scale that they were reported from one end of Latin America to the other. A Latin American news report on the activities of the CIA camp in Guatemala was soon picked up by the Soviet paper *Izvestia*; then, in turn, the Soviet mission at the UN released even more details of preparations for an invasion by Cuban exiles, charges the U.S. government promptly denied.

By October 1960, Nixon could stomach no longer the role of defending an ostensible U.S. policy of tolerating Castro. With just two weeks left until election day, Nixon finally secured Eisenhower's permission to publicly announce that official U.S. forbearance of Cuba's socialist infatuation had ended. On October 19 a full-scale economic embargo was announced. Meanwhile, in Cuba, Castro stepped up police surveillance; arrests mounted as he announced a blood drive in preparation for the coming invasion. But after John F. Kennedy's victory in the U.S. presidential election, the "lame duck" Eisenhower administration was reluctant to authorize an action that President Eisenhower felt should be directed by the new administration

THE FIRST HUNDRED DAYS: FALSE STEPS

Incoming president John Kennedy had started to become convinced that Castro's example in Latin America was a critical threat. To Kennedy, the problem was not so much the Cuban revolution itself but the possibility that other impoverished Latin American peoples would embrace the Cuban example. If that happened, Kennedy calculated, the result would be catastrophic for the American position in the Cold War.

Khrushchev's speech in early 1961 declaring that the Soviets would support "wars of national liberation" was the first required reading of the new Kennedy administration team. A year later, in January 1962, Kennedy reminded the National Security Council that it was "one of the most important speeches of the decade." The Soviets, Kennedy said, had made it clear that "military and paramilitary subversion" would be the order of the day in Russian foreign policy.[9] To Secretary of State Dean Rusk, Khrushchev's speech was nothing short of a Soviet "Mein Kampf."

The day before his inauguration Kennedy met with Eisenhower, who urged Kennedy to support ongoing plans for guerrilla operations against Castro "to the utmost." But it is doubtful if the Kennedy team needed the old general's encouragement. The new administration was pledged to action. Cuba was at the top of the agenda of the president; his national security advisor, McGeorge Bundy; and the president's closest advisor of all, his brother Robert, the attorney general.[10]

Many of Kennedy's other senior policy advisors, especially in the State Department, opposed the operation. Dean Rusk fretted that an air campaign against Castro would condemn the United States to diplomatic isolation despite whatever success the invasion might have. Rusk was not alone in his doubts. But neither the incoming secretary of defense, Robert McNamara, nor the chairman of the Joint Chiefs of Staff, General Lyman Lemnitzer, were successful in conveying their doubts.

Lemnitzer, according to one report, sent a memo to McNamara arguing that a single Cuban training craft could sink the entire invasion fleet. But there is no evidence that McNamara passed on the information to the president. A Marine colonel, detailed to be chief of the CIA's paramilitary staff, claimed he had predicted "flatly" in writing that if all of Castro's Sea Fury fighters and Lockheed T-33 jets were not destroyed, "a military disaster would occur."[11]

However, the question of air cover gave way to the new president's foremost concern—that U.S. involvement in the invasion be denied. Kennedy sought and somehow secured assurances that an amphibious assault involving 1,500 armed troops, several ships, and a squadron of bombers would be attributed not to the United States but to either disaffected Castroites or some kind of phantom exile movement that had sprung from the ether fully formed. In the end, the CIA-sponsored landing at the Bay of Pigs was neither well conceived nor well executed. And the failure was total. All but a handful of the invading team of Cuban exiles who made it to shore were killed or captured.

The Bay of Pigs Disaster

In assessing the fiasco later, the CIA inspector general noted that "plausible deniability" had become a "pathetic illusion":

The project had lost its covert nature by November 1960. . . . For more than three months before the invasion the American press was reporting . . . the recruiting and training of Cubans. Such massive preparations could only be laid to the U.S.[12]

Some CIA planners were so concerned about the plan and the lack of same-time air cover of the invasion that they went to the home of CIA deputy director Richard Bissell to tell him the operation was hopeless. Bissell did not argue but retorted, simply, that "it was too late to stop now," despite the fact that Kennedy had allowed for the possibility that he might disapprove the plan and abort the mission even as the troop ships set sail for Cuba.

Kennedy did not know that Bissell had become the chief enthusiast of his own operation. Nor did Kennedy know that the CIA was using maps of the invasion site that were charted in 1895.[13] Nor did the president know that Castro apparently had received advance word of the invasion and had ordered floodlights placed on the apartments overlooking the beach that would illuminate the entire beleaguered exile invasion force with one flick of a switch.[14]

The landing's ultimate vindication would have to be political. CIA agents reported that the Cuban people "would welcome the landing." CIA briefings argued that 1,000 CIA fighters were pre-positioned nearby in the Escambray Mountains. The CIA did not report to the president, as Castro revealed four decades later, that

some weeks earlier we had sent 40,000 troops to the Escambray Mountains, a relatively small territory, and there we had been able to reduce the irregular groups from their original number of more than 1,000 to less than 200.[15]

The few stragglers left to aid the invasion were denied hope when a botched air drop gave over their materiel to a surprised unit of Castro's men instead.[16]

The CIA's commando forces were in an impossible situation. They were forced to debark from their landing craft at a greater distance than they had planned and to wade in neck-deep water over coral that twisted their ankles and sent them under the swells as Castro's guns fired from the shore. Yet the brigade fought for three days. The messages from the beach literally made some CIA men vomit with shame: "We are out of ammo and fighting on the beach. Please send help." Later, from the water, came the last call: "Out of ammo. Enemy closing in. Help must arrive in next hour."[17] But the president had decided not to throw American forces into what appeared to be a failed undertaking.

Castro's superior inventory of weapons doomed the exile brigade. Even if air cover had been effective, the invading Cuban exiles stood little chance. Castro's order of battle included 300,000 fully mobilized militia armed with 125 tanks, 50 self-propelled SAU-100 guns, 428 artillery pieces, 170 antitank guns, 898 large machine guns, 920 anti-aircraft guns, 7,250 smaller machine guns, and 167,000 pistols and rifles.[18] If CIA pilots had knocked out the whole of Castro's air force with the full complement of sixteen B-26s, it was unlikely that such an inferior force would secure much territory against the vastly better armed defenders without some kind of American back-up.

The CIA's inspector general was unequivocal: "the fundamental cause of the disaster"[19] was the CIA planning, assumption, and execution of the doomed mission. At best the agency had chosen to gamble that the Kennedy administration would commit more resources once the invading brigade was at the beach and in trouble, or it had counted on a miracle of deliverance from the Cuban people.

Oddly, an after-action investigation conducted by Attorney General Robert Kennedy and presidential military advisor Maxwell Taylor found Director of Central Intelligence Allen Dulles backing away from what the Kennedy team had believed was the CIA's operant assumption: that an invasion would trigger an uprising.[20] Yet it was inconceivable that if the Cubans did not rise up, more than 1,000 men could simply slip into the jungle for which they had neither supplies nor training.

Later, Theodore Sorensen, who had been a special counsel to President Kennedy and a member of the National Security Council, remembered:

The day that the invasion [ended] . . . we walked around the garden in the back, and he [Kennedy] was more distraught than I'd ever seen him. "How could I have been so stupid?" he said. "How could I have let the experts so mislead me?" . . . [H]e had achieved what he had achieved in life by not relying on experts; and this time he had relied on them and they had let him down.[21]

After the crisis, there were many post-mortems investigating how such a disastrous course could have been counseled and approved. McGeorge Bundy offered an explanation framed in terms of domestic politics. The president, he opined, feared to cancel the operation and then face so early on in his tenure the inevitable Republican charge that an "antsy-pantsy bunch of liberals" did not have the "guts" to take back the patrimony of 1898 and James Monroe.[22]

President Kennedy blamed the military above all. "Those sons of bitches with the fruit salad on their chest just sat there nodding." Kennedy's bitterness matched that of the exiles stranded in Castro's jails and CIA professionals such as Bissell and Hunt, who downed massive quantities of whiskey to stifle their anger and shame.[23]

Outright Deception?

Dulles, as his post-invasion notes indicate, hoped that even if the invasion floundered it would be rescued by Kennedy.[24] And according to Bissell's military aide, Colonel Jack Hawkins, Bissell's personal briefings to the president just before the invasion were riddled with deliberate errors. What was the logic of offering a plan that could not succeed on its merits? Why not come up with a better strategy that did not sacrifice, or jeopardize, so many on the CIA payroll? And why were Dulles and Bissell so eager to get on with the invasion that they would misrepresent its changes for success? One clue might be the intelligence warning to the president that the "shelf life" of the Cuban unit in Guatemala "was getting precarious."[25] Or, as the CIA's internal report notes, the option of stopping the invasion seemed just too

embarrassing. The brigade . . . members would have spread their disappointment far and wide . . . the Agency's embarrassment would have been public. . . . The choice was between retreat without honor and a gamble between ignominious defeat and dubious victory.[26]

Later another, darker explanation emerged regarding Kennedy's repeated delays in rendering a "go" or "no go" directive to the invasion. This explanation also hints at why the CIA backed a plan with such a small chance of success when calculated in terms of the balance of forces. Perhaps Kennedy was waiting to see if Castro would be "taken out" by a CIA saboteur, in which case the island's political structure "would [then] be in an uproar."[27] Given the level of Mafia and CIA activity on the island, this does not seem far-fetched. And it does explain why a plan with so many evident flaws was offered and approved.

Ironically, Kennedy's domestic popularity rose in the wake of the Bay of Pigs disaster—perhaps, in part, because of the grace with which he embraced responsibility. Victory, he said, has a hundred fathers, and defeat is an orphan.[28] "[I]n a parliamentary system," Kennedy acknowledged privately to Bissell and Dulles, "I would resign. . . . But in our system, the President can't and doesn't. So you . . . must go."[29] Within months, Bissell and Dulles were gone. But the president's traditional honeymoon with those who followed foreign policy was at its nadir. Two Harvard historians recently wrote that "old fashioned nationalist . . . anti-Communist . . . [h]ard-line Cuban exiles" as well as "senior military officers" and officers in the CIA "never came close to forgiving him."[30]

Former president Eisenhower was peculiarly brutal:

Eisenhower: How could you expect the world to believe that we had nothing to do with it? Where did these people get the ships to go from Central America to Cuba? Where did they get the weapons? Where did they get all the communications and all the other things that they would need? How could you possibly have kept from the world any knowledge that the United States had been involved?

Kennedy, ruefully: No one knows how tough this job is until after he had been in it a few months.

Eisenhower: If you will forgive me, I think I mentioned that to you three months ago.[31]

Kennedy's respect for President Eisenhower and his sense that Eisenhower's views carried weight, not just by dint of his accumulated wisdom but with the public as well, remained intact. Indeed, the question "Will General Eisenhower back me?" remained important to Kennedy, especially during the Berlin and Cuban missile crises to come.[32]

NOTES

1. *Foreign Relations of the United States* (FRUS), Vol. VI (Washington, DC: U.S. Government Printing Office, 1991), pp. 861–66.

2. Ibid., p. 837. The Soviets put down a Hungarian revolution when the people of Hungary rose up and ousted the Communist authorities. The new government left the Warsaw Pact, but their experiment with freedom lasted only a few weeks. Thousands died, and 200,000 Hungarians fled West.

3. Department of State, Cuban Missile Crisis Collection, National Security Archive, "Principal Soviet Statements on Defense of Cuba" <http://cwihp.si.edu/cwihp>.

4. Cited in Martin Walker, *The Cold War* (New York: Henry Holt, 1994), p. 321.

5. Robert E. Quirk, *Fidel Castro* (New York: W. W. Norton, 1993), p. 248.

6. Ibid., p. 347.

7. Ibid., p. 349.

8. Michael R. Bechloss, *The Crisis Years* (New York: HarperCollins, 1991), p. 135.

9. Remarks in 496th meeting of the National Security Council, 18 January 1962, FRUS, Vol. VI, pp. 238–42.

10. Richard Reeves, *President Kennedy: Profile of Power* (New York: Simon & Schuster, 1993), pp. 31–32.

11. See Jack Hawkins, "An Obsession with Secrecy," *Military History* 15, no. 3 (1996): p. 10.

12. "Excerpts from Bay of Pigs Report," *New York Times*, 22 February 1998.

13. FRUS, Vol. X, Doc. 276.

14. Robert Smith Thompson, *The Missiles of October: The Declassified Story of John F. Kennedy and the Cuban Missile Crisis* (New York: Simon & Schuster, 1992), p. 105.

15. Fidel Castro, interview, CNN, March 1998. Internet transcript on CNN's Cold War Web site, The Cold War, 1998 Cable News Network <www.cnn.com/specials/cold.war/episodes/10/interviews/castro>.

16. Thompson, *Missiles of October*, p. 102.

17. FRUS, Vol. V, Doc. 145.

18. Alexander Fursenko and Timothy Naftali, *One Hell of a Gamble* (New York: W. W. Norton, 1997), p. 92.

19. Central Intelligence Agency, *Inspector General's Survey of the Cuban Operation—October 1961*. The National Security Archive secured a copy of the report in 1998 and put it on the Internet at <http://www.seas.gwu.edu/nsarchive/latin_america/cuba/ig_report/index.html>.

20. Luis Aguilar, ed., *Operation Zapata* (Frederick, MD: Aletheia Books, University Publications of America, 1981), p. 111–12.

21. <Http://www.cnn.com/SPECIALS/cold.war/episodes/10/interviews/sorensen/>.

22. Kai Bird, *The Color of Truth: McGeorge Bundy and William Bundy, Brothers in Arms* (New York: Simon & Schuster, 1998), p. 29.

23. Ernest R. May and Philip D. Zelikow, *The Kennedy Tapes: Inside the White House during the Cuban Missile Crisis* (Cambridge, MA: Harvard University Press, 1997), p. 28.

24. Bechloss, *The Crisis Years*, p. 134.

25. Central Intelligence Agency, *Inspector General's Survey of the Cuban Operation—October 1961*. On the other hand, notes taken by Major General Da-

vid Gray about a White House meeting at the end of March 1961 indicate that Bissell was clear that the guerrillas could not "fade away into the jungle" (as Kennedy had hoped) if they did not meet initial success and, instead, "would probably have to be withdrawn." Cited in Stephen Rabe, "John F. Kennedy and Latin America," *Diplomatic History* 23, no. 3 (1998), p. 550.

26. Central Intelligence Agency, *Inspector General's Survey of the Cuban Operation—October 1961.*

27. Bechloss, *The Crisis Years*, pp. 125–50. Also FRUS, Vol. X, Doc. 337.

28. Reeves, *President Kennedy*, p. 103.

29. Ibid.

30. May and Zelikow, *The Kennedy Tapes*, p. 26.

31. Bechloss, *The Crisis Years*, p. 136.

32. May and Zelikow, *The Kennedy Tapes*, p. 24.

6

Blowback and Berlin

The Bay of Pigs incident served, ironically, to solidify Fidel Castro's hold on power. Most Cubans, indifferent or hostile to Castro, either resigned themselves to accommodating the regime or schemed to leave. The American misadventure at the Bay of Pigs also marked the moment when the Kremlin firmed its bet on Castro, deciding to make Cuba a virtual model of Soviet largesse.[1] And the incident presented Soviet premier Nikita Khrushchev with the opportunity to realize an apparent validation of Russia's nuclear credibility.

As the fiasco unfolded, Khrushchev wrote to President Kennedy and immediately released the letter to the public, on April 18, 1961: "planes which are bombing Cuban cities . . . belong to the United States of America." Therefore, stated Khrushchev, the United States was plainly involved in an act of "[a]rmed aggression. . . . As far as the Soviet Union is concerned, there should be no mistake about our position: We will render the Cuban people . . . all necessary help."[2]

The administration hardly worried about what seemed to be another tiresome exercise in nuclear bluster, but there was concern over what the Soviet message portended for substantive problems elsewhere, especially because Khrushchev concluded that "it is hardly possible so to conduct matters that the situation is settled in one area and conflagration extinguished, while a new conflagration is ignited in another area."[3]

The president was depressed by Khrushchev's letter. It underscored the fact that the Bay of Pigs disaster had come at a terrible moment in terms of the other issues that the new administration hoped to work out with the Soviets. For notwithstanding all the harsh campaign rhetoric about closing the "missile gap" and standing firm against communist aggression, the Kennedy administration moved swiftly and eagerly to begin talks on banning the atmospheric testing of nuclear weapons. Moreover, the new president believed it was possible to iron out the differences with the Russians over Berlin and Laos. Berlin was the most serious issue of all because it was integral to peace in Europe.

The Republicans attacked the president on every foreign policy front. The general accusation that the new Administration was not as tough as its rhetoric especially smarted. Kennedy's response was to "up" the public language of confrontation. "We face a relentless struggle," he told the Society of American Newspaper Editors in the weeks following the Bay of Pigs incident, and he promised that the United States would meet the challenge "regardless of the cost and regardless of the peril" in all parts of the globe, "whether in Cuba or South Vietnam."[4]

The speech was intended to bolster the public impression that the administration had a firm sense of purpose. But Ambassador Llewellyn I. Thompson, Jr., cautioned from Moscow that there was a danger the rhetoric might fuel the very actions it was designed to combat.[5]

BALKAN BLOWBACK

Thompson's concerns were prophetic. A few days later, Khrushchev wrote to Kennedy a guarded indication that he considered Cuba in the same light as the West regarded states on the Soviet frontier. But unlike Cuba (which was a new addition to the Russian camp), Greece, Turkey, and Italy, being under the NATO umbrella, had been recently armed by NATO with nuclear weapons.

"We do not have bases in Cuba," Khrushchev noted pointedly, and "we do not intend to establish any." But the Soviet union would have "no lesser grounds" to act against Turkey, given U.S. missiles and bases there, than the United States had when it acted against Cuba. So, Khrushchev warned again, flames in one area might "kindle a new conflagration elsewhere."[6]

Khrushchev was obliquely touching U.S. policy at its rawest points: Berlin, the Western Alliance, and Cuba. What seemed to trouble Khrushchev was the asymmetry (or, as one of his advisors put it much later, "the unfairness"[7]) of a situation that enabled the Americans to place arms on Russian frontiers while retaining the Western Hemisphere as a sanctuary distant from any meaningful Russian reach. More than anything, it was the thought of American missiles just over the horizon from his resort dacha on the Black Sea in Turkey that obsessed Khrushchev. It was not that these "Jupiter class" missiles—as the American NATO strategists termed them— were especially important in themselves. They were out of date, known to be vulnerable to sniper fire, inaccurate, and slow to fire. The engines of the Jupiters were finicky and unpredictable.[8]

But to Russia's decision-makers, these missiles dampened the claim that they had reached a level of nuclear might sufficient to menace the United States. So concerned were Moscow's decision-makers with the installation of nuclear rockets across the Black Sea that at one point in 1960 the Soviets offered the financially strapped Turkish government a subsidy of half a billion dollars a year and an abundant supply of top-of-the-line weapons if the Turks would give up the Jupiter bases.[9]

BERLIN

For both Khrushchev since 1958 and Kennedy at the onset of his presidency, the overriding Cold War concern was Berlin.[10] As Khrushchev once told Senator Hubert Humphrey (D-Minnesota), Berlin was nothing short of a "bone in my throat." Berlin was to be the first item on the Russian itinerary, superseding "normalization" with Cuba, nuclear testing, or any other area of contention. The East German regime, misleadingly entitled the German Democratic Republic (GDR), was critical to Russia. As Eisenhower had discovered and Kennedy was to rediscover, the problem of Berlin was without an apparent solution for the United States.

Berlin was 110 miles deep into the Communist occupied zone of Germany. Berlin, like Germany, was divided. One half was controlled by the West and the other was under Soviet control. East Berlin was the only point of easy egress anywhere in the Communist bloc. Since 1949, some 2.6 million people had fled the East German zone through Berlin. Any professional, worker, or young person who was unhappy with his or her lot or future in East Germany could take a subway from East Berlin to the Western Allied Controlled sector of West Berlin to join the West. Senior Soviet officials joked that there would be nobody left in the GDR, except for its nominal leader, Walter Ulbricht. Surely Ulbricht's wife would go, but, they quipped, perhaps Ulbricht's mistress would stay on.

The only way for the Russians to stop the hemorrhage of talent was, as they had threatened for years, to sign a separate treaty with their German "Democratic" satrap. The Russians' logic was that then, given the legal warrant, the East German state would have the right to control its own frontiers.

If East German military forces controlled, for instance, the subway to the West, surely they would have the right to control traffic and the vast outmigration that was exceeding 1,000 people a day in good weather.

Khrushchev had threatened to sign a "final" accord with the East German leadership since 1858. But he knew that without the acceptance of the West, such an agreement could not be valid. For Russia was only one of the four Allied Powers of World War II that were designated by treaty to administer Germany. All four powers—France, Britain, America, and Russia—were guaranteed access to the other powers' "zones."

From his very first communications with the Soviets, Kennedy pushed Khrushchev for a bilateral summit meeting. After February, Kennedy let the issue lapse. But just five days before the Bay of Pigs invasion, he proposed a date in the first week of June. The date would be fewer than eight weeks after the CIA's effort in Cuba. Whether the adventure succeeded or failed, June turned out to be hardly a good choice to meet the Soviet premier for the first time, because three days before the Bay of Pigs operation the Soviets put a man in space—a feat the Americans had not considered possible within the limits of Soviet technology. Inexplicably, Kennedy waited until the Bay of Pigs debacle played out and then accepted a summit date for June.[11]

After the Bay of Pigs invasion it was unavoidable that comparisons would be made within the Soviet camp regarding Kennedy's real mettle and the willingness of the United States to pay for its European commitments in blood. After all, Khrushchev had gone ahead with an invasion of his own—Hungary in 1956—and the cost was some 32,000 dead. Hence the Bay of Pigs incident only reinforced the Russians' sense that they were riding a cresting wave of success.[12] Khrushchev was strengthened in his belief that Kennedy, unlike Eisenhower, was not "serious"; rather, as Khrushchev put it later, the president was a very young man in "short pants" without real experience in world.[13]

Khrushchev approached the June meeting in Vienna with confidence. He was buoyed by the Americans' failure at the Bay of Pigs and the sense that Kennedy would not risk war over the issue of the Soviet-occupied zone of Berlin coming under the nominal direction of the Russians' East German partner.

Kennedy's advisors held a uniform belief that Berlin was diplomatically intractable. The Joint Chiefs told the president that there was no conventional defense of Berlin and that the only way the city could be held was with the early and intensive use of nuclear weapons.[14]

Kennedy was willing to give and negotiate—on arms control, nuclear tests, Laos, and perhaps some kind of understanding regarding the necessity for caution in a nuclearized, bipolar world. But first he had to appear resolute to a man who would come to the meeting already harboring doubts about American will and leadership. However, given the shaky foundation of the recent U.S. experience in Cuba, it was unclear how Kennedy would establish a credible and firm position on Berlin.

The Vienna Summit

In retrospect, both leaders regarded the Vienna summit meeting in the first week of June as a test that Kennedy failed in every respect. The mood of the American delegation was captured by the portrait offered later by Kenneth O'Donnell, a good friend of the president, who saw the Soviet premier from a window. The two leaders had gone for a stroll in the garden below. Khrushchev was wagging his finger at Kennedy and "snapping like a terrier."[15]

By and large, Kennedy felt he had to take it. A bit later James Reston, the noted *New York Times* correspondent, commiserated with the president. "Pretty rough?" asked Reston. The president responded, "He just beat hell out of me. . . . It was one of the roughest things in my life."[16]

Most senior Soviets recalled that they were "amazed" that Kennedy had been so "affected and scared." "When you have your hand up a girl's dress, you expect her to scream, but you don't expect her to be scared."[17] The Soviet premier later recalled that Kennedy had looked not only anxious but deeply upset. "I would have liked very much for us to part in a different mood," Khrushchev remembered. But "[p]olitics is a merciless business."[18]

"He treated me like a little boy," the president raged in private. "Now we have a problem in making our power credible."[19] What bothered Kennedy most was that, largely privately, he was struggling to find a way to achieve a modus vivendi with Khrushchev. As Kennedy told O'Donnell:

it seems particularly stupid to risk killing millions of Americans about access rights on an Autobahn . . . or because Germans want Germany to be reunified. . . . If I am going to threaten nuclear war it will have to be for much bigger . . . reasons than that.[20]

At the final lunch in Vienna, Khrushchev told Kennedy that he was committed to building up Soviet forces in response to Kennedy's position on Berlin. Moreover, Khrushchev said, the United States would be able to claim special rights for only six months more. Then the situation would be liquidated. Khrushchev's December timetable for a treaty with East Germany was "firm and irrevocable." "I want peace," declared Khrushchev, "but if you want war, that is your problem." To which Kennedy replied, "it's going to be a cold winter."[21]

Kennedy sensed that he had two problems as a result of the meeting. The first was to figure out why Khrushchev had rebuffed the president's attempt at a dialogue. The second was to decide "what to do about it. I think the first part is pretty easy," Kennedy mused. "I think he did it because of the Bay of Pigs . . . he thinks I'm inexperienced and have no guts."[22]

Vienna and the Bay of Pigs conjoined in the minds of American policy-makers. On the afternoon of October 18, 1962, just before President Kennedy revealed the facts of the Cuban Missile Crisis to the world, the president ruminated on how the Russians could have believed the United States would tolerate Russian missiles in Cuba. It was "a consequence of the Vienna summit," claimed Kennedy. That was where Khrushchev had concluded he was weak and timid.[23]

If Vienna was the "roughest thing" Kennedy had ever faced, it was a remarkable statement for a man who had dealt with so much in war, health, and family tragedy.[24] But remarkably, acting on Secretary of State Dean Rusk's advice, Kennedy did not mention Khrushchev's December deadline on Berlin in his initial public comments about the summit meeting. Kennedy might have been trying to allow the Russians additional time to rethink the implications of a dangerous position, a tactic he employed again in the coming missile crisis. In any event, the Soviet news agency, Pravda, publicly revealed Khrushchev's demands, starkly and in full.

The tempo of Khrushchev's diplomatic offensive and campaign of intimidation accelerated. He had promised Kennedy that Russia would not be the first to resume nuclear testing.[25] But a month later, at a dinner with the Presidium (Soviet executive committee), Khrushchev announced that he was going to begin an extensive series of tests:

[W]e have to conduct our policies from a position of strength. . . . Our opponents don't understand any other language. . . . Look, we helped Kennedy last year. Then we met with him in Vienna. But what does he say? "Don't ask too much . . . [or] . . . I'll be turned out of office." Quite a guy! . . . [H]e comes to a meeting, but can't perform. What the hell do we need a guy like that . . . ? Why waste time talking to him?[26]

On July 8, Khrushchev announced that the Soviet union would increase its defense preparations by over three billion rubles.[27] Washington, in turn, struggled to find the means to appear prepared to confront the Soviets at any price. U.S. National Security Council staff aide Robert Kromer, for instance, recommended and got approval for

Stepping up the momentum in South Vietnam. I believe it is very important that this government have a major anti-Communist victory to its credit in the six months before the Berlin crisis is likely to get really hot. Few things would be better calculated to show Moscow and Peiping that we mean business than an obvious (if not yet definitive) turnaround in Vietnam.[28]

At the same time, Kennedy grew impatient with the slow, "stale, tedious, and negative phrases" of the State Department. The president also was not only eager for a more dynamic statement of the U.S. interest in Berlin but anxious to define a path by which the Soviets and the United States could both get what they needed in resolving the Berlin issue.[29] Thus, on July 25, 1961, Kennedy proclaimed the American interest and hinted at a possible means of getting out of a potentially disastrous conflict of interests.

"We cannot and will not permit the Communists to drive us out of Berlin," he announced to a nationwide television audience. To ensure that the United States was not "forced" to concede anything, he asked for six new combat divisions to prepare for European duty. He announced that the military draft would be doubled. The reserves—more than 150,000 men, veterans of Korea and World War II—were called up amid considerable grumbling. Kennedy responded, "life is unfair." He had reason to know it.

Kennedy also announced that 50 percent of "our missile power . . . and . . . bombers" would be put on "alert which would send them on their way with 15 minutes warning." Civil defense programs, given a huge boost in May, were enlarged again. The president proposed a national air-raid warning system and fallout detection systems. An additional $3.5 billion was requested to procure food, water, first-aid, and home radiation detection kits in order to protect Americans in home shelters.[30]

THE BERLIN WALL

In the same speech that aimed at convincing the Soviets that the United States was willing to go to war over Berlin,[31] the president deliberately hinted at a way out of the crisis for both parties. He emphasized that the United States would defend its legal rights in West Berlin and *access* to East Berlin. Whatever else the Soviets did in their occupied zone, he indicated, was up to the Russians to determine, not the West.

The president said today "the endangered frontier of freedom runs through divided Berlin."

The immediate threat to free men is in *West Berlin* . . . our basic rights . . . include both *our presence in West Berlin* and the enjoyment of *access across East Germany.* . . . Thus, *our presence in West Berlin, and our access thereto, cannot be ended* by any act of the Soviet government.[32] (emphasis added)

The point was clear, and it seems the Soviets understood. The president would not "challenge Soviet power in place."[33]

While Soviet foreign affairs experts correctly deciphered Kennedy's public iteration of the limits to American interests, the KGB learned that at an early August meeting of the United States, Great Britain, France, and West Germany, the allies proved unwilling to risk a war over Berlin unless any Soviet move there seemed to prelude to an advance on a wider front.[34]

It is an aphorism of diplomatic history that positions of strength, a bit like mirages, frequently recede just as they seem in hand.[35] A real position of strength is one thing. But some of Khrushchev's claims of strategic nuclear strength were exaggerated. Hence the KGB was authorized to dupe the West. A fictitious new generation of tanks "equipped with tactical nuclear weapons" was proffered to Western intelligence. Rumors were circulated of plans that were fifteen or twenty years in advance of the fact. Soviet rocket forces were said to have solid-fuel missiles that could be carried by mobile launchers. KGB experts also sought to make it appear that the Soviet Navy had an abundance of nuclear submarines with solid-fuel Polaris type missiles. Anti-aircraft defenses that did not yet exist were nonetheless covertly touted, as were fictitious aircraft carrying effective "air-to-air" and "air-to-ground" missiles with impressive operational range. The capstone of Soviet disinformation was to be word of a new "strategic bomber [program] with nuclear engines and unlimited range."[36]

The Russians campaigned during much of the Cold War not so much on achievement as on appearance and rumors of ever more in the wings. It was a chillingly risky habit. For if the West indeed became convinced that the Soviets were on the brink of achieving strategic superiority, there would be a logic to the occasional American impulse to take advantage of U.S. atomic superiority and strike first.

Behind the Russian bluff were real fears. First was the Soviet awareness that their rocket force was illusory, even less capable than the American estimates at the time. Second, the Soviets worried that their pivotal German ally might slip from its Soviet lead. The East German Communists threatened, for instance, to move on the rest of Berlin and capture it from NATO. Khrushchev was appalled. "[N]ot a millimeter further," he admonished the East German leadership. Khrushchev was also privately concerned that the Chinese might make diplomatic inroads in East Germany with fatal consequences for the unity of the Soviet Bloc. Most convincing to the Rus sians was the prospect that their position in East Germany might collapse. If that happened, Khrushchev acknowledged, it would mean that "the Bundeswehr [West German army] [would] move to the Polish border . . .

[then] to the borders with Czechoslovakia, [and then] . . . closer to our Soviet border."[37]

The East German tail of the Russian empire had the ability to manipulate the Soviet dog. The Soviets' German ally, the German Democratic Republic, was opposed to Khrushchev's plan "to seal every weak spot" the West "might look for." The East Germans wanted the much-promised final treaty and the ability to police the East zone of Berlin themselves. But, Khrushchev insisted that he only would meet the GDR's and the Soviet's minimum requirements on Berlin. Moreover, by remaining within the letter of the 1945 Potsdam accords, Khrushchev concluded that there might be "a thaw, and, more importantly, a cooling down" in East-West tension.[38] Khrushchev had discovered what he called a "compromise"; yet it was a solution that curiously seemed to have been pre-authorized by American policymakers.

On Sunday, August 13, 1961, at 2:00 A.M., construction of the Berlin Wall began. John C. Ausland, the State Department duty officer in Washington, remembered:

it became apparent that American leaders were taking a relaxed attitude toward events in Berlin. Secretary Rusk cam in at ten o'clock as planned. After conferring with Foy Kohler, the head of the Berlin Task Force, he issued a calming press release and went to a baseball game.[39]

The mayor of West Berlin, Willy Brandt, protested angrily to Kennedy about America's initial nonchalance about the Wall. But Kennedy did not call a formal meeting in the White House until Thursday, August 17. The closing of the border was "not a shooting issue," Kennedy concluded. Rather, it was an "opportunity" for the United States to "reap a large [propaganda] harvest."[40]

THE WALL AND THE MISSILE CRISIS

In fact, for the Kennedy administration the walling off of the Soviet sector of East Berlin was not only an obvious "out" to the problem with East German and Berlin, it may have been overtly suggested by Robert Kennedy in what came to be regular but highly secret meetings with the KGB agent residing in Washington, D.C. Indeed, as historian Michael Bechloss notes, it defies belief that the matter was not discussed in these meetings. If Bechloss is right, the diplomatic methodology used in the Berlin matter was to prove critical to the successful resolution of the Cuban Missile Crisis.[41]

For, as would happen in Cuba, Kennedy had reached a quiet understanding that led to the factual end of the Berlin question.[42]

This type of "back channel" diplomacy also seemed to promise a better relationship somewhere down the road. In the short run (as in Cuba, as Kennedy noted in 1961), the sheer brutality of the Berlin Wall presented itself as a useful "propaganda stick, which, if the situation were reversed, would be well used in beating us." In sum, the walling of Berlin—to Kennedy, at least in private—was a triumph of American diplomacy.[43]

Berlin Prelude to the Missile Crisis

On August 28, 1961, a huge Soviet nuclear explosion broke a long-standing nuclear moratorium honored by East and West alike. The test was the vivid repeal of a pledge that Khrushchev had given to Kennedy at Vienna to the effect that Russia would not be the first to test nuclear weapons in the atmosphere. When Kennedy's national security advisor, McGeorge Bundy, told the president of the test, Kennedy's response was clear outrage: "Fucked again!" he exclaimed.[44]

In number and yield, the Soviet tests between September 1, 1961, and November 4, 1961, were enormous. Thirty nuclear devices were detonated, including an enormous 58 megaton device. Andrei Sakharov, the renowned Russian physicist, was asked, "Why do we need to make 'cannibalistic' weapons like this?!" Sakharov replied that it was Khrushchev's idea to have "this device hang over the heads of the capitalists, like a sword of Damocles."[45]

Khrushchev's rejection of a ban on atmospheric tests was apparently aimed at intimidating the West. If he had thought more clearly about the long run, Khrushchev might have known that the explosions would lead to an acceleration of U.S. bomb development. But it was Khrushchev's calculation, as he told Cyrus Sulzberger of the *New York Times*, to prove that the USSR had "no lesser capability than . . . Western countries."[46]

The substance of the East-West crisis in Berlin may have been over, but Soviet nuclear testing and the ugly partition of Berlin did not augur well for East-West relations. Pressure on Kennedy to test in the atmosphere was so intense that on October 11, 1961, he ordered a resumption of atmospheric tests.[47] Two days later on Friday, October 13, 1961, General Lucius Clay, the former U.S. military governor general of Berlin, returned to the city he had done so much to save from Joseph Stalin's 1948 blockade.[48]

Clay was privately determined to see that the Berlin divide was tested and, if possible, breached. Unknown to the administration in Washington, D.C., General Clay began to practice breaching procedures and, in time, actually built a section of wall and tried out specially configured bulldozer tanks against it. A high-ranking U.S. intelligence official of the time, Raymond L. Garthoff, recently found documents proving that "Soviet military intelligence [had] learned of [Clay's practices] and had also found out that Clay's bulldozers were to be followed by U.S. tanks, then jeeps and finally foot soldiers."[49]

As Clay arrived in Berlin, the White House decided to send a 1,500-man battle group down the Autobahn to reinforce the American garrison in Berlin. The U.S. troops passed along the 110-mile corridor without incident. But a few days later, on Sunday evening, October 21, a senior American diplomat in Berlin, Allan Lightner, and his wife, crossing Checkpoint Charlie to go to the theater in East Berlin, were unexpectedly stopped by the East German police (*Volkspolizei*), who asked to see the Lightners' diplomatic passports. The Lightners were in their own private automobile, albeit with diplomatic plates. Hence the East German request might not have been that untoward. But the Americans refused and said they would only deal with Soviet officers. The East Germans refused. The American couple then began to drive, only to be stopped by more heavily armed police. Lightner then phoned from his car for an escort of American soldiers, who soon arrived with fixed bayonets, followed by four U.S. M-48 tanks. The East German border guards stepped aside.

"We didn't send Lightner over there to go to the opera in East Berlin," Kennedy muttered.[50] In fact, neither the State Department nor the Russians were inclined to make much of the Lightner incident. But General Clay believed the Lightner matter was either a deliberate test or an opportunity. Thus he ordered the Lightner scenario to be repeated. A series of American officials in civilian cars drove up to Checkpoint Charlie, where they were asked by the *Volkspolizei* for their credentials. Upon refusing the East German requests, the Americans were instructed to return with American soldiers. The odd and dangerous drama turned stale after a few days.

Clay then decided to make the point of American rights firm and definitive. On October 25, ten M-48 tanks appeared near Checkpoint Charlie, and at the same time one of the largest masses of U.S. soldiers since World War II was assembled at the rear of the tanks. Two days later an equal number of Soviet tanks moved to the East German side of the checkpoint. For the next sixteen hours, with engines running and occasionally revved up, American and Soviet tanks stood nearly muzzle to muzzle, separated by a span of three yards. Both sides were instructed to return fire in case of any sign of hostility.

Nuclear Coming Out

On the day the Lightner crisis began, Deputy Defense Secretary Roswell Gilpatric, in a formal and well-publicized speech, released many details of a CIA estimate that confirmed Soviet military inferiority. Noting that the missile gap, if there ever had been one, was now overwhelmingly in America's favor, Gilpatric outlined an American inventory of strategic weapons that would leave the United States with a larger strike force than Russia had, even after a Soviet nuclear bolt from the blue. As Gilpatric put it, "The fact is that this nation has a nuclear retaliatory force of such lethal power that an enemy move which brought it into play would be at an act of self-destruction on his part."[51]

According to Roger Hilsman, a senior State Department intelligence advisor at the time, the administration's rationale for underscoring America's strategic advantage was to ensure that Khrushchev was not "allowed to assume that we still believed the missile gap." Making public the truth that Khrushchev hoped dare not be spoken would prevent the Soviets from pushing an advantage that the Kennedy administration wanted the Russians to know they did not have. Khrushchev wanted to apply nuclear jujitsu; the Kennedy administration wanted to emphasize that in war, like in boxing, size matters.[52]

By late October 1961, President Kennedy decided not only that the Berlin tank standoff had gone on too long but that escalation was such a serious possibility that the crisis must be resolved soon. The problem for Kennedy was how to do it quickly with a leak-proof mechanism that would not disgrace his campaign of appearing to be strong and determined. His method—as was to occur two years later at the height of the Cuban Missile Crisis—was to bypass the president's own national security machinery, and closest advisors, and quietly enlist interlocutors who would not later go to the press. Using Georgi Bolshakov, a Russian intelligence officer officially detailed to the United States as a Soviet press attaché, the president sent word to Khrushchev that it was time for a mutual withdrawal.

But who should go first?

In his memoirs, Khrushchev remembered telling his tank commander:

I'm sure that within twenty minutes or however long it takes them to get their instructions, the American tanks will pull back, too. They can't turn their tanks around and pull them back as long as our guns are pointing at them. They've gotten themselves into a difficult situation, and they don't know how to get out of it. They're looking for a way out, I'm sure. So let's give them one. We'll remove our tanks, and they'll follow our example.[53]

Khrushchev informed Kennedy through Bolshakov that he would make the first move and withdraw tanks from the standoff first. At the same time, he announced that he was rescinding the Berlin ultimatum. "What counts most," he declared, "is not the particular date" of the settlement of the German problem, "but a businesslike and honest settlement."[54]

From General Clay's standpoint, and that of many American military observers at the time, the United States had exposed yet another Russian bluff.[55] However, the analysis of Secretary of State Dean Rusk at the time and later was different. Rusk, and most senior civilians including Kennedy, felt that even if the Wall were breached at one point, it could always be erected again. "Those who believed," wrote Risk, "that the East Germans and Russians would simply back down upon a slight show of force were not prepared to face up to second, third and fourth steps if the backdown did not occur." Moreover, noted Rusk, "no NATO government (including the Federal Republic of Germany) favored the use of armed force to break through the barbed wire."[56]

Although the United States had done nothing about the Berlin Wall, indeed, had encouraged it, Soviet power had been depreciated. Kennedy may have had little choice in the timing of the revelation of Soviet weakness. If he had chosen not to confront the Russians with the truth, any subsequent compromise made with the Russians would appear at home—and, as important, in Russia—as if the Americans had been forced to yield to an impression of Russian strength. But because the announcement of American preponderance in strategic weapons came at the apogee of an immensely dangerous moment in the Cold War, Americans came to believe that the United States could regain the momentum in the Cold War.

To the Soviets, in retrospect the tank standoff seemed a point at least as dangerous as the Cuban Missile Crisis.[57] Khrushchev might take comfort in the sheer enormity of Soviet nuclear bombs. The Soviet leader could point out to the disbelieving Chinese and the ever edgy Germans that Western acquiescence to the Berlin Wall implied a permanent division of Germany and prepared the ground for future German leaders to live with the results of World War II, as, in fact, occurred in 1970.[58] Khrushchev could also claim that he had "forced Kennedy and the Western Allies to swallow a bitter pill," just as he would later claim that Russian might had secured Cuba from an American invasion.[59] But these claims were bluster, and the Soviet and American officials alike knew it.

The Berlin crisis, like the missile crisis in Cuba later, confirmed to American policymakers that nuclear preponderance would dictate foreign policy outcomes. Indeed, in narratives of the Kennedy era the policy of preponderance appears to displace other approaches for dealing with Russia. In reality, however, diplomacy had never been in full eclipse during the Berlin crisis. Like the Cuba crisis later, the Berlin standoff ended with private American concessions, initiated and conveyed privately. The public interpretation in the United States was that events had quieted as a function of Soviet concessions or retreat in the face of American determination. In fact, both crises were defused by means of a species of classic negotiations, that is, compromise. To be sure, there was a Cold War twist: the normal perception of mutual give-and-take common to classic diplomacy was skewed by Kennedy's domestic political needs and perhaps his personal needs as well; after all, Kennedy and the senior members of his administration were obsessed by the drive to appear "tough."

NOTES

1. See on this James G. Blight and Peter Kornbluh, eds., *Politics of Illusion* (Boulder, CO: Lynne Reinner, 1998), passim.

2. *Foreign Relations of the United States* (FRUS), Vol. VI (Washington, DC: U.S. Government Printing Office, 1996), Doc. 9.

3. *Department of State Bulletin*, 8 May 1961, p. 662.

4. Michael R. Blechloss, *The Crisis Years* (New York: HarperCollins, 1991), pp. 128–29.

5. Ibid., p. 129.

6. Ibid., p. 131.

7. *CNN Perspectives Presents the Cold War: Cuba, 1959–1962, Vol. 4, The Cold War*, CNN, 1998, Film No. 10, ISBN 0–7806–2390–8.

8. Nur Bilge Criss, "Strategic Nuclear Missiles in Turkey: The Jupiter Affairs, 1959–1963," *Journal of Strategic Studies* 20, no. 3 (1997): pp. 102–3.

9. Ibid., p. 113.

10. See Vladislav Zubok, "Khrushchev and the Berlin Crisis (1958–62)," *Cold War International History Project*, Working paper no. 6 (Washington, DC: Woodrow Wilson International Center for Scholars) <www. cwihp.si.edu>.

11. Alexander Fursenko and Timothy Naftali, *One Hell of a Gamble: Khrushchev, Castro, Kennedy, and the Cuban Missile Crisis, 1958–1964* (London: Pimlico, 1999), p. 88.

12. Oleg Troyananovsky interview by Vladislav Martinovich Zubok, in Criss, "Strategic Nuclear Missiles in Turkey."

13. Zubok, "Khrushchev and the Berlin Crisis (1958–62)."

14. Dwight D. Eisenhower, *Waging Peace: The White House Years, 1956–1961* (New York: Doubleday, 1965), pp. 338–39.

15. Bechloss, *Crisis Years*, p. 199.

16. Ibid., p. 224.

17. Cited in ibid., p. 234.

18. Nikita S. Khrushchev, *Khrushchev Remembers: The Last Testament* (Boston: Little, Brown, 1974), pp. 500–1.

19. Stanley Karnow, *Vietnam: A History* (New York: Penguin, 1983), p. 248.

20. Kenneth O'Donnell and David F. Powers, *Johnny We Hardly Knew Ye: Memoirs of John Fitzgerald Kennedy* (Boston: Little, Brown, 1972), pp. 296–300.

21. Bechloss, *Crisis Years*, p. 224.

22. *New York Times*, 5 June 1961.

23. Bechloss, *Crisis Years*, p. 457.

24. Kennedy's family history is painful. His brother died in a World War II air action; his sister was born retarded and spent her life in a mental institution; and his own health was precarious.

25. Richard Ned Lebow and Janet Gross Stein, *We All Lost the Cold War* (Princeton: Princeton University Press, 1994), p. 36.

26. Andrei Sakharov, *Memoirs*, trans. Richard Laurie (New York: Random House, 1990), p. 217.

27. "Speech by Comrade N. S. Khrushchev at Reception for Graduates of Military Academies of U.S.S.R. Armed Forces, July 18, 1961," *Current Digest of the Soviet Press* 13 (August 2, 1961): p. 5.

28. Theodore C. Sorensen, *Kennedy* (New York: Bantam, 1966), p. 587.

29. Arthur M. Schlesinger Jr., *A Thousand Days: John F. Kennedy in the White House* (New York: Fawcett Crest, 1967), p. 406; Sorensen, *Kennedy*, p. 587.

30. Fursenko and Naftali, *One Hell of a Gamble*, p. 137.

31. The speech seems to have been drafted by McGeorge Bundy. See McGeorge Bundy, "The Wall: 1958–63," interview, *The Cold War*, film no. 9, CNN, 1998.

32. McGeorge Bundy, *Danger and Survival: Choices about the Bomb in the First Fifty Years* (New York: Random House, 1988), pp. 385–89ff.

33. Ibid.

34. Vladislav M. Zubok, "Spy vs. Spy: The KGB vs. the CIA, 1960–1962," *Cold War International History Project*, Bulletin 4 (Washington, DC: Woodrow Wilson International Center for Scholars, 1995) <www.cwihp.si.edu>.

35. Coral Bell, *Negotiation from Strength* (New York: Greenwood, 1977).

36. Zubok, "Spy vs. Spy."

37. "Soviet Foreign Policy During the Cold War: A Documentary Sampler," *Cold War International History Project*, Bulletin 3 (Washington, DC: Woodrow Wilson International Center for Scholars, n.d.) <www.cwihp.si.edu>.

38. Hope Harrison, "Ulbricht and the Concrete 'Rose': New Archival Evidence on the Dynamics of Soviet–East German Relations and the Berlin Crisis, 1958–61," *Cold War International History Project*, Working paper no. 5 (Washington, DC: Woodrow Wilson International Center for Scholars, 1993) <www.wwics.si.edu>. The Potsdam accords was a conference held at the end of World War II in Europe where Stalin set a date to enter the war against Japan. The conference fixed the occupation zones within Germany and Berlin and detailed Allied access rights.

39. John C. Ausland, "When the Allies Split Berlin, Washington Was Asleep," *International Herald Tribune*, 14 November 1989.

40. See *Foreign Relations of the United States* (FRUS), Vol. XV (Washington, DC: U.S. Government Printing Office, 1994), pp. 333–34, 347–49.

41. Bechloss, *Crisis Years*, p. 281.

42. Ibid., p. 314.

43. Ibid., p. 275.

44. Ibid., p. 291.

45. Lebow and Stein, *We All Lost the Cold War*, p. 36.

46. For Cyrus Leo Sulzberger's account of his interview with Khrushchev, see Cyrus Leo Sulzberger, *The Last of the Giants* (New York: Macmillan, 1970), pp. 788–803.

47. FRUS, Vol. V, p. 119ff.

48. The Berlin blockade arose from an attempt by the Soviet Union to force the Western Allies to abandon their post–World War II jurisdictions in West Berlin. When the Soviets closed land-access routes to Berlin, the Allies supplied the city by airlift. In the end, the blockade was lifted, and the United States decided to join in an Atlantic Alliance to opposed Soviet power.

49. Raymond L. Garthoff, "Berlin 1961: The Record Corrected," *Foreign Policy*, no. 5 (Fall 1991): pp. 142–56.

50. According to McGeorge Bundy, Kennedy was willing to talk of compromise at any stage during the Berlin crisis. See Bundy, *Danger and Survival*, p. 385.

51. "Address by Roswell Gilpatric, Deputy Secretary of Defense, before the Business Council at the Homestead, Hot Springs, Virginia, October 21, 1961," *Documents on Disarmament* (Washington, DC: U.S. Department of State, 1961), pp. 544–45.

52. See Roger Hilsman, *To Move a Nation* (Garden City, NY: Doubleday, 1967), p. 163.

53. Khrushchev, *Khrushchev Remembers*, pp. 506–7.

54. "Speech by Comrade N. S. Khrushchev at Reception for Graduates of Military Academies of U.S.S.R. Armed Forces, July 18, 1961," p. 5.

55. Garthoff, "Berlin 1961: The Record Corrected," pp. 142–56.

56. Dean Rusk, "Review of Honore M. Catudal's 'Kennedy and the Berlin Wall Crisis,' " *American Journal of International Law* 77, no. 3. (July 1983): p. 775.

57. Garthoff, "Berlin 1961: The Record Corrected," pp. 142–56.

58. The frontiers of post–World War II Poland were disputed by West Germany. The East German state was not recognized by any Western power, including West Germany. After a 1970 initiative by West German Chancellor Will Brandt, West Germany recognized East Germany and came to terms with Poland's western frontier.

59. Nikita S. Khrushchev, *Khrushchev Remembers*, eds. Edward Crankshaw and Strobe Talbot (London: Deutsch, 1971), p. 509.

U.S. President John F. Kennedy (left) and Soviet Premier Nikita Khrushchev (right) leave the Soviet Embassy in Vienna, Austria on June 4, 1961, following their final talk. The two leaders finished their private talks in solemn fashion, shaking hands without smiling. © Bettman/CORBIS

Soviet Premier Nikita Khrushchev (right) and Cuban Premier Fidel Castro (left) shake hands at Grand Kremlin Palace after signing a joint Soviet-Cuban declaration on May 23, 1963. © Bettmann/CORBIS

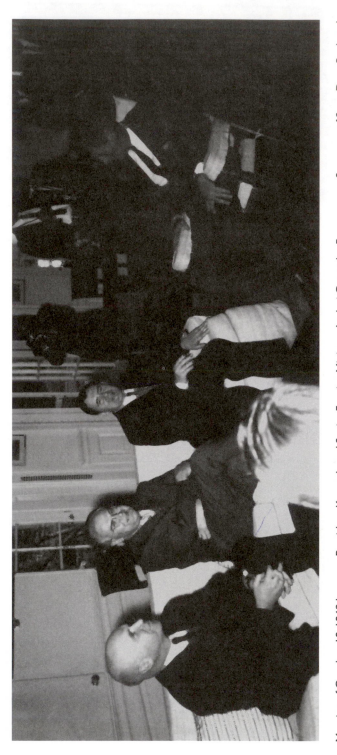

Meeting of October 18, 1962 between President Kennedy and Soviet Foreign Minister Andrei Gromyko. Present were Secretary of State Dean Rusk and Soviet Ambassador to the United States Anatoli Dobrynin. The meeting was designed by the President to allow the Soviets to believe that their deception regarding the placement of missiles in Cuba had gone undetected. Courtesy of The JFK Library.

October 22, 1962. At 7:00 PM. President Kennedy went on national television to advise the American people and the world that a crisis was at hand over the secret Soviet nuclear build-up in Cuba. Courtesy of The JFK Library.

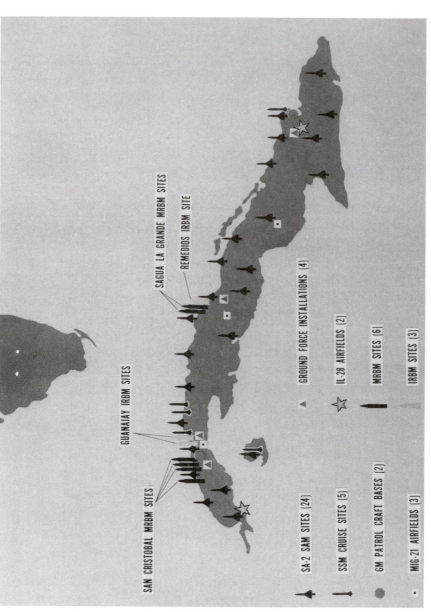

A composite diagram released by the Pentagon showing Soviet military deployments. The position of Soviet deployments and forces was derived from U-2 reconnaissance photos taken from October 14th on. Despite the intense reconnaissance, the number of Soviet forces was underestimated. The Soviet tactical nuclear armaments were unknown until the late 1980s. Courtesy of The JFK Library.

October 23, 1962. President Kennedy, Secretary of State Dean Rusk, Secretary of Defense Robert McNamara, with Press Secretary Pierre Salinger looking on the President's signing of a proclamation limiting items that can be carried by Seato Cuba. Courtesy of The JFK Library.

President Kennedy signing a proclamation on October 23, 1962, which limited the number of items that could be carried by sea to Cuba. Courtesy of The JFK Library.

MRBM LAUNCH SITE 1
SAN CRISTOBAL, CUBA
23 OCTOBER 1962

CABLE

MISSILE ERECTOR

MISSILE SHELTER TENT

TRACKED PRIME MOVERS

OXIDIZER TANK TRAILERS

FUEL TANK TRAILERS

October 23, 1962. MRBM launch site. One of a number of U-2 photographs of one of the several hastily constructed missile and bomber bases being put in service by Soviet technicians. Courtesy of The JFK Library.

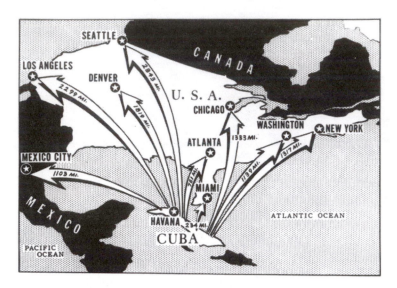

President Kennedy flatly rejected Soviet Premier Khrushchev's offer on October 27, 1962, to take Soviet missiles out of Cuba if the United States would remove its rockets from Turkey. This map shows approximate distances from Cuba to various key U.S. cities and Mexico City. © Bettmann/CORBIS

The Soviet ship *Divinogorsk* departs Cuba on November 5, 1962, with four missile transporters, each with a canvas-covered missile, lashed to its deck. © Bettmann/CORBIS

7

Cuba: "The Top Priority in the United States Government— All Else Is Secondary"

At the time the Berlin crisis was being played out, the Kennedy administration was upping the ante in Cuba. Berlin was a matter of cohesion in the Western Alliance and focused on a key element of Cold War contention: the political structure of Germany and Europe. But Cuba was integral to the American self-image in general as the benefactor of the Western Hemisphere. Even more, it was central to the initial position the president had staked out for himself and the nation as dynamic, resolute, and above all, successful. The Bay of Pigs was a signal failure. It demanded a counterstroke.

To Undersecretary of State Chester Bowles, the disaster of the Bay of Pigs left the president personally and politically shattered. The president, observed Bowles, had a "long career" unmarked by "political setbacks."[1] To Bowles, Kennedy's attitude toward Cuba after the Bay of Pigs fiasco became a matter of personal dignity and honor, almost a vendetta.

But the personal stain on the Kennedy image was peppered with serious concerns of statecraft. Both President John Kennedy and Attorney General Robert Kennedy felt that the American failure at the Bay of Pigs would embolden Fidel Castro and the Russians in their mutual determination to export revolution to the Americas. A "forceful and determined" effort aimed at the "downfall of Castro" had become a matter of supreme national interest. Indeed, both Kennedys were insistent that the "survival" of the United States as a bulwark of democracy had become the stake in relations between Cuba and the United States.[2] The attorney general made it clear that this was:

[t]he top priority in the United States government—all else is secondary—no time, money, effort, or manpower is to be spared. There can be no misunderstanding on the involvement of the agencies concerned nor on their responsibility to carry out this job.[3]

President Kennedy was determined not to have the Bay of Pigs disaster be his political obituary. There were two essential tracks to American planning. The first was to create a situation whereby another invasion would seem a natural outgrowth of deteriorating relations between Cuba and the United States. Perhaps, the attorney general suggested, the United States "might have to blow up the [U.S.] Consulate [building] in Cuba" in order to provide the rationale for another U.S. invasion.[4] Later, on November 30, 1961, Robert Kennedy oversaw another track: Operation Mongoose, a campaign to "use our available assets . . . to help Cuba overthrow the Communist regime."[5] A part of these plans involved the assassination of Castro by means of Mafia "assets."

Castro had done nothing to lull or mollify the United States. In fact, there were points at which he seemed to provoke the United States deliberately. On December 1, 1961, for instance, he made a radio declaration that he was a "Marxist Leninist" and would remain so "until the last day of my life."[6] Then came indications that Castro might put on trial all the exiles from Brigade 2506, the invasion group captured at the Bay of Pigs. Upon conviction, there was the risk of mass executions. Indeed, some five members of Brigade 2506 had been summarily and publicly dispatched months earlier. Moreover, Cuba's military position had improved dramatically. The Cuban New Year's Day parade in 1962 gave the CIA its first extensive look at Soviet Bloc arms deliveries. The Cuban Revolutionary Air Force had become startlingly impressive, including sixty Soviet-built MIG-15s, MIG-17s, and MIG-19s along with helicopters and transport aircraft.

COUNTERING CASTRO

The campaign to counter Castro proceeded along multiple tracks. Diplomatically, the Cuban regime was isolated. At a vote of the Organization of American States (OAS) held in Uruguay at the end of January 1962, Cuba was ousted from the OAS, an action without precedent. Another resolution was adopted that prohibited OAS members from selling arms to Cuba and authorized a series of collective defense measures against Cuban activities in the hemisphere.[7]

In the shadow world of covert operations, Brigadier General Edward G. Lansdale was made Operation Mongoose's director. Lansdale had become a famous Cold War protagonist at the forefront of anti-Communist campaigns in the Philippines and Vietnam. And in an extraordinary act of self-promotion, he had arranged to become the hero of two novels and two films in five years before being tapped by Robert Kennedy to direct the effort against Cuba.

Lansdale's task was to develop a "strongly motivated political action movement" within Cuba capable of generating a revolt that would lead to the downfall of the Castro government. The plan was to push Cuba toward chaos and revolution. In the final stages, the U.S. government would be prepared to offer large-scale uniformed military forces to abet Castro's undoing.[8] "Plausible deniability" would no longer be the issue. In the end, it would be an undisguised American hand at the edge of the cliff that would give Castro the final shove.

The open evidence of the intention to unseat Castro was a unilateral trade embargo. The president stated that the embargo was to be total—with the exception of certain foodstuffs, medicines, and medical supplies. The intent of the embargo, the president stated on February 3, 1962, was to reduce the economic capacity of the Castro government to engage in acts of aggression or subversion or any other activities endangering the security of the United States and other nations of the hemisphere.

By January 1962, Lansdale was supervising thirty-two planning groups for Operation Mongoose. By February 1962, Mongoose planners had fixed October 1962 as the "target," but "not a rigid time-table," for the last stage of the operation. Stage VI would mark the culmination of the "plan for the overthrow of the Communist regime in Cuba, by Cubans from within Cuba, with outside help from the U.S."[9]

The use of open U.S. force to aid the Cuban people in winning their liberty was the sine qua non of Lansdale's effort. "Will the U.S. respond promptly within military force to aid the Cuban revolt?" Lansdale asked rhetorically. The answer, he said, had to be resounding "yes!"[10]

Robert Kennedy forwarded his approval for Lansdale to go ahead with Operation Mongoose at the start of 1962. When Roger Hilsman, the State Department's director of intelligence and research, got wind of Lansdale's suggestion that a small uprising be accompanied by a large-scale American intervention, he wrote a heartfelt complaint. Hilsman agreed that it would be nearly impossible to "unseat the present regime in Havana by anything short of outright military intervention" and that "[t]here exist . . . contingency plans for taking Cuba over in a matter of days." "What does not exist," cautioned Hilsman, "[is] an analysis of the possible consequences of intervention." If the approval of Lansdale's plans remained in effect, Hilsman wrote, "I am afraid we may be heading for a fiasco that could be worse for [the] U.S. than the ill-fated operation of last year."[11]

President Kennedy's real position was unclear. On the one hand, Robert Kennedy would hardly authorize Lansdale to proceed without clearing it with the president. On the other, the president himself—along with Secretary of State Dean Rusk, National Security Assistant McGeorge Bundy, and Secretary of Defense Robert McNamara—paused before the prospect of any further over-the-beach invasions. As the notes of one National Security Council meeting indicate, "The President . . . expressed skepticism that in so far as can now be foreseen circumstances will arise that would justify and make desirable the use of American forces for overt military action."[12]

Later, McGeorge Bundy argued that Operation Mongoose was a self-administered "psychological salve" on the wounded ego of the Kennedy administration.[13] Because "open war" with Castro was "not advisable," Bundy felt that all the president and his closest aides were doing was making the administration feel better by planning tough actions they knew they would never use. If this was, indeed, the president's tactic of the day, it proved useful later when some parts of the senior leadership of the Kennedy administration planned massive actions against Russia while a smaller coterie of intimates plotted the means for a negotiated settlement of the Cuban Missile Crisis.

But if the president's real purpose was to use the Mongoose plans as an instrument of psychological reinvigoration, the new CIA director, a longtime Republican business leader, John McCone, disagreed. "National policy was too cautious," he declared. Officials should "review . . . policy and . . . decide upon more aggressive action including direct military intervention." Once again, however, the State Department demurred. Undersecretary U. Alexis Johnson "raised [the] question of loss of friends and support of other South American countries." McCone retorted that "maybe a show of [U.S.] strength would assist us to win friends rather than lose them."[14]

McCone was a man to take seriously in the U.S. bureaucracy. In interagency deliberations he had become more influential than Rusk ever since being selected by Kennedy to bring some discipline to the CIA at the start of 1962. Early in his tenure, with a strange prescience he later admitted was no more than a hunch, McCone asked if "we now [should] develop a policy for action if missile bases are placed on Cuban soil?" Interestingly, a similar question was raised by Robert Kennedy on March 22, 1962, at the Special Group (Augmented) that supervised Operation Mongoose: "[W]hat would be an . . . action . . . in the event . . . the Soviets establish[ed] a military base in Cuba[?]"

In May 1962, Lansdale echoed a concern that the Soviets might place ballistic missiles in Cuba:

This would act to prevent any future U.S. decision to intervene with U.S. military force. . . . [E]stablishment of a military base(s) in Cuba would [allow the Soviets to] simply taking a page from our book, and would remove their base(s) from Cuba if we would remove ours from Berlin, Turkey or Formosa.[15]

At the start of 1962 the Joint Chiefs of Staff, like the CIA, adopted as a "first priority" the completion of contingency plans to unseat the Cuban government. Oplan 314-16 involved U.S. "assaults against Cuba" that would begin "four days following the initial air strikes"; therefore, the "entire Naval Task Force" would have to be fully loaded and ready at sea in order to meet "the requirement of troop readiness."[16] In other words, if the Russians caught wind of these plans, they might well believe the dispatch of a large number of troops to the Atlantic was the tell-tale signal of an imminent invasion.

U.S. PLANNING AND SOVIET MISSILES

If the Russians did not learn of this planning by means of their own espionage, they could readily adduce them from other "signals" intended for Russia, U.S. allies, Congress, and perhaps Castro himself. For example, a huge mock Caribbean invasion exercise, named Lantphibex-62, was initiated in April 1962. With the president and the visiting shah of Iran looking on over a North Carolina beach, some 40,000 men boarded 84 ships to head out for the largest exercises ever conducted in the Caribbean. Away from the ceremonies, an even larger invasion exercise took place at Vieques Island, a part of Puerto Rico.[17] Soon another ten-day military exercise ensued, designated Whip Lash. At the conclusion of Whip Lash another exercise, Jupiter Springs, was announced.

Khrushchev got the message. He was alarmed that Russia had no ability to protect Cuba from what he and the Cubans were certain would be a vastly more serious replay of the Bay of Pigs invasion. As the Soviet leader remembered, "[O]ne thought kept hammering away at my brain, what will happen if we lose Cuba?"[18] Not that the Soviets had specific intelligence. Indeed, Khrushchev recalled years later, "not . . . [that] . . . we had documentary proof that the Americans were preparing a second invasion. . . . We didn't need documentary proof . . . to expect the worst."[19]

In the early spring of 1962, U.S. Jupiter missiles in Turkey were reported "ready and manned" by U.S. personnel. At the same time, Khrushchev approved the first shipment of Soviet surface to air missiles (SAMs) to Cuba. At the end of May, while vacationing in the Crimea, Khrushchev began to ruminate with Rodin Malinowsky, the Soviet defense minister and a World War II hero, whether it would be wise to follow up the SAM shipments to

Cuba with a fleet of ballistic missiles. Strolling around the vacation compound, Malinowsky noted that must across the sea the Russians now faced America's missiles in Turkey. Khrushchev then asked, "Why do the Americans have such a possibility? They have surrounded us on all sides, and we have no possibility to do the same."[20] Answering his own question, Khrushchev declared, "[W]hy not throw a hedge hog at Uncle Sam's pants?" Malinowsky and Khrushchev knew it would take ten years for Russia to catch the Americans in long range missile deployment. But Soviet intermediate range missiles were reliable and abundant. What about putting them in Cuba, Khrushchev wondered. Would it not only save Cuba, but, perhaps, right the nuclear balance?[21]

Spring 1962: The Shadow of Power

Like Kennedy and Eisenhower, the Russians were worried not so much of their power but of the shadow that power casts. Much of the Cold War was configured around concerns about prestige, no less for the Russians than the Americans. The Kennedy administration fretted perpetually that the loss of Cuba "would gravely diminish our stature in the world."[22] Not to be dismissed, however, was Khrushchev's virtual obsession that the Soviet Union be seen and acknowledged as a "great power" on the same plane as the United States. The decision to place missiles in Cuba thus can be attributed to several motives. First, it was to lock Cuba into the Soviet orbit. Second, it was to rectify the nuclear balance of power and give evidence that the Soviets were a serious nuclear power, something they had attempted to demonstrate for years with space shots, boasts, and parades. Third, the missile deployment would buttress deterrence, making the Americans afraid to use their projected advantage in long range nuclear delivery vehicles. As Khrushchev explained to his colleagues, "Every idiot can start a war, but it is impossible to win this war [with nuclear weapons]. Therefore these missiles [are] . . . to scare them, to restrain them. . . . [and] give them back some of their own medicine."[23]

Fidel Castro accepted the Russian arguments that Cuba needed to accept missiles for its self-defense. Castro did not accept the logic but, as a member of the Soviet Bloc, felt Cuba had a duty to sustain socialism and render aid to Russia. As Castro reminisced in a 1998 interview on CNN television,

On May 29, 1962 . . . they raised the possibility of installing 42 of those missiles. . . . I didn't very much like the idea . . . because of how it would affect the image of the Cuban Revolution. . . . But then . . . [i]f we expected the Soviets to fight on our behalf . . . it would be immoral . . . to refuse to accept . . . those missiles . . . which would improve the balance of power in favor of the . . . socialist camp.[24]

During this interview, which was broadcast on American and British television, Castro remembered that he was not eager to host a Soviet rocket base. But in a 1997 interview he had recalled that when Soviet advisors came to Cuba to discuss the deployment, he was deeply upset when he learned how few missiles were to be installed. It was Castro's earnest suggestion that the Kremlin deploy a thousand missiles, not just forty-two.[25]

From the end of 1961, the Cubans had been receiving Soviet, Czech, and East German intelligence "indicating the United States was planning a full scale" attack on Cuba. Perhaps, one former Cuban intelligence official speculates, the Soviets skewed these reports toward an extreme interpretation of U.S. intentions so as to make it easier for Castro to accept Soviet missiles once they were offered.[26] Cuban intelligence professionals were skeptical of reports that the United States was readying an attack, but Castro was a believer. He accepted Soviet missiles with alacrity out of "socialist duty" and because he was convinced that the United States would not rest until he was out of power or dead. One Cuban plan, tellingly labeled Operation Boomerang, reflected Castro's views: in the case of an invasion, Cuba would authorize sympathetic Cubans in the United States to bomb military and civilian targets in New York and other major U.S. cities.[27]

Summer 1962: U.S. Plans Stall

For all the exercises and all the plans, Operation Mongoose was failing. Castro was not intimated, nor were the Soviets scared away. As Raúl Castro came to Moscow for secret talks about a new defense treaty that would include a Russian missile deployment in Cuba, the CIA's planners despaired of ever getting Mongoose off the ground.[28] But Lansdale vigorously defended his program. Even though there were few "successes," he felt the United States was obligated to do more, especially before October; after that, unfavorable weather might cause another season of delay during which "people inside Cuba will lose hope."[29]

The covert Cold Warriors found that plans for the death of Castro and the infiltration of exile saboteurs were insufficient. As one CIA planning paper noted, Castro's death would have to be combined with "certain . . . considerations" such as an "outbreak of rebellion" followed by a Cuban government "reign of terror." Only after that might the United States find sufficient warrant in the Cuban population's "desire for vigorous action" to take armed action against Cuba. Intervention in Cuba would then proceed, the report concluded, even though there would be serious "penalties" under the best of circumstances, not the least of which would be the "violation of U.S. international commitments."[30]

Meanwhile, the Defense Department had become a cheerleader of its own contingency planning. Exasperated that more than two years of invasion planning and practices were being squandered, Pentagon planners argued that it would be wise to carry out a U.S. intervention sooner rather than later, because "[i]n the future the Castro-Cuban capability for counteraction will improve."[31]

Brigadier General Lansdale was also eager to get on with the work of finishing off Castro directly. It seemed to prompt him to raise again the issue of a Soviet base being established in Cuba. The State Department's response was that "the possibility was too remote to waste time on."[32]

Despite energetic arguments by the Pentagon, Lansdale, and McCone, only a "somewhat more aggressive program" was finally approved. Robert Kennedy "ruled out those which would commit [the] U.S. to deliberate military intervention."[33] Operation Mongoose was floundering. But the chances for an invasion, and war, were increasing dramatically.

NOTES

1. *Foreign Relations of the United States* (FRUS), Vol. X (Washington, DC: U.S. Government Printing Office, 1997), pp. 304–14ff.

2. Ibid., pp. 304, 313–14.

3. Ibid., pp. 484–88.

4. Ibid., pp. 635–41.

5. Ibid., pp. 270, 336.

6. The speech must be put in context. On December 1, 1961, President Kennedy issued a proclamation under the provisions of section 408(b) of the Sugar Act in which he put the sugar quota for Cuba at zero. Later that day, Fidel Castro stated: "I am a Marxist Leninist and I will continue to be a Marxist Leninist until the last day of my life." The translated text of Castro's speech is printed in the *New York Times*, 3 December 1961.

7. Theodore C. Sorensen, *Kennedy* (New York: Bantam, 1966), pp. 669–70.

8. FRUS, Vol. X, Doc. 304.

9. Ibid., Doc. 303.

10. Ibid.

11. Ibid., Doc. 305.

12. Ibid., Doc. 314. See "Special Group Augmented. Guidelines for Operation Mongoose, Washington, March 14, 1962."

13. Robert S. McNamara, James G. Blight, and Robert K. Brigham, with Thomas J. Biersteker and Herbert Y. Schandler, *Argument without End: In Search of Answers to the Vietnam Tragedy* (New York: Public Affairs, 1999), p. 215.

14. FRUS, Vol. X, Doc. 319.

15. Ibid., Doc. 341.

16. Ibid., Doc. 306.

17. For public coverage of the maneuvers, see: "Big Maneuver Opens," *New York Times*, 10 April 1962; "President Joins Fleet Maneuvers," *New York Times*, 14 April 1962; "President Sees Atlantic Fleet Hunt and Destroy 'Enemy' Submarine" and "9,000 Marines Land," *New York Times*, 15 April 1962; "10,000 Marines in Sea Games," *New York Times*, 16 April 1962; "Marines Maneuver on Isle," *New York Times*, 25 April 1962.

18. Nikita S. Khrushchev, *Khrushchev Remembers*, trans. Strobe Talbot (Boston: Little, Brown, 1970), p. 493.

19. Nikita S. Khrushchev, *Khrushchev Remembers: The Last Testament*, trans. Strobe Talbot (Boston: Little, Brown, 1974), p. 511.

20. Michael R. Bechloss, *The Crisis Years* (New York: HarperCollins, 1991), p. 381.

21. Alexander Fursenko and Timothy Naftali, *One Hell of a Gamble* (New York: W. W. Norton, 1997), p. 167.

22. Khrushchev, *Khrushchev Remembers: The Last Testament*, p. 493.

23. Fursenko and Naftali, *One Hell of a Gamble*, p. 182.

24. <http://cnn.com/SPECIALS/cold.war/episodes/10/interviews/castro/>, March 1998 interview.

25. "Castro Loved Missiles," *Minneapolis Star Tribune*, 16 August 1997, p. 8.

26. Domingo Amuchastegui, in James G. Blight and David A. Welch, eds., *Intelligence and the Cuban Missile Crisis* (London: Frank Cass, 1998), pp. 96, 97ff.

27. Ibid., p. 99.

28. The CIA was aware that Raúl Castro was in Moscow but did not know what the talks were about and, in fact, assumed they had failed. See Raymond Garthoff, *Reflections on the Cuban Missile Crisis*, rev. ed. (Washington, DC: Brookings Institution, 1989), p. 67.

29. FRUS, Vol. X, Doc. 360.

30. Ibid., Doc. 275.

31. Ibid., Doc. 368.

32. Ibid., Doc. 370.

33. Ibid., Doc. 380.

8

August 1962: Spotting the Buildup, Planning for the Worst

At first, the CIA concluded that Raúl Castro's visit to the Soviet Union in July 1962 to solicit arms and aid was not successful because there was no communiqué issued at the end of his trip. By September, it was becoming clear that the CIA had been wrong. But how wrong was not yet evident. From 3,000 to 5,000 Soviet personnel were spotted on the island by U.S. intelligence sources; these personnel were actually a fraction of some 42,000 that were on the island by October 1. Twenty Soviet vessels had been counted coming into Cuba since late July, and five more were reported on the way by mid-August. All Soviet shipping to the island, the CIA now concluded, involved "dual use" military and civilian goods. It was oddly ominous that when Soviet military personnel were sighted, they were dressed as tourists. The net effect, said the CIA, was to indicate the quiet yet "most extensive campaign to bolster a non-bloc country ever undertaken by the U.S.S.R."[1]

The true extent of the buildup was not known until 1988.[2] Inexplicably, notwithstanding abundant eyewitness reports of large, crew-cut blonde, Russian-speaking "tourists" bedecked in nearly identical Hawaiian shirts traveling in platoon-sized groups, the CIA never figured there were more than 16,000 Russian personnel on the island—not even at the peak of the crisis with extensive reconnaissance and heightened monitoring of other intelligence sources.[3]

A U-2 reconnaissance mission flown over Cuba on August 29, 1962, revealed that the Soviets were developing a huge military base in Cuba protected not only by MIG fighters, light bombers, and cruise missiles for coastal defense but also by a ring of surface to air missiles. The size of the buildup was large, but still grossly underestimated. Not noted then or later were either the 100 tactical nuclear weapons or the squadron of Russian submarines with nuclear payloads already on the island. Nor were the Soviet ballistic missiles spotted until they began to be placed on launch pads ten days after they were off-loaded in Havana harbor on October 3, 1962.

So massive was the Soviet deployment that Cuban intelligence was "amazed and baffled by the failure of the CIA, the Pentagon, and even a majority of members of Congress to acknowledge or respond" to the huge influx of men and materiel. "Either the CIA was truly ignorant," the Cubans calculated, "or it was deliberately withholding its knowledge." Perhaps, the Cubans puzzled, "the CIA did not want to tell the president something he did not want to hear" and was "unwilling to see what the Kennedy administration did not want to see," at least until after the 1962 mid-term election. Or perhaps, speculated the Cubans, the CIA was simply "incompetent."[4]

The scale of the Soviet buildup—though not known in even a fraction of its particulars—was enough to convince the director of the CIA, John McCone, that Cuba would soon be a home base for Soviet medium range ballistic missiles (MRBMs). McCone got high-level Kennedy advisors to discuss hypothetical remedies that were actually later used. These included "blockades of Soviet and Bloc shipping into Cuba or alternatively a total blockade of Cuba."[5]

Robert Kennedy and McGeorge Bundy demurred. The president's closest advisors were reluctant to push the discussion to any means that would threaten escalation. Not knowing that nuclear missiles were already in Cuba, the Kennedy administration was not willing to risk a blockade. But Robert Kennedy was now prepared to become more proactive against Cuba. "[W]hat other aggressive steps could be taken[?]" the attorney general asked; he suggested that planners consider "provoking an action against Guantánamo which would permit [the] U.S. to retaliate."[6]

On August 23, 1962, McCone met President Kennedy and his most senior foreign policy advisors at the White House. Again, McCone stated the United States was on the cusp of a national emergency. The administration had to mobilize "sufficient armed forces to occupy [Cuba], destroy the regime, free the people, and establish in Cuba a peaceful country which will be a member of the community of American states."[7] The meeting resulted in the highly restricted "Top Secret" National Security Action Memorandum No. 181 [NSAM 181].[8]

NSAM 181 reflected the president's guess that if there were MRBMs in Cuba, they would be linked (as it turned out to be the case) with U.S. deployments on Soviet borders. Hence the National Security Council was ordered to look for actions that "can be taken to get Jupiter missiles out of Turkey." In addition, the president urged existing Operation Mongoose plans to "be developed with all possible speed." The president also requested a "study . . . of the advantages and disadvantages of action to liberate Cuba by blockade or invasion or other action beyond Mongoose."

The Defense Department was ordered to "study . . . military alternatives . . . to eliminate any installations in Cuba capable of launching [a] nuclear attack on the U.S. What would be the pros and cons, for example, of pinpoint attack, general counter-force attack, and outright invasion?"[9] Kennedy seemed to want, at last, to give the Mongoose plans the muscle its directors had longed for from the onset. The president also wanted[10] to have an augmented repertoire to meet the worst—proof that the Russians were making Cuba a base for offensive nuclear missiles.[11]

GAUGING PUBLIC OPINION AND COVERT INTELLIGENCE

At the end of August 1962, President Kennedy and his closest advisors were beginning to contemplate the worst while discounting it in public as a figment of the imagination of disgruntled Cuban exiles and, especially, congressional Republicans who were eager to discredit Kennedy before the mid-term elections. The domestic imperative of American politics seemed to explain to the Russians, like the Cubans, why Kennedy appeared to be coy about the missiles after the disclosures of Senator Kenneth Keating on the Senate floor in August and September that he had proof positive of Soviet missiles in Cuba (which, however, he was unwilling to share with one of his closest friends, CIA director McCone).

Keating, a New York Republican on the Senate Foreign Relations Committee, had risen on the floor of the U.S. Senate to make ten speeches claiming there was alarming evidence of Soviet "rocket installations in Cuba."[12] But it was six weeks before he found much support among his colleagues or among professionals in the administration.

However, as campaign season began for the mid-term elections, the charges proliferated about the administration being soft on Cuba. The chairman of the Republican National Committee jabbed at Kennedy's most sensitive spot—his concern for foreign policy resolve: "If we are asked to state the issue in one word, that word would be Cuba—symbol of tragic irresolution of the administration."[13] On August 27, 1962, Republican senator Homer E. Capehart of Indiana declared, "It is high time that . . . President Kennedy quit 'examining the situation' and start protecting the interests of the United States."[14] Former vice president Richard Nixon, on the gubernatorial campaign stump in California, proposed that Cuban Communism be "quarantined" by a naval blockade.[15] The pressure mounted. As the political campaign began, one observer spotted a sign at a Kennedy rally in Chicago that read, "Less Profile—More Courage."[16] The widely respected and conservative London *Economist* reported that America had become "obsessed" by the "problem" of Cuba.[17]

As congressional excitement grew—there were six congressional resolutions on Cuba, implying that the administration was not alert to the increasing military challenge there—the bureaucracy continued to insist that its well-worn explanation of Soviet behavior was still valid. Congress had begun to ring with reports, published and unpublished, of a huge Soviet buildup in Cuba. Yet the Kennedy administration tried to discredit Senator Keating's military sagacity in Congress.[18]

The extant intelligence wisdom that the Soviets would not make Cuba a missile base was so powerful that many of the earliest intelligence reports seem to have been diminished or even shredded, unread by high-level administration officials.[19] Later, the intuition of McCone and Republicans such as Keating proved an embarrassment to the administration. Indeed, the reasons why McCone's suggestions and needling were not acted on with more alacrity take explaining. Seven possible reasons can be proposed.

First, from Pearl Harbor to the Persian Gulf War, Americans have had experience with gathering the right intelligence and then not taking it seriously because it does not conform to the collective mindset of the hour. In the Cuban crisis there was a consensus, starting with the top of the U.S. government (and reinforced by abundant later studies), that the Soviets had no reason and were too sober-minded to take such a risky move as putting offensive nuclear weapons in Cuba. It is hard enough, as any student of psychology knows, to get individuals who have invested much in a position to change their mind. It is doubly hard to secure a re-evaluation of an opinion if the belief is underpinned by evident "rationality."

Second, within bureaucracies there is a syndrome known as "not invented here"—that is, material that does not come from a source that has already gained credibility within, say, the U.S. intelligence community has a limited chance of carrying weight in the councils of government.

Third, as one student of intelligence has noted,

[T]he accuracy and usefulness of intelligence can only be improved so far. . . . [T]here is a performance limit to intelligence assessment. Misperceptions that result from perfectly normal . . . psychological needs are, for analysts and policy makers alike, a professional hazard.[20]

Fourth, the president's Republican critics were frequently fierce, and an election was nearing. The charges that there were offensive missiles in Cuba were almost exclusively leveled by Republicans, chiefly Senator Keating. These charges were echoed in private by his good friend, CIA director John McCone, also a Republican, who seemed therefore (to the Kennedy team) somewhat tainted by witting or unwitting bias.

Fifth, the appearance of surface to air missiles (SAMs), by themselves, was not alarming to many intelligence professionals. Indeed, it had been predicted because the Russians already had placed SAMs in Egypt, Indonesia, and Syria. Even the surreptitious introduction of SAMs in Cuba, unlike their overt introduction to Soviet clients elsewhere, was explicable to U.S. intelligence given the fact that the Russians were aware of American political sensitivities and the skittishness of the largely Catholic Cuban public to any overt alliance with international Bolshevism.

Sixth, the mere fact that SAMs were deployed at the island's periphery, and not at airfields, did not seem especially meaningful to the CIA's professionals. But McCone sensed that because the SAMs were not at known military installations, the missiles must be shielding something else. To the CIA and DIA (Defense Intelligence Agency), the island's size and topography explained the position of the SAMs better than did the conjecture that McCone was offering.[21]

Seventh, the Russians had gone out of their way to reassure the Kennedy team at the highest level that they would not introduce offensive ballistic missiles into Cuba. There were personal assurances transmitted by Ambassador Anatoly Dobrynin and a number of private emissaries from Khrushchev that he would do nothing to upset the Democrats' chances before the elections.[22] The assurances allowed the White House to issue a statement on September 4 asserting that Soviet offensive missiles in Cuba would be a critical threat to American security. The statement referred to the installation of anti-aircraft defense missiles and a number of Soviet support technicians—some 3,500; but, Kennedy added, there was no evidence of Soviet combat forces in Cuba, nor any evidence of military bases with an offensive capability such as ground-to-ground missiles. "Were it to be otherwise, the gravest issues would arise."[23]

Nonetheless, speculation about missiles in Cuba continued and begged a response from the administration. In a press conference at the Department of State on September 13, 1962, Kennedy underscored what the United States would do if missiles were to be placed in Cuba. Such a Russian action, said the president, would be cause for an American military response. Kennedy began his remarks by noting that the American press had recently speculated that an invasion of Cuba by the United States was in the offing.

The president dismissed the speculation, not as rumors of ongoing planning and exercises (as was actually the case) but as a "frantic effort" by Castro and his backers to bolster a troubled regime. Military action by the United States against Cuba would be triggered, Kennedy states, only if Cuba posed a threat to any other nation in the hemisphere, or if Cuba became an offensive military base for the Soviet Union.

President Kennedy warned:

If at any time the Communist build-up in Cuba were to endanger or interfere with our security in any way, including our base at Guantánamo, our passage to the Panama Canal, our missile and space activities at Cape Canaveral, or the lives of American citizens in this country, or if Cuba should ever attempt to export its aggressive purposes by force or the threat of force against any nation in this hemisphere, or become an offensive military base of significant capacity for the Soviet union, then this country will do whatever must be done to protect its own security and that of its allies.[24]

Kennedy later ruefully recalled his remarks of September 4 and September 13. It would have been better, reflected the president, as the Cuban Missile Crisis unfolded, either to have said nothing or to have said that any Russian introduction of medium range missiles to Cuba would mean nothing to the balance of power. Kennedy mused:

Last month I said we weren't going to [allow it]. Last month I should have said . . . that we don't care. But when we said we're not going to [tolerate them] and then they go ahead and do it, and then we do nothing, then I should think that our risks increase.[25]

Unknowingly and uncomfortably, Kennedy had managed to find himself on a perch from which a retreat seemed all but impossible. His exposed position was only cemented by Soviet assurances that it would not place offensive weapons in Cuba. One of the most important of these came on September 11, two days before Kennedy's press conference; it was, in fact, the primary warrant for Kennedy's advisors to draft his remarks.

Later Andrei Gromyko, the soviet foreign minister, and his deputy, Anastas Mikoyan, stated that Kennedy had known of the missiles all along and had chosen not "to speak [publicly] about the missiles until after the congressional elections."[26] But it was clear then and later that Soviet deception was a deliberate and consistent effort to allow Khrushchev to plan the surprise announcement of his move during his scheduled visit to the UN in the late fall, after the U.S. mid-term elections. Khrushchev was convinced that in the end Kennedy would simply have to get used to being uncomfortably in the sights of nuclear weapons just minutes away.

DECEIT UNMASKED

By mid-September, a torrent of American press stories reported the massive Soviet arms buildup in Cuba. Later, some people speculated that the source of the leaks was none other than CIA director McCone.[27] Notwithstanding Khrushchev's personal assurances, McCone relentlessly pursued his singular but powerful hunch that the worst fears of the administration, offensive missiles in Cuba, were in the offing. At every opportunity the director demanded a systematic regime of overflights to ferret out the missiles. Even on his honeymoon, which began on Labor Day 1962, McCone's drumbeat of messages reverberated throughout the CIA's headquarters. But his constant suggestion for surveillance of Cuba seemed an especially poor idea to both Secretary of State Dean Rusk and Secretary of Defense Robert McNamara. Rust and McNamara were mindful of an earlier incident in May 1960 when a U-2 was shot down over Russia, causing an emerging Soviet-American détente to fail. The U-2 incident dogged Washington for years. Rusk and McNamara were worried that U.S. surveillance flights over Cuba might provoke an incident that would complicate relations between the United States and Russia.

Rusk faced a snide and aggressive Robert Kennedy, who already had formed an impression of the ever courtly Rusk as a "relic" unsuited to the fast and hard politics of the New Frontier, especially in matters of security. Rusk argued for the use of only peripheral surveillance flights over international waters near Cuba, if there were to be augmented reconnaissance flights at all, in order to minimize the risk of losing a plane. Kennedy listened to the secretary's explanations, the most important of which was that a U-2 had been shot down over China just days earlier and that the Soviet SAMs in Cuba were operational. The attorney general then tossed a series of increasingly pugnacious barbs toward Rusk, a man with nearly double his years and experience. Kennedy's sally ended with a question that spoke volumes regarding the administration's attitude toward force and diplomatic experts, of whom Rusk seemed emblematic: "What's the matter, Dean?" asked Robert Kennedy of the secretary, a man who could recall making his way in secret military operations through Burma's jungles during World War II. The younger Kennedy answered his own question with another: "No guts?"[28]

Later, partisans of the Kennedys noted that the slant angle of the photographs produced by the U-2 were unhelpful in adducing Soviet activities in Cuba. But it is uncertain if the Soviets would have been far enough along in the construction and deployments for any earlier flights to have revealed their purposes.[29] And if a U-2 had been brought down, the diplomatic fallout might have delayed subsequent overflights and discovery of the missiles. However, it must be added, if the overflights had been delayed much past mid-October, Soviet rocket installations would have been complete and the missiles probably would have been on the same alert that other Soviet rocket forces had been on since mid-September. Then, it would have been much harder to get out the Russian MRBMs by any means.[30]

Responding to McCone's urging, the CIA issued Special National Intelligence Estimate (SNIE) 85-3-62 on September 19, 1962. But the CIA stuck to its guns. Although there was now some intelligence indicating the ongoing deployment of nuclear missiles to Cuba, the reports were called neither compelling nor compatible with Soviet interests and past behavior; moreover, the CIA insisted, the Soviets "would almost certainly estimate that this could not be done without provoking a dangerous U.S. reaction."[31]

Additional arrivals of Soviet jets, tanks, and artillery, as well as reports by Cuban refugees of huge cylindrical objects being trucked through Havana in the dead of night, might have augured a Soviet endeavor that was not typical of other deployments in the Middle East and Asia. But the heads of nearly all U.S. agencies, with the exception of a few mavericks like McCone, insisted that the Soviet deployments were defensive.[32]

Khrushchev's letter to President Kennedy on September 28, 1962, reinforced the administration's sense that the Soviets were undertaking only defensive deployments in Cuba. Khrushchev protested Kennedy's recent call-up of 150,000 U.S. military reserve forces, a step directed not so much in reality toward Cuba as toward Berlin. Khrushchev knew the true purpose of Kennedy's move but nonetheless fixed on the problem of Cuba. Was the United States trying to show it "has the right to attack Cuba whenever it wishes?" asked Khrushchev. If so, he said, it constituted "a step [that made] the atmosphere red-hot."[33]

One of Khrushchev's aides subsequently recalled a meeting at which Khrushchev was receiving reports on the initial missile deployments. "Soon," the Soviet leader predicted to an aide, all "hell will break loose." The aide replied, "I hope the boat does not capsize, Nikita Sergeyevich." Khrushchev thought for a moment, then answered, "Now it's too late to change anything."[34]

HEDGING BETS

Meanwhile, U.S. contingency plans proliferated throughout the highest levels of government. There were even some exercises and preliminary redeployments. Given later intelligence, definitive only in mid-October, that the Soviets were installing *offensive* ballistic missiles in Cuba, the long and perhaps provocative planning of the Pentagon and CIA may have conjured the worst; but in the end they also helped prepare the administration to deal with that threat once it did occur. To historian James Hershberg, it seems clear that the "Kennedy Administration believed it was headed toward, let alone desired, a military confrontation with Cuba in the immediate future, just before news of the missiles."[35]

In any case, the long season of exercises and plans was about to pay off. Secretary of Defense Robert McNamara, in a meeting with the Joint Chiefs of Staff on October 1, 1962, directed the chiefs to have in place, by October 20, a capability at the ready to invade Cuba. He listed a number of circumstances that would warrant an invasion:

1. [A] Western response [to a move in Berlin] . . .
2. Evidence that the Castro regime has permitted the positioning of bloc offensive weapon systems on Cuban soil . . .
3. An attack against . . . U.S. planes or vessels . . .
4. A substantial popular uprising in Cuba, the leaders of which request assistance in recovering Cuban independence . . .
5. Cuban armed assistance to subversion in other parts of the Western Hemisphere . . .
6. A decision by the President that affairs in Cuba have reached a point inconsistent with continuing U.S. national security.[36]

The comment about a popular uprising is interesting because U.S. intelligence records and those of the Kennedy administration's National Security Council meetings reveal no evidence of discontent on the part of the Cuban population that might have led to open rebellion. Perhaps this was an allusion to the possibility that one of the two squads sent by the United States to Cuba in order to eliminate Castro might yet find success.

At the same time that McNamara was asking "the views of the Chiefs" as to "(a) the removal of the threat to U.S. security of Soviet weapon systems in Cuba, or (b) the removal of the Castro regime and the securing in the island,"[37] the commander-in-chief of the Atlantic Fleet announced a "training exercise" called PHIBRIGLEX-2 to practice landing U.S. Navy personnel and Marines in order to liberate a Caribbean island from a mythical despot named Ortsac (*Castro* spelled backwards). Asked about the coincidence of heightened U.S. military preparations and the stepped-up Operation Mongoose activities of the CIA just before Soviet missiles were discovered, Admiral George W. Anderson Jr., the chief of naval operations during the

Kennedy years, told Hershberg in 1987 that Kennedy's chairman of the Joint Chiefs, Maxwell Taylor, believed McNamara ordered the increased operations so as to spark an upheaval on the island.[38]

To Hershberg it seems possible that the Kennedy entourage, and perhaps the president himself, wanted to carry out an "October Surprise" timed to counterbalance the Bay of Pigs embarrassment and turn Cuba into an asset instead of an electoral albatross just before the nation went to the polls on November 6, 1962.[39]

Overall, despite a congressional atmosphere that favored some kind of action against Cuba, President Kennedy and his secretary of defense seemed to pull back from any offensive action. In the weeks before missiles were discovered and the crisis blossomed, McNamara argued for restraint; indeed, on the afternoon of October 15, 1962, hours before U-2 photos would prove that the Soviets were placing MRBMs in Cuba, McNamara informed the Joint Chiefs of Staff that the "President wants no military action [against Cuba] within the next three months."[40]

On balance, most of the evidence indicates that the White House was only trying to hedge its bets domestically and internationally and that all the exercises and preparations were largely a defensive reaction to congressional alarms led by the indefatigable Kenneth Keating, who had just announced to the Senate chamber that there were now exactly six IRBM bases under construction in Cuba. The president's national security assistant, McGeorge Bundy, responded: "there is no present evidence and I think there is no present likelihood that the Cuban government and the Soviet government would, in combination, attempt to install a major offensive capability" in Cuba.[41]

NOTES

1. *Foreign Relations of the United States* (FRUS), Vol. XI (Washington, DC: U.S. Government Printing Office, 1997), Doc. 363.

2. Raymond Garthoff, in James G. Blight and David A. Welch, eds., *Intelligence and the Cuban Missile Crisis* (London: Frank Cass, 1998), p. 29.

3. Beth A. Fisher, in ibid., p. 159.

4. Domingo Amuchastegui, "Cuban Intelligence and the October Crisis," *Intelligence and National Security*, vol. 13, no. 5 (1998), pp. 101–3.

5. FRUS, Vol. XI, Doc. 382.

6. See Graham T. Allison Jr., ed., *The Secret Cuban Missile Crisis Documents of the Central Intelligence Agency* (Washington, DC: Brassey's, 1994), p. 13.

7. FRUS, Vol. XI, Doc. 385.

8. Ibid., Doc. 386.

9. Ibid., Doc. 386.

10. McGeorge Bundy in ibid.

11. McGeorge Bundy in ibid.

12. John Prados, *The Soviet Estimate* (New York: Dial Press, 1982), p. 135.

13. Thomas Halper, *Foreign Policy Crisis: Appearance and Reality in Decision Making* (Columbus, OH: C.E. Merrill Publishing, 1971), p. 132.

14. *U.S. News & World Report*, 10 September 1962, p. 45.

15. *New York Times*, 19 September 1962.

16. Quincy Wright, "The Cuban Quarantine of 1962," in *Power and Order*, eds. John G. Stoessinger and Alan Westin (New York: Harcourt, Brace and World, 1964), p. 186.

17. *Economist*, 6 October 1962, p. 15.

18. Edward Wedintal and Charles Bartlett, *Facing the Brink* (New York: Scribner's, 1967), p. 69.

19. Robert E. Quirk, *Fidel Castro* (New York: W. W. Norton, 1993), p. 418.

20. Beth Fischer, "Perception, Intelligence Errors, and the Cuban Missile Crisis," *Intelligence and National Security* 13, no. 3 (Autumn 1998): p. 157ff.

21. Blight and Welch, "Introduction," *Intelligence and the Cuban Missile Crisis*, p. 5.

22. Anatoly Dobrynin, *In Confidence: Moscow's Ambassador to America's Six Cold War Presidents* (New York: Times Books, 1995), p. 70ff. Most notably, Georgi Bolshakov (ostensibly a press attaché, presumably an intelligence officer) had been used as a go-between to deliver a personal assurance from the Soviet leader that only defensive weapons were being shipped to Cuba.

23. For text, see Department of State, *Bulletin*, 24 September 1962, p. 450.

24. *Public Papers of the Presidents of the United States: John F. Kennedy, 1962* (Washington, DC: U.S. Government Printing Office, 1979), pp. 674–75.

25. Ernest R. May and Philip D. Zelikow, eds., *The Kennedy Tapes: Inside the White House during the Cuban Missile Crisis* (Cambridge, MA: Harvard University Press, 1997), p. 92.

26. Garthoff, in Blight and Welch, *Intelligence and the Cuban Missile Crisis*, pp. 45–65.

27. Robert Smith Thompson, *The Missiles of October* (New York: Simon and Schuster, 1992), p. 163.

28. FRUS, Vol. X, Doc. 421.

29. Blight and Welch, "Introduction," *Intelligence and the Cuban Missile Crisis*, p. 6.

30. See Garthoff, in Blight and Welch, *Intelligence and the Cuban Missile Crisis*, pp. 53, 59 fn38.

31. Central Intelligence Agency, "National Intelligence Estimate: The Military Buildup in Cuba, 9/19/62", in *CIA Documents on the Cuban Missile Crisis, 1962*, ed. Mary S. McAuliffe (Washington, DC: Central Intelligence Agency, 1992).

32. Doc. 398. Telegram from the Embassy to the Soviet Union to the Department of State, Moscow, August 31, 1962, 6 P.M. See John Prados, *The Soviet Estimate* (New York: Dial Press, 1982), pp. 134–38.

33. For text, see FRUS, Vol. VI, pp. 152–61; Vol. V, Doc. 241.

34. Oleg Troyanovsky, "The Caribbean Crisis: A View from the Kremlin," *International Affairs* [Moscow], April–May 1992, p. 150.

35. See James Hershberg, "More New Evidence on the Cuban Missile Crisis: More Documents from the Russian Archives," *Cold War International History Project*, Bulletin 8–9 (Washington, DC: Woodrow Wilson International Center for Scholars, 1997) <www.cwihp.si.edu>.

36. James G. Hershberg, "Before 'The Missiles of October': Did Kennedy Plan a Military Strike against Cuba?" in *The Cuban Missile Crisis Revisited*, ed. James Nathan (New York: St. Martin's Press, 1992), pp. 237–80.

37. Yale Law School Web Site <http://www.yale.edu/lawweb/avalon/diplomacy/forrel/cuba/cuba004.htm>.

38. Anderson (October 1987), in Hershberg, "Before 'The Missiles of October.' "

39. On October 4, for example, presidential pollster Louis Harris advised Kennedy that 62 percent of voters had a negative view of his handling of the Cuban issue.

40. "Notes Taken from Transcripts of Meetings of the Joint Chiefs of Staff, October–November 1962, dealing with the Cuban Missile Crisis (handwritten notes were made in 1976 and typed in 1993)," released under the Freedom of Information Act. Copy made available by the National Security Archive, Historical Division of the Joint Chiefs of Staff, April 1981; see Hershberg, "More New Evidence of the Cuban Missile Crisis: More Documents from the Russian Archives."

41. Weintal and Bartlett, *Facing the Brink*, p. 59.

9

Thirteen Days on the Brink of War: The Cuban Missile Crisis

On October 14, 1962, the very day National Security Assistant McGeorge Bundy was trying to calm the domestic alarm over Cuba, a U-2 aircraft flying a reconnaissance mission over the western part of Cuba produced the first verified evidence of the existence of Soviet offensive missile sites on the island. Analysis and interpretation of the 928 photographs taken during the flight revealed three medium range ballistic missile sites near San Cristobal, in Pinar del Rio Province. U.S. analysts counted eight large MRBM transporters and four erector launchers already in firing positions. But it was unclear—in fact, it was unclear throughout the entire crisis—how many of the missiles could actually be fired.

At 8:30 P.M. on Monday, October 15, the CIA reported to Bundy the conclusive evidence of the administration's worst fears having been verified. To Bundy, "It was a hell of a secret, and it must remain one." Yet he chose not to tell the president the startling news that evening. As he explained to President Kennedy later, the president had "had a strenuous campaign weekend" and was "returning from Niagara Falls and New York City at 1:40 Monday morning." So Bundy "decided that a quiet evening and a night of sleep" would be best for the president. Bundy asked, "What help would it be to you to give you this . . . news and then tell you nothing could be done about it till morning?"[1]

On the morning of October 16, McGeorge Bundy notified President Kennedy that what had formerly been hypothetical conjecture was now real. Soviet offensive missiles had been discovered in Cuba.

By the time Kennedy convened his advisors, it was discovered that the Russians had placed forty-two medium range missiles in Cuba. The president's advisors, an ad hoc committee of top officials, considered the options. After a week of deliberations, essentially only two alternatives emerged. As had been rehearsed and planned earlier, (1) the United States could launch air strikes on the Russians' offensive missile sites and follow up with a massive U.S. invasion, or (2) the United States could institute a blockade of the island coupled with a demand that the missiles be removed. If the demand was not met, then an air strike and an invasion would follow.

All the previous Soviet assurances—that there were no offensive missiles in Cuba and that the Soviets would not, in the near future, make Kennedy's domestic or international position difficult—had been revealed as duplicitous. The sense of personal betrayal on the part of Kennedy and his immediate entourage was palpable: "He can't do that to me," Kennedy is said to have complained to Bundy on hearing the news on October 16. Kennedy was more disturbed by the audacity of the move than he was bothered by the arithmetic of likely mutual atomic damage. He was also affronted.

I can't understand their viewpoint, if they're aware of what we said at the press conferences [at which the administration warned in September against placing missiles in Cuba]. . . . I don't think there is any record of the Soviets ever making this direct a challenge, ever, really.[2]

To Kennedy, it seemed as if Soviet premier Nikita Khrushchev was both "rubbing [the president's] nose in the dirt" and being reckless.[3] To Kennedy, therefore, the sum of the Soviet action constituted both a national and a personal test. On October 22, President Kennedy announced to a national television audience that the United States was imposing a blockade around Cuba that would be removed only if the missiles were taken out by the Soviets. He told the American people the "secret, swift, and extraordinary" decision to base strategic missiles for the first time outside of Soviet soil was "a deliberately provocative and unjustified change in the status quo which cannot be accepted by this country if our courage and our commitments are ever to be trusted again by friend or foe."[4]

During the next four days, some ships carrying Russian goods were stopped and searched and some Soviet vessels carrying missiles toward Cuba turned back, but the crisis intensified. Blockades, in international law, are clear acts of war. The Russians might well have challenged the American blockade of Cuba with force had it not been for the remarkable and quiet diplomatic labors of Secretary of State Dean Rusk. He called a special session of the OAS in Washington and managed to garner the concurrence of twenty states with no dissent for the American blockade, thus giving it an added veneer of legality and international weight. At the same time, U.S. diplomats in Guinea and Senegal negotiated with those governments to close their airspace to Russian cargo planes en route to Cuba that had previously used Guinea and Senegal as refueling spots. Similar public efforts at arguing the case in the UN, as well as private briefs shared with NATO allies, turned a dangerous and legally dubious maneuver into a successful effort to buy time.

Fortunately, the mechanism of a blockade was available. The legal preparatory work had begun early in October, and much of the Atlantic Fleet was already at sea. One of the contingent maneuvers the Atlantic Command had set to practice was, in fact, a blockade. Moreover, the idea of a blockade of Cuba had been part of the public debate for some time. Direct intervention had never been popular. But an early October 1962 poll, commissioned by the White House, showed the public favoring a blockade by an 8 to 1 margin. Moreover, the precautionary measures of early October had included a National Security Action Memorandum that closed all U.S. ports to ships that were involved in Soviet Bloc trade with Cuba.

On October 26, Khrushchev sent an emotional private message to Kennedy indicating a willingness to remove the missiles if the United States would guarantee that it would not invade Cuba. The next day, however, a more formal and much tougher message was delivered to Kennedy demanding that the United States remove its missiles from Turkey in exchange for the removal of Soviet missiles from Cuba. After the crisis, the public story was that the crisis was resolved at a meeting between U.S. attorney general Robert Kennedy and Soviet ambassador Anatoly Dobrynin on October 27. The agreement they hammered out held that the Russians would remove the missiles in return for the U.S. non-invasion pledge. In the initial reports, Robert Kennedy only ambiguously alluded to the fact that missiles were scheduled to leave Turkey if and when Turkey and the rest of the NATO allies agreed; but this understanding was not a promise and was in no way linked to the Soviet withdrawal from Cuba, which had to be immediate and separate from anything that would happen in Turkey. On the next day, October 28, the Soviets announced on radio that the missiles would be removed. The world exhaled.

THE REAL STORY

In Khrushchev's apt description, it was a time when "a smell of burning" hung heavy in the air.[5] President Kennedy's apparently controlled and masterful way of forcing Khrushchev to withdraw the missiles in the thirteen-day crisis has become a paradigmatic example of the way force can be harnessed to a policy by an elaborate manipulation of threats and gambits, negotiation and intimidation. Instead of seeing Kennedy's actions as largely an intuitive response to a threat to his administration's electoral future, pride, and strategic posture, academic and government analysts have viewed Kennedy's response as a highly calibrated dissection of alternatives as worked out by a skilled group of advisors. As Hans J. Morgenthau, an eminent scholar and a critic of the Kennedy administration, concluded, "The Cuban Crisis of 1962 . . . was the distillation of a collective intellectual effort of a high order, the like of which must be rare in history."[6]

After the crisis was over, Kennedy's national security team felt that they had mastered the merger of politics and force as an instrument of policy. The ad hoc grouping of advisors—self-labeled the Executive Committee of the President ("ExCom" for some purposes, but meaningfully code-named "Elite" by the U.S. Secret Service)— thought they had developed a capacity to precisely oversee and orchestrate force. Indeed, "crisis management" became the coin of an exclusive realm. National security managers occupied a narrow circle with few apprentices and still fewer fully accredited practitioners. As the State Department's senior intelligence officer, Roger Hilsman, put it, crisis management in foreign affairs had become "like blue cheese . . . [an] acquired taste," gained by rarefied experience and apprenticeship at the top of—or even astride—the national security bureaucracy.[7]

The common characterization of the ExCom was that it was a paragon of organizational effectiveness. One student of decision making, Thomas Halper, wrote:

The Executive Committee was important in helping plumb the reality of the situation. . . . The men chosen were calm, rational, and frank. . . . [T]he Committee was the scene of intellectual conflict . . . and not emotional quarreling arising from interpersonal friction. . . . [The ExCom] permitted . . . the freedom essential for effective dissuasion . . . and made the best use of available time. . . . [T]he information and skills brought to bear to the task were additive. Both in scope and depth, the President and his advisors had a decisive edge over the President alone.[8]

But the ExCom conversations, as now disclosed in declassified transcripts, hardly show a cool delineation of alternatives or a deliberate dissection of well-gamed actions. The voices are halting. The sentences are incomplete. Thoughts ramble. Memories slip and options ooze into the ether. At several points, Secretary of Defense Robert McNamara's distraction is abundantly clear. One of McNamara's senior aides subsequently remembered him being nearly hysterical: "He turned absolutely white [when he got the news of the stray U-2] and yelled hysterically, 'This means war with the Soviet Union.' "[9]

The meetings were long, inconclusive, and terrifying. Robert Kennedy recalled, "The strain and hours without sleep were beginning to take their toll. . . . That kind of pressure does strange things to human beings, even to brilliant, self-confident, mature, experienced men."[10] There were reports that one assistant secretary was so disconcerted and fatigued that he drove into a tree at 4:00 in the morning.[11] The initial judgment on the meetings by the acid-tongued former secretary of state, Dean Acheson, are confirmed by the transcripts. Called from retirement to advise with other senior members of the administration, Acheson soon found that the ExCom meetings were "repetitive" and "leaderless"; he stopped attending them because they were "a waste of time."[12]

The ExCom transcripts do make clear that President Kennedy tended to favor a trade of the Jupiters, as the second public message of Khrushchev suggested. Although a trade might appear reasonable at home and overseas, it could also have constituted something of an embarrassment within NATO and an opening to right-wing critics at home. But Kennedy was also aware that if a trade was not made and war broke out, even if it was "limited," then there would be bitter recriminations. How could the carnage of battle be justified when the price of avoiding it was the small change of obsolete, vulnerable missiles that the administration was hoping to stand down soon in any case? Kennedy said, "We can't very well invade Cuba with all its toil [sic], and as long as it's going to be, when we could have gotten them [the Soviet missiles] out by making a deal on the missiles in Turkey. If that's part of the record, I don't see how we'll have a very good war."[13]

By the afternoon of October 27, the president told his advisors that "we will get the Soviet strategic missiles out of Cuba by invading or trading."[14] But even while he had earlier sent his brother to explore with Dobrynin a pull-out of the Jupiter missiles from Turkey in exchange for a withdrawal of Soviet missiles from Cuba, on the evening of October 27 the president indicated to the ExCom that he was moving closer to a military solution: if "our reconnaissance planes are fired on tomorrow . . . then we should take out the SAM sites in Cuba by air action."[15]

In fact, Kennedy was indeed planning to trade Jupiter missiles recently activated in Turkey for the Soviet missiles in Cuba. And if a private understanding would not achieve an agreement, the president was prepared to make the offer public at the UN. What now seems clear is that President Kennedy was negotiating with both the Soviets and his own advisors. To most of the advisors, Kennedy wanted to appear as resolute as possible. Hence only at the eleventh hour, and then only to a small circle of intimates, was he willing to show some of the flexibility that he had apparently come up with on his own.

The truth is that on "Black Saturday," when the Joint Chiefs of Staff were pressing for a strike and invasion within forty-eight hours, Kennedy convened a smaller group—a fraction of the ExCom advisors: Rusk, McNamara, Robert Kennedy, George Ball, Roswell Gilpatric, Llewellyn Thompson, Theodore Sorensen, McGeorge Bundy. This group decided to authorize Robert Kennedy to tell Ambassador Dobrynin that the missiles in Turkey would come out after the crisis had been resolved.[16] Moreover, not knowing whether Khrushchev would accept this private deal offered to Dobrynin regarding a swap of the Jupiters for the missiles in Cuba, Rusk and President Kennedy worked on further measures to end the crisis via a quid pro quo. The secretary of state was given authority to act on a signal from the president; Rusk and the UN secretary general would then announce in public the American willingness to exchange U.S. missiles in Turkey for the removal of Soviet missiles from Cuba.[17] In sum, if the private message to Khrushchev forwarded through Dobrynin failed to either reach or impress Khrushchev, the public acceptance of virtually all the Soviet demands was authorized.

It was a complex game. Informally and quietly, the president had authorized his brother to see if Ambassador Dobrynin would accept a "private understanding" (already broached in discussions with Dobrynin some days earlier) with Khrushchev to exchange the Jupiters for the missiles in Cuba. In addition, the United States offered to guarantee publicly that the Cubans would be free from American invasion. Formally, the United States offered a "no invasion" pledge in exchange for removal of the missiles from Cuba. Informally, there was more that was traded. If the arrangement Robert Kennedy was offering the Soviets were to be made public, the attorney general stated, it "would damage the relationship."[18]

KEEPING THE FACTS UNDER WRAPS

What was not known until the end of the 1980s was that if Khrushchev rejected Robert Kennedy's offer, the president was prepared to go forward with the offer of a public trade. Meanwhile, the vast majority of the president's advisors were wholly in the dark about the president's "back-channel" negotiations.

The reasons that Kennedy was forced to negotiate behind his advisors' backs may be more understandable than the long silence his closest advisors kept about the arrangements afterwards. For the only real alternatives the ExCom had settled on were an air strike and invasion, or some other kind of forceful action.

By Saturday, October 26, McNamara subsequently recalled, the atmosphere of the ExCom had heightened:

tension had really increased and there was a tremendous sense of urgency. . . . [Chairman of the Joint Chiefs of Staff] Maxwell Taylor . . . always displayed terrific judgment and professionalism to me—but Taylor was absolutely convinced we had to attack Cuba. The pressure was on. . . . I left the White House that evening through the Rose Garden, and it was reported that I said I thought I might never see another Saturday. . . . It was because there was so much pressure for action . . . that night the preponderance of opinion was in favor of an air strike and invasion that week. . . . President Kennedy had not finally decided to invade. But there was great uncertainty—a tremendous amount of uncertainty.[19]

Yet the Kennedy administration was saved from the domestic and international embarrassment of a public trade, for on October 28 Khrushchev responded via Radio Moscow, accepting Robert Kennedy's offer without mentioning (as the attorney general had insisted) the imminent American withdrawal of the Jupiter missiles from Turkey. President Kennedy was thus relieved of the inevitable criticism that would have attended the initiation of a public swap, even though the deal was known to the president's most intimate advisors for twenty-five years.

While being questioned before the Senate Foreign Relations Committee in 1963, Rusk was asked by Senator Bourke Hickenlooper to confirm that a "deal" or "trade" had in "no way, shape or form, directly or indirectly been connected with the settlement . . . or had been agreed to?" Rusk replied, "That is correct, sir."[20]

In 1963, McNamara told the House Appropriations Committee that "without any qualifications whatsoever there was absolutely no deal . . . between the Soviet Union and the United States regarding the removal of the Jupiter weapons from either Italy or Turkey."[21]

Bundy wrote of the swap in the late 1980s: "As far as I know, none of the nine of us told anyone else what had happened. We denied in every forum that there was any deal."[22] As a result of muting the elements of negotiation in the untangling of the nuclear Gordian knot, the lesson of the crisis to all but a select group of Kennedy intimates was that Kennedy had determined events by dictating a virtual ultimatum.

In public and in the lore of the national security literature of the ensuing decades, it seemed that Kennedy had stood firm. He was tough. And he prevailed. The crisis was portrayed as a test of will that highlighted the Soviet transgression of the political-nuclear status quo. The chroniclers of the 1960s claimed that the Soviets merely capitulated. This was the sum of Robert Kennedy's ultimatum to Dobrynin: "We had to have a commitment by tomorrow. . . . [I]t was a statement of fact. . . . [I]f they did not remove those bases, we would remove them."[23] Roger Hilsman, the senior State Department intelligence officer in the crisis, reached the only conclusion possible based on the "facts" as they were portrayed at the time: Khrushchev simply "backed down."[24] Dean Rusk's phrase, recalling a childhood game, "we were eyeball to eyeball, and the other fellow blinked," was said to have told it all.

NOTES

1. This memorandum appears in McGeorge Bundy, *Danger and Survival: Choices about the Bomb in the First Fifty Years* (New York: Random House, 1988), pp. 684–85.

2. Transcript of "Off the Record Meeting on Cuba, October 16, 1962, 6:30–7:45 P.M," JFK Library, p. 78.

3. Arthur M. Schlesinger Jr., *A Thousand Days* (New York: Fawcett Crest, 1967), p. 363.

4. Text in Roger Hilsman, *To Move a Nation* (Garden City, NY: Doubleday, 1967), pp. 210–11.

5. Roger Hilsman, *To Move a Nation* (New York: Dell, 1967), pp. 48, 157.

6. Hans J. Morgenthau, *Truth and Power: Essays of a Decade, 1960–1970* (New York: Praeger, 1970), p. 158.

7. Cited in John McDermitt, "Crisis Manager," *New York Review of Books* 60 (September 14, 1967): p. 8.

8. Thomas Halper, *Foreign Policy Crisis* (Columbus, OH: Charles E. Merrill, 1971), pp. 189–93.

9. David Detzer, *The Brink* (New York: Thomas Y Crowell, 1979), p. 281.

10. Robert F. Kennedy, *Thirteen Days: A Memoir of the Cuban Missile Crisis*, afterword by Richard Neustadt and Graham T. Allison, 2d. ed. (New York: W.W. Norton, 1971), p. 48.

11. Robert Kennedy was reported to have believed that Dean Rusk "had a virtual complete breakdown mentally and physically." It was totally false, but Schlesinger neither withdrew the statement nor apologized to Rusk. Arthur M. Schlesinger Jr., *Robert Kennedy and His Times* (New York: Ballantine, 1978), pp. 546–47.

12. Dean Acheson, "Dean Acheson's Version of Robert Kennedy's Version of the Cuban Missile Crisis," *Esquire* (February 1969): p. 77.

13. ExCom Meetings, October 13, 1977 <www.cnn.com>.

14. JFK Library Audio File, October 27, 1963 <www.hpol.org/JFK/Cuban>.

15. Ibid.

16. Bundy, *Danger and Survival*, pp. 432–33.

17. The letter was revealed for the first time at the Hawks Cay Conference, Rusk to Blight, February 25, 1987; David Welch, ed., *Proceedings of the Cambridge Conference on the Cuban Missile Crisis, October 11–12, 1987*, p. 131.

18. Schlesinger, *Robert Kennedy and His Times*, p. 564.

19. Welch, *Proceedings of the Cambridge Conference*, pp. 86–87.

20. "Briefing on Cuban Developments, January 25, 1963," *Executive Sessions of the Senate Foreign Relations Committee (Historical Series)* 15 (1982): pp. 105–6, 111.

21. U.S. House Appropriations Committee, Department of Defense Appropriations for 1964, 88th Cong., 1st Sess., 1963, pt. I, p. 57. This was also McNamara's position in 1968 when he wrote in an introduction to Robert Kennedy's memoir: "Perhaps his [JFK's] most difficult decision was the refusal, against the advice of his weaker brethren . . . to bargain the security of the Western world by yielding to the specious Russian offers of a face saving accommodation at the expense of America's allies." Robert Kennedy, *Thirteen Days* (New York: New American Library, 1969), p. 18.

22. Bundy, *Danger and Survival*, p. 434.

23. Kennedy, *Thirteen Days*, p. 108.

24. Hilsman, *To Move a Nation*, p. 226.

10

The Nuclear Dimension

In battle, well-trained troops frequently act under pressure without giving much heed to the consequences; only later does the shock settle in and linger. Similarly, many members of the ExCom,[1] the high-level ad hoc group assembled at the time of the missile crisis, discounted the possibility of nuclear war.[2] At first, some of the most influential advisors were not even sure if the United States faced an urgent situation; they would deem it important only if the American officials appeared preoccupied by the situation of Soviet ballistic missiles being installed in Cuba. Others thought it was a political problem that could be finessed. Most, however, believed the missiles would at least have radical consequences in the perception of the balance of power. But decades later, most of the bravest looked back and quaked. The missiles of both nations were not controlled as well as had been thought. In hindsight, it was realized that the situation had come very close to nuclear war.

CUBA AND THE CREDIBILITY OF THE NUCLEAR THREAT

"The whole problem with the nuclear age," Henry Kissinger once put it, is that "until power is used, it is . . . what people think."[3] Several times at the height of the Cuban Missile Crisis, Kennedy's advisors noted the domestic political dimensions of the fact that the Democratic Kennedy administration has "allowed" the Soviets to place missiles in Cuba. The ExCom was hardly insulated from domestic considerations in its deliberations. One Republican member of the ExCom sent Theodore Sorensen, Kennedy's alter ego, a note that read: "Ted—have you considered the very real possibility that if we allow Cuba to complete installation and operational readiness of missile bases, the next House of Representatives is likely to have a Republican majority?"[4] Similarly, McGeorge Bundy wondered, when the missiles were first reported, whether action could be deferred until after the 1962 mid-term election.[5] If the missile installations were completed before the election, there would be both a strategic and an electoral problem facing the administration.

To Robert McNamara, it seemed that "a missile is a missile. It makes no great difference whether you are killed by a missile from the Soviet Union or from Cuba."[6] Roswell Gilpatric confirmed the debatable meaning of the missiles: "I don't believe that we were under any greater threat from the Soviet Union's power, taken in totality, after this than before."[7] President Kennedy told his advisors that he had erred when he told the nation in a September speech, "I should have said . . . that we don't care. But when we said we're not going to [tolerate them] and then they go ahead and do it, and then we do nothing, then . . . our risks increase. They've got enough to blow us up now anyway. I just think it's just a question of . . . a political struggle as much as [a] military issue."[8] McNamara joined the conversation with his own underscore: "[T]his is a domestic political problem."[9]

Similarly, Theodore Sorensen wrote in a memorandum to the president on October 17, 1962—five days before the blockade was ordered—that the presence of missiles in Cuba did not "significantly alter the balance of power." Sorensen explained, "They do not significantly increase the potential megatonnage capable of being unleashed on American soil." He confessed, in conclusion, that "Soviet motives were not understood."[10]

However, to Soviet and American strategists, the missiles in Cuba were hardly a trivial addition to the Soviet strategic arsenal. Well before the crisis, McNamara had abandoned "static" measures of nuclear advantage reckoned in terms of raw megatonnage delivered to an ever more expansive list of targets.[11] Undoubtedly this "bean counting" was somewhat surreal and its impact was largely "psychological," as one of the participants in the ExCom deliberations put it. According to U.S. analysts at the time, however, the twenty-four MRBMs and some twelve to sixteen IRBMs discovered in Cuba did raise the number of targets the Soviets could lethally cover in the United States by 40 percent.

On the merits of what was known and thought about nuclear weapons in strategic circles beyond the confines of the ExCom deliberations, the missiles in Cuba severely eroded the possibility of an unanswered U.S. first strike against the Soviets.[12] This point had been central to U.S. Air Force planners but was not critical in the mind of the secretary of defense, who believed, before the crisis, that a disarming first strike was a chimera.[13] Clearly, however, the missiles in Cuba seemed to give the Soviets some of the leverage they had lost when the missile gap was revealed as a myth in 1961.

Yet if the administration did not fully understand Khrushchev's sensitivity to a "loss" of Cuba, it did understand that the appearance of a radical revision in the strategic equation was serious. Because deterrence rests as much on a psychological relationship as it does on the balance of force, a shift from the well-advertised "missile gap in reverse" of 1961 to a position where, as Kennedy fretted, "they look like they're coequal with the U.S.," was bound to be unsettling—especailly if the most well advertised component of containment had been reversed by a strategic short-cut. As Kennedy summed up the experience in public a few months later, if the Soviets had succeeded in keeping their missiles in Cuba, "it would have politically changed the balance of power. It would have appeared to, and appearances contribute to reality."[14]

FEARFUL OPTIONS AND NUCLEAR CREDIBILITY

Later, McNamara claimed that U.S. plans detailing strategic nuclear exchanges were "unreal."[15] But at the time of the crisis in Cuba, the U.S. military was under the impression that "it might be necessary to make a compensatory attack against the U.S.S.R." as a follow-on to an invasion of Cuba.[16] Although there were doubters in the ExCom, even among the "Doves," most seemed to feel that if Cuba were invaded then the Soviets would be forced to move in an area where the Russians had an equivalent preponderance and where the United States had an equivalent exposure.[17] Indeed, the losses to the Soviets and the Americans in the event of an invasion of Cuba would have been substantial. The Soviets were prepared to defend their two combat divisions, their missiles, and their planes with an array of short range tactical weapons. The United States, in turn, was prepared to deal with Soviet submarine harassment of the U.S. invading fleet with atomic depth charges, then stored at Guantánamo Bay in Cuba at the U.S. base on the island.[18] The enormity of the Soviet and American "order of battle"—that is, the true inventory of men and materiel that both sides were preparing to commit—was not known until more than thirty-five years later.

An invasion was expected, at least as Robert Kennedy's memoirs have it, "by Monday or Tuesday," October 9, 1962, or the next day.[19] It is possible that an invasion could have been mounted and that the Soviets, even though suffering high numbers of casualties and a significant strategic and political loss, might not have done much in response, as some analysts and some of the participants in the crisis now maintain.[20] But an equivalent riposte was expected. And if the memoirs of Soviet leaders are to be taken seriously, it seems likely that the Russians would have defended Cuba.

Dean Acheson argued convincingly that the U.S. missiles based in Turkey would be lost, and he proposed a follow-on nuclear strike within the Soviet Union after the Soviets struck Turkey.[21] Some in the ExCom were willing to "write off" an attack on Turkey if a Soviet attack were confined to the Jupiter sites. "We were going to let him [Khrushchev] have his strike in Turkey, as I understood it last week," said Bundy. "Yeah, that's right," replied McNamara. But if Allied forces in Berlin were squeezed, it raised prospects so frightening that McNamara said he was not "prepared to address" them.[22]

By October 27, the ExCom had become convinced that the Soviet missiles' ultimate strategic meaning, their symbolic meaning, was both unmistakable and no longer tolerable. The longer the missiles stayed in Cuba, the more irretrievable the situation would become. The longer there were operational missiles in place, the more certain it was that they changed the Soviet bargaining position vis-à-vis the United States and diminished the standing of the United States in the world.[23] Further, if the crisis persisted, the majority in the ExCom feared that the high-voltage stasis could not be sustained. Shooting could start anywhere, and then the United States would have put in jeopardy not just its control of events but control of the rhythm of combat as well. Considering all the dangers, the Joint Chiefs of Staff and Chairman Maxwell Taylor were clear with their recommendation in favor of a strike no later than Monday, October 29, 1962, if for no other reason than that thereafter the military would start to lose its edge. Planes and men would wear down under the strain of peak readiness, and with each surveillance flight more planes and pilots would be exposed to hazards.[24]

NEAR MISSES AND MISADVENTURES

At the height of the tension, a U.S. Air Force U-2 surveillance flight was shot down over Cuba with the subsequent loss of a pilot. General Maxwell Taylor, the one military man who commanded real respect in the Kennedy camp, argued, "[W]e must not fail on surveillance. We can't give up twenty-four hours at this stage." McNamara seconded Taylor's insistent observation. He "fully agreed," and President Kennedy added his assent.[25] Reconnaissance planes would scour the island in runs at two-hour intervals.[26] But it was expected that U.S. planes would be attacked.[27] The momentum of events, it was clear in the ExCom discussions, pointed to striking Soviet surface to air missiles.

A small-scale strike at just one offending air defense battery, the ExCom advisors realized, would kill Soviets; and perhaps in the melee a medium range ground-to-ground nuclear-tipped missile would be fired on the United States. The Joint Chiefs, therefore, wanted an all-out coordinated air strike launched at Cuba "right away" but agreed to a limited, single strike first, with the understanding that if another attack on U.S. aircraft occurred, then there would be a thoroughgoing extirpation of all the Soviet SAMs.[28]

Two thousand sorties would then cover an estimated 16,000 troops, but in fact there were over 45,000 Soviet personnel and their equipment, including tactical nuclear weapons and operational submarines with nuclear torpedoes. The invasion of some 180,000 Americans that would follow some days later would have run into fierce resistance, much greater than anticipated, and might well have failed unless followed by reinforcements and, as likely, the use of tactical nuclear missiles and weapons in exchange.[29] Oblivious to the real order of battle, McNamara conceded part of the argument to the military. "Invasion," he affirmed, would be "inevitable" once military hostilities began.[30]

The throbbing press of events wore on the deliberants. Secretary Rusk, on contemplating the reaction of the "Hawks" to the news of the downed U-2, found his eyes brimming with tears. Acheson brought him up sharply: "Pull yourself together, Dean, you're the only Secretary of State we have."[31]

Robert Kennedy wrote about the time left in terms of hours:

The President was not optimistic nor was I. He ordered twenty-four troop carrier squadrons of the Air Force Reserve to active duty. They would be necessary for invasion. The expectation was that there would be a military confrontation by Tuesday, possibly tomorrow.[32]

For his part, President Kennedy put the odds for war at between one in three and even.[33] Clearly, most of the participants in the events found them harrowing. Robert Kennedy reported that he felt, on October 25, that "we were on the edge of a precipice with no way off. . . . President Kennedy had initiated the course of events, but he no longer had control over them."[34] The sense of dread was soon superseded by the elation that accompanied success. However, years later researchers Raymond Garthoff and Scott Sagan assembled a lengthy list of worrisome (but at the time unapprehended) near misses and communication and control failures that could have triggered an inadvertent chain of events taking the United States and the Soviets over the edge of war and into the abyss.

1. American intelligence operatives learned that their premier informant, Colonel Olaeg Penkovsky, had been arrested by the KGB on October 22. Penkovsky's arrest had dangerous implications. The Soviets, Garthoff suggests, might have inferred that the information that Penkovsky relayed to the United States verified that the United States did, indeed, have sufficient nuclear punch to exercise the Joint Chiefs' preferred first strategic option, a devastating coordinated first strike.

In addition, Penkovsky had been given some coded signals:

> one to be used in the ultimate contingency: imminent war. When he was arrested, he ... chose to use the signal for imminent Soviet attack! ... . [A]bout to go down, he evidently decided to play Samson and bring the temple down on everybody else as well.[35]

Penkovsky's provocative signal was suppressed within the CIA. Neither the CIA director nor the ExCom were told of his dire last call.

2. Orders to cease U-2 flights near the Soviet boarders were either not received or ignored.[36] In one incident, an authorized U-2 entered Soviet airspace in Siberia.[37] Soviet MIGs scrambled to shoot the spy plane down. The U-2's SOS alerted Galena Air Force base in Alaska, and a group of American fighter aircraft rose to escort the errant plane back to base. Not known at the time in the White house was the fact that the American fighter group that scrambled to rescue the U-2 some 100 miles into Soviet airspace was armed with nuclear weapons that could be fired on each pilot's own authority.[38]

3. The commander-in-chief of the U.S. Strategic Air Command, in an uncoded signal given on the afternoon of October 22, 1963, alerted all his units to the highest peacetime alert, Defcon 3. Most of the actions relevant to this alert would have been picked up in due course, but the Soviets must have been puzzled by the bravura with which the moves were broadcast.[39] This unprecedented intensification of peacetime readiness for war was taken openly so that the Soviets could pick up the message and be suitably daunted.[40] "[T]his remarkable display of American power," writes Garthoff, "was unauthorized and unknown to the President, the Secretary of Defense, the Chairman of the Joint Chiefs, and the ExCom as they so carefully calibrated and controlled action in the intensifying confrontation."[41]

4. In the same heated hours, the FBI informed the White House that the Soviet mission in New York had prepared to burn its archives. Some analysts took this as preparation for war, notwithstanding the fact that none of the Soviet strategic forces within the Soviet Union had been put on alert.[42]

5. An Atlas ICBM was test-launched from Vandenberg Air Base in California on the afternoon of October 26, 1962. The missile that was tested sat side by side with others that were fully loaded, already on alert. At best, the

test flight might have appeared as a nuclear "stray" had the Soviets been able to observe it.[43] At worst, it might have been regarded as a precursor to an all-out attack.

6. At the height of the crisis, at least one CIA covert action team was roaming Cuba. Operation Mongoose activities were suspended apparently, only as an afterthought, on October 30, 1962, by Robert Kennedy.[44] Nonetheless, the CIA-sponsored unit decided on its own authority to blow up a Cuban factory on November 8.[45] One can only speculate what might have happened if any of the clandestine units operating in Cuba had decided to fire on Soviet missiles, vulnerable as they were reported to have been to rifle fire. It is equally frightening to conjecture what might have happened if a CIA-backed team had attempted to kill Castro or his close associates, or if they had killed any of the high-level Soviet officials on the island at the time.

7. According to one controversial report, two F100 jet fighters, armed with nuclear weapons, took off from Homestead Air Force Base in Florida in the direction of Cuba on October 25. The unusual flight was begun at 4:00 A.M. and apparently was recalled only at the last moment.[46]

8. In another controversial revelation, a Soviet-era source has indicated that the crisis came even closer to war than anyone suspected. At the fifth in a series of conferences on the Cuban Missile Crisis held in Havana in January 1992, General Anatoly I. Gribikov asserted that Soviet field commanders had, on their own authority, the ability to launch up to six short range nuclear missiles at any invading U.S. forces if the United States tried to take the island. The CIA had no knowledge that ninety short range, tactical warheads were on the island and would be used if the United States launched an invasion.[47]

9. Castro seemed to have a different sense of history and nuclear war than either Khrushchev or Kennedy. Castro fully expected an invasion and "was certain . . . that . . . we would pay the price. . . . [W]e would disappear. . . . Would I have been ready to use nuclear weapons[?] . . . I would have agreed."[48]

10. The main instrument of U.S. control of the tempo of pressure was the blockade run by the U.S. Navy. McNamara, sensing that the Navy might not be responsive to what the president had in mind, went to the Naval Operations Center, where he could talk to ship commanders directly. McNamara's colloquy with the chief of naval operations, Admiral George Anderson, has been often told:

McNamara: When that ship reaches the line, how are we going to stop it?

Anderson: We'll hail it.

McNamara: In what language—English or Russian?

Anderson: How the hell should I know.

McNamara: What will you do if they don't understand?

Anderson: I suppose we'll use flags.

McNamara: Well, what if they don't stop?

Anderson: We'll send a shot across the bow.

McNamara: Then what if that doesn't work?

Anderson: Then we'll fire into the rudder.

McNamara: What kind of ship is it?

Anderson: A tanker, Mr. Secretary.

McNamara: You are not going to fire a single shot at anything without my express permission, is that clear? Do you understand that?

Anderson: The Navy has been running blockades since the days of John Paul Jones and if you and your deputy will go to your offices, the Navy will run the blockade.

[McNamara wheeled to return to his office.]

Anderson: Don't worry, Mr. Secretary, we know what we are doing here.[49]

In fact, all six U.S. submarines near the quarantine line were shadowed. Unknown to the ExCom, one sub was "surfaced" by a low-level depth charge and disabled. The Soviets were not informed of where the quarantine was supposed to be until October 27, 1962—Black Saturday, the worst moments of the crisis. On that date Undersecretary of State George Ball suggested to the president that the Russians be notified as to where U.S. surface ships were on patrol.[50]

If the Soviets were informed, the information might not have been very close to the reality of the quarantine. The Navy had established the quarantine at a distance of 500 miles from Havana and Cape Maysi.[51] The president ordered the Navy to draw the line closer in to shore in order to give the Soviet ships heading toward Cuba more room and time to turn away instead of submitting to the American interdiction, but the Navy kept the quarantine where it was until well after Khrushchev's last open communication to Kennedy signaled the end of the crisis.[52] All during the crisis, the quarantine had a flexible definition in practice. Notwithstanding the secretary of defense's order to recall a pursuing American destroyer, a Soviet freighter loaded with nuclear weapons, the *Poltava*, was designated the Navy's "first target" and shadowed ahead of the official quarantine line by a U.S. warship.[53]

Ever since the Bay of Pigs disaster, President Kennedy's substantial distrust of the military had deepened. During the crisis, every effort was made to keep nuclear forces and commanders on as short a leash as possible. But so vast was the modern machinery of war that the effect proved elusive. It should have been a salutary lesson, but most of the failures remained hidden for years beneath reports and a veil of secrecy. Only the diligent research of scholars and the sober recollections of the participants made it clear, later, how close the world had come to as great a catastrophe as it might ever see at the hand of humankind.

NOTES

1. The Executive Committee of the President was an ad hoc group assembled on short notice consisting of around fifteen individuals, most of whom had high-level responsibilities. Their numbers included: George W. Ball, Undersecretary of State; McGeorge Bundy, Special Advisor to the President on National Security Affairs; C. Douglas Dillon, Secretary of the Treasury; Roswell L. Gilpatric, Deputy Secretary of Defense; U. Alexis Johnson, Deputy Undersecretary of Defense for Political Affairs; Robert F. Kennedy, Attorney General; Edward M. Martin, Assistant Secretary of State for Inter-American Affairs; John H. McCone, Director of the CIA; Robert S. McNamara, Secretary of Defense; Paul Nitze, Assistant Secretary of Defense for National Security Affairs; Dean Rusk, Secretary of State; Theodore C. Sorensen, Special Counsel to the President; General Maxwell D. Taylor, Chairman of the Joint Chiefs of Staff, Lieutenant General Joseph F. Carroll, Director of the Defense Intelligence Agency; Lyndon B. Johnson, Vice President; Adlai E. Stevenson, Ambassador to the United Nations; Llewellyn E. Thompson, Ambassador-at-Large and former Ambassador to the Soviet Union; Donald Wilson, Deputy Director of the United States Information Agency; and for a while, Dean Acheson, former Secretary of State.

2. McGeorge Bundy, *Danger and Survival* (New York: Vintage, 1988), p. 385ff.

3. Cited by Jonathan Schell, *The Time of Illusion* (New York: Alfred A. Knopf, 1967), p. 354.

4. Theodore C. Sorensen, *Kennedy* (New York: Bantam, 1969), p. 688.

5. Alexander George et al., *The Limits of Coercive Diplomacy* (Boston: Little, Brown, 1971), p. 89.

6. Roger Hilsman, *To Move a Nation* (Garden City, NY: Doubleday, 1967), p. 195.

7. *New York Times*, 12 November 1962.

8. *Foreign Relations of the United States* (FRUS), Vol. XI (Washington, DC: U.S. Government Printing Office, 1997), Doc. 21.

9. Ibid., p. 89.

10. *Wilmington Morning News*, 25 January 1974.

11. Raymond Garthoff in David Welch, ed., "Transcript of the Proceedings of the Hawk's Cay Conference," Harvard University, April 1988, p. 142.

12. Ibid., pp. 31, 53.

13. Scott Sagan, *Moving Targets: Nuclear Strategy and National Security* (Princeton: Princeton University Press, 1989), p. 29.

14. FRUS, Vol. XI, Doc. 21.

15. *Transcript of the Proceedings of the Hawk's Cay Conference*, p. 31.

16. Frank Sieverts, "The Cuban Crisis," 1962, Box 49, National Security Files. Prepared for the ExCom in early 1963 on McNamara's request and declassified on November 14, 1984 (eyes only Top Secret), Box 49, National Security Files, JFK Library, pp. 75–76.

17. Transcript, Presidential Recordings, ExCom meetings, Cuban Missile Crisis, October 27, 1962, JFK Library, p. 46.

18. Robert Burns, "Pentagon Reveals Weapons Locations," 19 October 1999. Associated Press, Internet edition.

19. Robert F. Kennedy, *Thirteen Days* (New York: Norton, 1969), p. 109.

20. *Transcript of the Proceedings of the Hawk's Cay Conference*, p. 141ff.

21. Sorensen, *Kennedy*, p. 773.

22. Ibid.

23. *Transcript of the Proceedings of the Hawk's Cay Conference*, p. 71. The point is Raymond Garthoff's.

24. Transcript, Presidential Recordings, Cuban Missile Crisis, October 27, 1962, pp. 26, 45; *Transcript of the Proceedings of the Hawk's Cay Conference*, p. 110.

25. Transcript, Presidential Recordings, Cuban Missile Crisis, October 27, 1962, p. 46.

26. Sieverts, "The Cuban Crisis," 1962, p. 186.

27. Transcript, Presidential Recordings, Cuban Missile Crisis, October 27, 1962, p. 42.

28. This is McGeorge Bundy's recollection in *Transcript of the Proceedings of the Hawk's Cay Conference*, p. 95.

29. Transcript, Presidential Recordings, Cuban Missile Crisis, October 27, 1962, p. 39. Troop estimates are in Raymond Garthoff, *Reflections on the Cuban Missile Crisis* (Washington, DC: Brookings Institution, 1989), p. 34.

30. Transcript, Presidential Recordings, Cuban Missile Crisis, October 27, 1962, p. 42.

31. Thomas J. Schoenbaum, *Waging Peace and War: Dean Rusk in the Truman, Kennedy, and Johnson years* (New York: Simon & Schuster, 1988), p. 321.

32. Robert F. Kennedy, *Thirteen Days* (New York: New American Library, 1969), p. 109.

33. Sorensen, *Kennedy*, p. 705.

34. Kennedy, *Thirteen Days*, pp. 70–71.

35. Garthoff, *Reflections on the Cuban Missile Crisis*, pp. 64–65.

36. Graham Allison, *Essence of Decision* (Boston: Little, Brown, 1971), p. 141.

37. Hilsman, *To Move a Nation*, p. 221.

38. Sagan, *Moving Targets*, p. 147.

39. Garthoff, *Reflections on the Cuban Missile Crisis*, p. 62; Scott Sagan, "Nuclear Alerts and Crisis Management," *International Security* 9, no. 4 (Spring 1988): p. 109.

40. Raymond Garthoff in *Transcript of the Proceedings of the Hawk's Cay Conference*, p. 118.

41. Garthoff, *Reflections on the Cuban Missile Crisis*, p. 62.

42. John Newhouse, *War and Peace in the Nuclear Age* (New York: Knopf, 1989), p. 178.

43. Scott D. Sagan, "The Limits of Safety: Organizations, Accidents, and Nuclear Weapons" (Princeton, NJ: 1933, manuscript), p. 167.

44. Sagan, "Nuclear Alerts and Crisis Management," p. 122, n64.

45. Garthoff in *Transcript of the Proceedings of the Hawk's Cay Conference*, p. 149.

46. Ed Offey, "Two Fighters Launched during '62 Cuban Crisis," *Seattle Post Intelligencer*, 4 November 1992, p. 6.

47. Gribikov's tale is not fully accepted. See John Newhouse, "A Reporter at Large," *The New Yorker*, 27 April 1992, p. 70ff.

48. Robert S. McNamara, James G. Blight, and Robert K. Brigham, *Argument without End: In Search of Answers to the Vietnam Tragedy* (New York: Public Affairs Press, 1999), p. 11.

49. Elie Abel, *The Missile Crisis* (Philadelphia: J.B. Lippincott, 1966), pp. 285–86.

50. J. Anthony Lukas, "Class Reunion: Kennedy's Men Relive the Cuban Missile Crisis," *New York Times Magazine*, 30 August 1987, p. 51.

51. Sieverts, "The Cuban Crisis," 1962, p. 188.

52. Garthoff, *Reflections on the Cuban Missile Crisis*, p. 68, fn 110; Sagan, "Nuclear Alerts," p. 110, n26.

53. Garthoff, *Reflections on the Cuban Missile Crisis*, p. 68.

11

Conclusion

The Cuban Missile Crisis accelerated the arms race and made the world considerably more dangerous notwithstanding the post-crisis desire of both President John Kennedy and Premier Nikita Khrushchev to reach an overall settlement. The American policy community was excited by the Cuban Missile Crisis and propelled by a heady steam of triumphalist certainty. Policymakers, as a result, tended to discount many of the classic accouterments of diplomacy: allies, international law, negotiation, and a cautious definition of the national interest.

The Cuban Missile Crisis stands as more than a signpost on the road to the looming disaster of Vietnam; it was a cause. Like many triumphs in politics and history, the missile crisis generated a hubris that defeated whatever fleeting success American arms and determination were said to have generated. Apiece with this tragedy was the long-hidden essence of the confrontation: the ultimate settlement was a compromise, which is the essence of the diplomatist's craft.

THE DANGERS AHEAD

Before the fall of 1962, Khrushchev's strategic policy "amounted to settling for a second-best strategic posture."[1] However, the missile crisis demonstrated Soviet strategic weakness and exposed other Soviet debilities that Khrushchev's verbal proclamation of superiority had previously covered.

After the events in Cuba the Soviet military, responding to the humiliating American stimulus, demanded a higher priority for strategic arms and a cutback on the agricultural and consumer sectors of the Soviet economy. For the Soviet Union had come to the same conclusion as the United States—that a preponderance of military power was the sine qua non of the successful exercise of political will.

Although Khrushchev and Kennedy moved toward a relaxation of tensions—best symbolized by the signing of the nuclear test ban accords in mid-1963—many in the Kremlin saw this as but a breathing spell in which the Chinese might be isolated and Soviet arms development could catch up with that of the United States. Soviet naval preparations, especially the building of a Russian version of America's Polaris submarines, were intensified. Amphibious landing capability, something in which the Soviets had shown little interest before, was expanded. Worldwide "blue water" Soviet submarine patrols were initiated, and a decision was made by Khrushchev's successors to extend the Soviet navy to "remote areas of the world's oceans previously considered a zone of supremacy of the fleets of the imperialist powers."[2]

Only a handful of ICBMs—perhaps as few as four—had been deployed in the first blush of Soviet rocket successes, from the launch of *Sputnik* in 1957 to the time of the Cuban crisis.[3] But after the Cuban Missile Crisis, the pace of deployment picked up. The Soviets could count some 200 ICBM launchers at the time Khrushchev was removed from office in 1964.[4] The Russians worked furiously on ICBM production, and by September 1968 they commanded a larger force than the United States did.[5]

In November 1962, John McCloy, representing President Kennedy, hosted Soviet deputy foreign minister V. V. Kuznetsov. McCloy's mission was to secure a confirmation from Kuznetsov that the Soviets would indeed observe their part of the agreement to remove the missiles and bombers from Cuba. Kuznetsov reaffirmed the Russian commitment but warned, "Never will we be caught like this again."[6]

The Soviets were to yield again to U.S. strength. In Vietnam, they tempered their assistance to Ho Chi Minh, Communist leader of North Vietnam, with diplomatic intercessions on behalf of a settlement in 1972; and in the Middle East in the early 1970s, Soviet influence was all but eliminated by the skillful maneuvers of Secretary of State Henry Kissinger. Yet in each instance the strategic leverage of the United States grew weaker. Thus the structure of the international system and international stability was shaken in three ways.

First, the United States became confident that its power would prevail because global politics had become "unifocal" or "unipolar." In truth, American military primacy began to erode as soon as it was proclaimed, when the Soviets fought to gain at least a rough strategic parity.

Second, as Kennedy admitted later, referring to the Cuban Missile Crisis, "You can't have too many of those."[7] Just as Kennedy feared that he had appeared callow and faint-hearted in the Bay of Pigs and successive Berlin crises and thus had to be tough regarding Castro and the missiles in Cuba, the Soviets were likely to calculate that they must appear as the more rigid party in future confrontations.

Matters were made worse by the Chinese, who, for weeks after the missile crisis, broadcast throughout the globe their charges of Russian stupidity and weakness. The Chinese labeled Khrushchev an "adventurist" as well as a "capitulationist" and therefore not fit for world Communist leadership. The Russian answer was to accuse the Chinese of being even "softer" still for tolerating the Western enclaves of Macao and Hong Kong. The charge of who was the most "capitulationist," the Chinese or the Russians, grew almost silly, but these puerile exchanges had their own dangers in terms of deterrence.

Third, once a threat is not carried out—even after an appearance of willingness to carry it out has been demonstrated—the ante is usually upped. Hans Morgenthau described this two-step process of nuclear gamesmanship as involving

diminishing credibility of the threat and ever bolder challenges to make good on it. . . . [T]he psychological capital of deterrence has been nearly expended and the policy of deterrence will be close to bankruptcy. When they reach that point, the nations concerned can choose one of three alternatives: resort to nuclear war, retreat, or resort to conventional war.[8]

Morgenthau's observation captured the dilemma of American policymakers after the crisis in Cuba. The problem was that nuclear superiority had been useful but each succeeding threat (because no nuclear threat has ever been carried out) would necessarily be weaker than the last. Yet how could security managers translate military power into political objectives without such threats? Daniel Ellsberg recalled the quandary of U.S. security managers:

[U.S. secretary of defense] McNamara's tireless and shrewd efforts in the early sixties . . . [were to] gradually control the forces within the military bureaucracy that pressed for the threat and use of nuclear weapons. [He had] a creditable motive for proposing alternatives to nuclear threats. . . . [I]n this hidden debate, there was strong incentive—indeed it seemed necessary—for the civilian leaders to demonstrate that success was possible in Indochina without the need either to compromise Cold War objectives or to threaten or use nuclear weapons.[9]

CUBA AND VIETNAM

After the Cuban Missile Crisis, the option of low-level violence became more and more attractive. Conventional and limited deployments of force became increasingly necessary as conventional force was considered less forbidding than the nuclear abyss. After all, the symbolic or psychological capital of deterrence rested on the notion of resolve. And one way to demonstrate political will was through the resurrection of conventional force as an instrument of demonstrating commitment—a commitment whose alternative form was a threat of nuclear holocaust. The latter was bound to deteriorate with the advent of a viable Soviet retaliatory capability and the knowledge that the Soviets had collapsed once under a nuclear threat and might not be quite so passive again. Many national security managers found they could navigate between the Scylla of nuclear war and the Charybdis[10] of surrender with the serendipitous discovery of the lifeboat of the 1960s—limited war. In Vietnam, it would not prove to be a sturdy craft.

Of course, the assumptions of the U.S. planners of limited war, as they emerged victorious from the Cuban crisis, were as old as the Cold War. They dated from the Truman Doctrine's presentation of a bipolar global confrontation in which a gain to one party necessarily would be a loss to the other. A world order of diverse centers of power with elements of superpower cooperation, where gains and losses would be less easily demonstrable, was not so demanding of military remedy. A multipolar world would be less congenial to the belief that the only options available to policymakers were either military force or retreat. Maneuver and negotiation, in such a world, would again become part of diplomacy. But such a development was to come about only after the tragic failure of the military remedy had been demonstrated in Vietnam.

THE ECLIPSE OF DIPLOMACY

The American concern with the appearance of strength was a mark of the Kennedy administration. One White House aide recalled that especially after the failure at the Bay of Pigs, "nobody in the White House wanted to be soft. . . . Everybody wanted to show they were just as daring and bold as everybody else."[11] In the Cuban crisis, the Cold War ethic of toughness exacerbated the discrepancies between the necessities of force and the necessities of diplomacy and negotiation. As a result, diplomacy was almost entirely eclipsed. In fact, it was hardly even explored in the ExCom. According to Adam Yarmolinsky, an inside observer of the Executive Committee of the National Security Council, no negotiations were considered by the ExCom advisors when they met as a group. Nor were economic pressures ever suggested by the foreign affairs bureaucracy. Only a series of military plans emerged, and they varied from a blockade to a preemptive strike.[12]

As result of the crisis and the way it was depicted in official and unofficial narratives, force and toughness became enshrined as instruments of policy. As George Kennan left forty years of diplomatic service, he observed:

There is no presumption more terrifying than that of those who would blow up the world on the basis of their personal judgment of a transient situation. I do not propose to let the future of mankind be settled, or ended, by a group of men operating on the basis of limited perspectives and short-run calculations.[13]

In spite of occasional epistles from the older diplomatist, the new managers who proliferated after the Cuban crisis routed those who most favored negotiations. In an especially shameful article in the *Saturday Evening Post*, Adlai Stevenson, one of the last moderates of the Kennedy administration, who would have been an essential conduit for negotiations had the last overture of Attorney General Robert Kennedy with Ambassador Anatoly Dobrynin failed, was savaged for advocating "a Munich." The source of the story, it was widely rumored, was President Kennedy himself, an odd payback to an old rival who was close to saving America and the Soviet Union from the precipice of thermonuclear war.[14]

As the policy of toughness became dogma, nonmilitary solutions to political problems were routinely excluded. A moderate in this circumstance was restricted to suggesting limited violence. Former undersecretary of state George Ball explained his later "devil's advocacy" in Vietnam, in which he suggested that there be a troop ceiling of 70,000 men and that bombing be restricted to South Vietnam:

What I was proposing was something which I thought had a fair chance of being persuasive . . . if I had said let's pull out overnight or do something of this kind, I obviously wouldn't have been persuasive at all. They'd have said "the man's mad."[15]

This peculiar search for the middle ground of a policy defined in terms of force was abetted by the sudden sense on the part of Kennedy's national security managers that the military was filled with Dr. Strangeloves. There was some warrant for this fear. Time and time again, during the Cuban Missile Crisis, the military seemed obsessed by the opportunity to demonstrate its potential. When asked what the Soviet reaction would be to a surgical raid on their missiles and men, General Curtis Le May snapped, "There will be no reaction." When the crisis ended on Sunday, October 28, one of the Joint Chiefs suggested that they go ahead with a massive bombing on the following Monday in any case. "The military are mad," concluded President Kennedy. Robert Kennedy recalled acidly that "many times . . . I heard the military take positions which, if wrong, had the advantage that no one would be around at the end to know."[16]

CHANGING VIEWS OF THE MILITARY

In part, it was as a result of the Cuban crisis that the civilians of the American defense and foreign policy bureaucracy grew to despise the military. The State Department's director of intelligence and research, Roger Hilsman, for instance, delighted in telling a story about General Lyman Lemnitzer, chairman of the Joint Chiefs of Staff, who once briefed President Kennedy on Vietnam: "This is the Mekong Valley." The general's pointer tip hit the map. Hilsman, watching, noticed that the spot the pointer touched was not the Mekong Valley in Vietnam as claimed. It was the Yangtze Valley in China.[17] Hilsman's recollection of the general's error became a common office story.

Ironically, while the military was increasingly thought to be rather loutish and ill prepared, civilians started to rely more and more on the application of military instrumentalities by those who were not trained and had a second-rate command structure at best. Civilian crisis managers believed, after Cuba, that they should have control and that the military could not be trusted.

To many observers as well as to these managers, the failures of the Cuban Missile Crisis were not failures of civilian judgment but of organizational responsiveness. The intelligence establishment, for instance, had not discovered the Soviet missiles in Cuba until the last minute. McNamara had never really secured control over the navy. U-2 flights had been sent near the Soviet Union to excite Soviet radar at the height of the crisis. U.S. alert messages had been sent "in the clear"; and until Kennedy ordered their dispersal, American fighters and bombers had been wing to wing on the ground, almost inviting a preemptive Soviet blow. Moreover, American tactical nuclear weapons and nuclear-tipped IRBMs in Turkey and Italy had been discovered to be unlocked and lightly guarded. All this led observers and policymakers to believe that crisis management demanded the president's organizational dominance and control, because the military and intelligence organizations were inept and their judgment was not reliable or, at times, even sane.

Years later Peter Rosen, a defense analyst, reflected on the consequence of the Kennedy team's distrust in Vietnam:

It must be said that the generals were and are often wrong. Their advice was often bad. The military, however, was fighting the war and had the data and personal experience that was crucial. Bad relations meant the civilians and the soldiers were less likely to work together to develop good strategy. Instead, the civilians were inclined to turn to limited war theory. It enabled them to make strategy of a sort without help from the generals. It gave them power over the generals.[18]

The new security managers believed they had discovered a modern alchemy of melding force to diplomacy. Subnuclear, and indeed subconventional, violence could, in the right admixture, be instrumental overseas and supportable at home.[19] Later, these confident assumptions were placed on a vast testing ground in Southeast Asia. In a rare and self-revelatory rumination, McNamara said years later:

Americans are always putting people in positions of high authority . . . who have almost nothing in the way of prior qualifications, and that carries risks. . . . It's very dangerous to bring the President of Ford Motor Company—or even worse, General Motors [laughter]—to be Secretary of Defense. . . . I really think it is vitally important to have people in top administration positions who have some prior expertise in national security matters.[20]

But the new national security managers were not overseeing an alien institution. Many of them had great success in military organizations, serving with heroism and distinction. During World War II, McGeorge Bundy had worked on the planning for D-Day with Admiral Kirk and General Bradley. When hostilities were winding down in Europe, he transferred to the infantry in order to be in on the invasion of Japan. McNamara was an Air Force planner in the war working with Robert Lovett in bringing the latest life-saving business management techniques to supply and support the Air Force. Hilsman, a West Point graduate, was a guerrilla fighter in the Burma theater.

The Kennedy national security clique's evident disdain for the military did not stem from a "know nothing" ignorance of armed force, but from their affection for the appealing theory that they had mastered a great secret of avoiding the Hobson's choices presented by nuclear war. Yet as Rosen points out, all those theories—abstracted from the "pauses" and "squeezes," "signals" and "messages" that were adduced from the blockade—to any extent that they may have succeeded in the Cuban Missile Crisis, manifestly failed in Vietnam.

It is unclear, moreover, how "clear" those signals were in execution and, most important, how accurately they were interpreted in Moscow or in Havana. The once ebullient crisis manager Robert McNamara told his former associates in a kind of coda of the crisis managing craft: there ought to be a "law" that

[i]t is impossible to predict with a high degree of confidence what the effects of the use of military force will be because of accident, miscalculation, misperception, and inadvertence. You can't manage crises; it's a dangerous metaphor, because it's misleading.[21]

THE DECLINING ROLE OF INTERNATIONAL LAW

Other effects were related to the exuberant reaction to the Cuban Missile Crisis. The United Nations, which came so close to being a vital forum for settlement of the crisis, instead was used only as a platform where Adlai Stevenson, the eloquent American representative, could deal "a final blow to the Soviet case before world opinion."[22]

As the United States began to feel that power and force were successful solvents to the more sticky problems of the Cold War, the role of international law declined precipitously. Participants in the crisis knew the blockade was an act of war that had little basis in international law. After the crisis was over, even lawyers began to regard law as but another instrumentality of American policy. The conclusion reached by American academics was that

international law is . . . a tool, not a guide to action. . . . It does not have a valid life of its own; it is a mere instrument available to political leaders for their own ends, be they good or evil, peaceful or aggressive. . . . [The Cuban Missile Crisis] merely reconfirms the irrelevance of international law in major political disputes.[23]

Dean Acheson, the former secretary of state, summarized the code of the Cold War as it was confirmed by the Cuban experience: "The power, prestige and position of the United States had been challenged. . . . Law simply does not deal with such questions of ultimate power. . . . The survival of states is not a matter of law."[24]

George Ball, former undersecretary of state, wrote:

No one can seriously contend that we now live under a universal system or, in any realistic sense, under the "rule of law." We maintain the peace by preserving a precarious balance of power between ourselves and the Soviet Union—a process we used to call "containment" before the word went out of style. It is the preservation of that balance which, regardless of how we express it, is the central guiding principle of American foreign policy.[25]

Epitomized by Cuba, crisis after crisis pointed out the stark irony: Americans, who had so long stroked the talisman of international law, now seemed to do so only when their interests were not jeopardized. Otherwise, law became merely a rhetorical flourish of U.S. policy. International law was still a part of the admonition that armed aggression and breaches of the peace cease and desist. Behind these legalistic and moralistic injunctions, the armed cop became more and more apparent. As French president Charles DeGaulle had observed earlier, the conclusion that American idealism was but a reflection of the American will to power became almost inescapable after the Cuban crisis. Few obeisances about the need for law in international society disguised the sense that America had abandoned its ancient, liberal inheritance in the zesty pursuit of world order.

GREAT POWERS

Not only were the weapons of great-power diplomacy increasingly inaccessible to other states, but the other tools of statecraft also receded from the grasp of those with modest resources. The spy, for instance, was largely replaced by satellite reconnaissance. Intellectual musings on great-power conflicts became differentiated from other strategic thinking. Gradually, the Soviets and the Americans created a shared private idiom of force, and a curious dialogue began between the congressional budget messages of the secretary of defense and the periodic revisions of *Military Strategy* by Marshal V. D. Sokolovsky (a Soviet era military officer who often argued the Soviet strategic position in print).

Another effect of the crisis was to differentiate the great powers—the United States and the Soviet Union—from other states, which were literally frozen out of a significant role in structuring global politics. After all, the major chips of big-power poker were simply not accessible to other governments, even those with modest and nominally independent nuclear forces. No other nations had the capability of making even plausible calculations of either preemptive or second-strike blows against a great power, much less basing national strategies on such possibilities. As a result, Europeans were offered the appearance of some control in their nuclear lot with the ill-fated multilateral force, although the nuclear trigger was still in the hands of the United States, as was the final squeeze.

The habit of unilateralism was baptized in the Cuban crisis. When, in 1963, French president Charles DeGaulle attempted to retrieve the deteriorating American position in Asia by brokering a conference conferring legal neutrality in the region, the U.S. officials wavered between indifference and hostility to the suggestion.[26]

Regardless of the motive for Khrushchev's moves in Cuba, the Chinese were enraged. Any attempts the Soviets had made to dissuade the Chinese from assuming a nuclear role prior to October 1962 lost their validity when it became obvious that the Russians would not risk their own destruction for an associate. Allies had become mere appurtenances of power after the Cuban crisis. Their purpose, in the emerging duopolistic structure of international society, was increasingly symbolic. Thus, for example, the Organization of American States was asked to validate the U.S. blockade at the same time the American quarantine was announced.[27] Similarly, Dean Acheson flew to Paris to see France's redoubtable Charles DeGaulle and to visit other European capitals to confer with American allies about the coming confrontation over Cuba.

"Your President does me great honor," DeGaulle said, "to send me so distinguished an emissary. I assume the occasion to be of appropriate importance." Acheson then presented President Kennedy's letter, with the text of the speech to be delivered at 7:00 P.M. Washington time. He offered to summarize it. DeGaulle raised his hand in a delaying gesture that the long-departed kings of France might have envied. "May we be clear before you start," he said. "Are you consulting or informing me?" Acheson confessed that he was there to inform, not to consult. "I am in favor of independent decisions," DeGaulle acknowledged.[28]

For the Europeans, Gaullists and leftists alike, there appeared a high likelihood of nuclear annihilation without representation. In spite of European gestures of support, the NATO alliance received a shock from which it did not recover. The British, in the midst of a vicious domestic debate about whether to abandon nuclear weapons, decided they were necessary to buy even minimum consideration from their American allies. The French did not debate; they accelerated their nuclear weapons program while withdrawing from a military role in the alliance in 1964. Henceforth NATO would be, in Henry Kissinger's words, a "troubled partnership."

On the Soviet side, it was equally apparent that Russian interests would not be sacrificed to fellow socialist states. Castro was plainly sold out. The weak promise tendered by the Kennedy administration not to invade the island was probably cold comfort as Castro saw his military benefactors beat a hasty retreat from American power. Embarrassingly, Castro began to echo the capitulationist theme of Chinese broadcasts. Privately, Castro said that if he could, he would have beaten Khrushchev to within an inch of his life for what he had done. Soviet foreign minister Mikoyan was dispatched to Cuba and stayed there for weeks, not even returning to the bedside of his dying wife, but Castro's fury was unabated.

THE CUBAN MISSILE CRISIS, THE AMERICAN CENTURY, AND THE ROAD TO VIETNAM

Nearly forty years later, Robert McNamara was still contending that the Cuban crisis was "the best managed crisis of the last half century," even though "it made the road to Vietnam all the much easier."[29] The Cuban Missile Crisis revived the sense of the American mission. Time-Life publisher Henry R. Luce once rhapsodized in a widely circulated editorial that Americans must

accept wholeheartedly our duty and opportunity as the most powerful and vital nation in the world and in consequence to exert upon the world the full impact of our influence for such purposes as we see fit, and by such means as we see fit.[30]

Despite President Kennedy's determination not to gloat after the crisis, some of the administration's decision-makers found celebration irresistible. To Arthur Schlesinger, the Cuban Missile Crisis displayed to the "whole world"

the ripening of an American leadership unsurpassed in the responsible management of power. . . . [a] combination of toughness . . . nerve and wisdom, so brilliantly controlled, so matchlessly calibrated that [it] dazzled the world.[31]

After Cuba, confidence in the ability of U.S. armed superiority to command solutions to crises in a way that would favor American interests expanded in such a way that Americans again began to speak of the American century. For a period before the crisis, there had been a national re-examination. People feared national decline in the face of startling Soviet economic growth. Advances in Russian rocketry had led Americans to believe that not only were they in a mortal competition with the Soviets but that the outcome was uncertain. Now, however, most of these doubts seemed to dissipate. Columbia University professor Zbigniew Brzezinski, for instance, then a member of the planning council of the Department of State, proclaimed that American paramountcy was the lesson of Cuba. Brzezinski explained, "The U.S. is today the only effective global military power in the world."[32]

In contrast to the United States, Brzezinski declared, the Soviets were not a global power. Although Khrushchev may at one time have believed otherwise, the Cuban crisis demonstrated the limits of Soviet capabilities.

The Soviet leaders were forced, because of the energetic response by the United States, to the conclusion that their apocalyptic power [nuclear deterrent power] was insufficient to make the Soviet Union a global power. Faced with a showdown, the Soviet Union didn't dare to respond even in an area of its regional predominance—in Berlin. . . . It had no military capacity to fight in Cuba, or in Vietnam, or to protect its interests in the Congo.

No doubt the historic American sense of divine purpose and the almost Jungian need to be the guarantor of global order received a strong fillip from the Cuban crisis. Brzezinski concluded:

What should be the role of the United States in this period? To use our power responsibly and constructively so that when the American paramountcy ends, the world will have been launched on a constructive pattern of development towards international stability. . . . The ultimate objective ought to be the shaping of a world of cooperative communities.[33]

The dreams of Woodrow Wilson had thus, in the Cuban crisis and for the rest of the century, been resurrected. From the mid-1960s on, a world order of liberal democratic states seemed just within reach, if only Americans could persevere in their obligations to take the American experience abroad.

NOTES

1. Thomas W. Wolfe, *Soviet Power and Europe, 1945–1970* (Baltimore: Johns Hopkins University Press, 1970), p. 134.

2. Fleet Admiral V. Kasatonov, "On Battle Watch," *Krasnaia Zvezda*, 30 July 1967, cited in Wolfe, *Soviet Power and Europe*, p. 446.

3. This is according to Russian experts; see Bill Keller, "Eclipsed [on the space race]," *New York Times Magazine*, 27 June 1999, <http://search.nytimes.com>.

4. Wolfe, *Soviet Power and Europe*, pp. 182–183.

5. Secretary of Defense Clark M. Clifford, "The Fiscal Year 1970–1974 Defense Program and Defense Budget" (statement by Department of Defense, January 15, 1969), p. 35.

6. John Newshouse, *Cold Dawn: The Story of SALT* (New York: Holt, Rinehart and Winston, 1973), p. 68.

7. Cited by K. J. Holsti, *International Politics*, 2nd ed. (Englewood Cliffs, NJ: Prentice-Hall, 1972), p. 325.

8. Hans J. Morgenthau, *A New Foreign Policy for the United States* (New York: Praeger, 1969), pp. 212–213.

9. Daniel Ellsberg, *Papers on the War* (New York: Simon & Schuster, 1972), pp. 292–293.

10. Scylla and Charybdis were two sea monsters who lived in caves on opposite sides of the Straits of Messina, separating Italy and Sicily. These sea monsters devoured sailors from passing ships. Scylla, originally a beautiful nymph, had been loved by Glaucus. When Glaucus asked Circe to give Scylla a love potion, the jealous sorceress instead gave her a poison that turned her into a monster with six heads, twelve feet, and heads of baying dogs surrounded her like a belt on her hips. Charybdis personified a dreadful whirlpool, sucking in and spewing out the sea three times a day.

11. Hugh Sidey, *John F. Kennedy, President* (New York: Atheneum, 1964), p. 127.

12. Adam Yarmolinsky, *The Military Establishment* (New York: Harper & Row, 1971), p. 127.

13. Arthur M. Schlesinger Jr., *A Thousand Days* (New York: Fawcett Crest, 1967), p. 397.

14. Richard J. Walton, *Cold War and Counter Revolution* (Baltimore: Penguin Books, 1972), pp. 103–143.

15. Leslie Gelb and Morton Halperin, "The Ten Commandments of the Foreign Affairs Bureaucracy," *Harpers* 244 (June 1972): p. 36.

16. Schlesinger, *A Thousand Days*, p. 831.

17. David Halberstam, *The Best and the Brightest* (New York: Random House, 1971), p. 255.

18. Stephen Peter Rosen, "Vietnam and the American Theory of Limited War," *International Security* 7, no. 2 (Fall 1982): p. 99.

19. As McNamara put it later: "If you read Toynbee, you realize the importance of a democracy learning to cope with limited war. The greatest contribution Vietnam is making—right or wrong [is] beside the point—is that it is developing in the United States an ability to fight a limited war without developing public ire." Douglas Kiker, "The Education of Robert McNamara," *Atlantic Monthly* 219, no. 3 (March 1967): p. 53.

20. McNamara in David Welch, ed., *Transcript of the Proceedings of the Hawk's Cay Conference*, Harvard, April 1988, p. 163. The seriousness of this sentiment is apparent when one notes that McNamara made this point twice in four days—once at the opening of the retrospective and once at the closing. See p. 13.

21. Ibid., p. 162.

22. Schlesinger, *A Thousand Days*, p. 824.

23. William P. Gerberding, "International Law and the Cuban Crisis," in *International Law and Political Crisis: An Analytic Casebook*, eds. Lawrence Scheinman and David Wilkinson (Boston: Little, Brown, 1968), pp. 209–10.

24. Dean Acheson, "Dean Acheson's Version of Robert Kennedy's Version of the Cuban Missile Affair," *Esquire* 71, no. 2 (February 1969): p. 77.

25. Richard J. Barnet and Marcus Raskin, *After Twenty Years* (New York: Random House, 1965), p. 229; George Ball, "Slogans and Realities," *Foreign Affairs* 47 (July 1969): p. 624.

26. See Gareth Porter, *Peace Denied: The United States, Vietnam and the Paris Agreements* (Bloomington: Indiana University Press, 1975), p. 45ff; George McT. Kahin, *Intervention: How the United States Became Involved in Vietnam* (New York: Anchor Press, 1986), pp. 109–10ff; and McNamara's comments in Robert S. McNamara, James G. Blight, and Robert K. Brigham, *Argument without End* (New York: Public Affairs Press, 1999), p. 452, n22.

27. On October 23 the Council of OAS passed, with one abstention, a resolution called for by Rusk. For its text, see "American Foreign Policy," *Current Documents*, 1962, pp. 408–10.

28. Elie Abel, *The Missile Crisis* (Philadelphia: J. P. Lippincott, 1969), p. 112.

29. *Transcript of the Proceedings of the Hawk's Cay Conference*, pp. 13, 162.

30. Henry Luce, *The American Century* (New York: Farrar and Reinhardt, 1941), p. 23; *Life*, 17 February 1941, p. 63.

31. Schlesginer, *A Thousand Days*, pp. 840–41.

32. "The Implications of Change for United States Foreign Policy," *Department of State Bulletin* 57 (July 3, 1967): pp. 19–23.

33. Zbigniew Brzezinski, background remarks to a conference for editors and broadcasters, May 22, 1967, cited in Morgenthau, *A New Foreign Policy for the United States*, p. 19.

Biographies: The Personalities behind the Cuban Missile Crisis

McGeorge Bundy (1919–1996)

Bundy was President John F. Kennedy's principal national security advisor during the Cuban Missile Crisis. Educated in America's elite schools of the day, he had a public remoteness that was reflective, in part, of his temperament and, in part, of the sociology of his associations.

In what was once a profession of the well born and well connected, few national security officials could top McGeorge Bundy. His father, Harvey Hollister Bundy, was assistant secretary of state during the Hoover administration, among several prominent national posts he held. His mother, Katherine Lawrence Putnam Bundy, was the daughter of Harvard president A. Lawrence Lowell. McGeorge Bundy grew up with men like Supreme Court Justice Felix Frankfurter, journalist Walter Lippmann, poet and administrator Archibald MacLeish, and statesman Henry Lewis Stimson, President Hoover's secretary of state and Presidents Franklin D. Roosevelt's and Harry Truman's secretary of war. McGeorge also married the daughter of Dean Acheson, secretary of state in the Truman administration.

Bundy studied mathematics at Yale, earning a B.A. with highest honors in 1940. In 1941 he became a junior fellow of Harvard's Society of Fellows, turning his attention to the study of foreign relations. In 1942 Bundy left Harvard and served briefly in the Office of Facts and Figures under Archibald MacLeish. He then joined the U.S. Army, having memorized the eye chart to hide his nearsightedness. He rose from private to captain, serving on the staff that helped draw up plans for the invasion of Europe during World War II.

At the age of 28, McGeorge Bundy ghost-wrote a rather misleading rendition of Henry Stimson's memoirs, *On Active Service in Peace and War* (1948), a book that affirmed the American obligation to maintain world order as well as the need to use the atomic bomb to end the war with Japan. The book earned Bundy a position at Harvard, where he taught a course on U.S. foreign policy. His ability to mimic the key participants at the infamous 1938 Munich conference grew famous and was also well known for its punch line: only military force makes effective diplomacy possible.

Bundy rose rapidly, becoming a full professor in 1954. From 1953 to 1961 he served as dean of Harvard College, a remarkable position for a man with no earned Ph.D.

Because Bundy was a Republican who had supported Dwight Eisenhower in 1952 and 1956, it surprised some of his more liberal colleagues when he was chosen by the Kennedy transition team to be the new president's national security advisor. But at times, Bundy seemed less motivated by his nominal Republican affiliation, or even the lessons of Munich, than by a politically pragmatic fear of what he called "the wild men in the wings" (i.e., conservative Republicans). In explaining his decision to appoint Bundy, Kennedy said that his new national security advisor would be "helping me to strengthen and to simplify the operations of the National Security Council [NSC]."

The new model of the NSC seemed more like Harvard than anything in government before: Bundy was dean, and Kennedy was president of the university and chairman of the Board of Trustees. Bundy delegated much less than any of his predecessors did and often took over jobs previously performed by at least five senior White House aides during the Eisenhower years.

The design of the NSC under Kennedy made it a kind of shadow State Department. In the new scheme of policy-making, Secretary of State Dean Rusk was seen by the Kennedy circle as something of a second-rate rival. By controlling the president's schedule Bundy arranged to have daily access to the president whereas Rusk did not.

The Cuban issue preoccupied the new administration. Bundy endorsed plans by the Central Intelligence Agency and Defense Department for an invasion of Cuba. When the subsequent Bay of Pigs operation proved a fiasco, Bundy offered to resign. Instead, Kennedy moved the NSC staff from the Old Executive Office Building to the basement of the West wing, only a few steps from the Oval Office.

Later, just before the Cuban Missile Crisis, a reporter noticed that together with the usual "In" and "Out" boxes on Bundy's cluttered walnut desk were two other boxes, one marked "President's Box" and the other "Cuba."

Bundy was an important advisor on Berlin, Laos, and other issues, but as the president's national security advisor he was consumed with dealing with Castro. He chaired the Special Group approving Operation Mongoose, the effort to unseat Castro. Bundy also recruited Brigadier General Edward G. Lansdale to run the covert Mongoose operation.

During the Cuban Missile Crisis, Bundy seems to have been on every side of every option; and his famed "razor" intellect seems (at least in White House transcripts of the time) to have failed to grapple clearly with events. Nonetheless he was one of the handful of participants whom President Kennedy trusted with the details of the settlement that was hammered out with Soviet premier Nikita Khrushchev.

Bundy stayed on as national security advisor in the first years of Lyndon Johnson's presidency. He was an influential voice in the formation of U.S. policy on Vietnam, advocating a strategy of "sustained reprisals" in response to the guerrilla activity of the Viet Cong. But Bundy fared poorly. Johnson was unimpressed by his cultivated demeanor and strove to humiliate him at every opportunity. Once the president reportedly demanded that Bundy deliver his foreign policy briefing while Johnson attended to his own bathroom ablutions.

After Bundy resigned in 1966, he continued to support the Vietnam War until the Tet offensive in late February 1968. Then, the Washington consensus that Bundy helped sustain cracked.

Bundy left the White house to become president of the Ford Foundation and served for eleven years, shifting the charity's work from largely overseas to domestic priorities. His financial management of the Ford fortune was controversial because it was not as successful as other great charitable trusts. Bundy retired in 1979 to write *Danger and Survival* (1988), a thoughtful and useful work on the impact of the atom bomb on the Cold War.

During the last ten years of his life, while teaching at New York University, Bundy was a key advisor to scholarly projects on the Cuban Missile Crisis and on the Vietnam War. On three occasions he was asked to participate in conferences outside the United States. He accepted an invitation in 1989 to the Moscow conference on the Cuban Missile Crisis but refused to go to Havana in 1992, saying that "Fidel was only a bit player." Bundy also refused a 1996 invitation to participate in a 1997 conference in Hanoi, saying there was nothing to talk to Vietnamese about either. It was a curious position for a university professor, but for all his intellect, Bundy seemed never to cultivate the intellectual's appreciation of novel ideas.

When he died, McGeorge Bundy was working on a book about the Vietnam War. The still unpublished message was that the U.S. effort in Vietnam was a terrible mistake. Bundy was also a vigorous advocate of arms control and an outspoken critic of the Clinton White House as being a "sense-free" zone that paid only halting and ineffective attention to foreign affairs.

Bundy died of a massive heart attack at his home in Manchester-by-the-Sea, north of Boston, in September 1996.

Fidel Castro Ruz (1926–)

The communist leader of Cuba, Fidel Castro precipitated the Cuban Missile Crisis when he agreed to host Soviet missiles in Cuba in 1962. The missiles could not defeat an American invasion, so Castro would rather have had more weapons or a Soviet conventional base in Cuba. However, Castro accepted the missiles as much to right the international balance of power as in any hope that the missiles would deter an invasion of Cuba by the United States.

Fidel Castro was born on May 13, 1926, on his family's sugar plantation near Biran in Oriente Province. Fidel and his brother, Raúl, were the illegitimate sons of a cook and a man who had emigrated to Cuba from Galicia, Spain, as a migrant laborer. The elder Castro ultimately became owner of a 23,000-acre plantation in an area that had long been dominated by estates of the American-owned United Fruit Company.

As a boy, Castro attended Jesuit institutions. In 1945 he enrolled at the University of Havana's Faculty of Law. While at the university he joined several radical student organizations. His university career was marked by stormy leftist protest that included burning buses, working in an abortive plot to overthrow the dictatorship of Rafael Trujillo in the Dominican Republic, and participating in urban protest in Bogotá, Colombia.

Once in law practice, Castro mostly devoted himself to practicing labor law and defending the poor. He also tried out for the American major league baseball team, the Washington Senators, with no success.

Castro intended to campaign for a parliamentary seat in the election of 1952, but General Fulgencia Batista overthrew the Cuban government in a coup d'état and canceled the election. Therefore Castro went to court and charged the dictator with violating the Cuban constitution. The court rejected Castro's petition.

Castro then organized a revolutionary cell, using his own money to buy weapons. On July 26, 1953, Fidel and his brother, Raúl, and their band of revolutionaries staged an attack on the Moncada Barracks in Oriente Province. The attack failed. About half of the 160 attackers were killed; Castro and his brother were taken prisoner. Castro's words at the end of his defense were, "history will absolve me." A transcript of his trial remarks, published under the title *History Will Absolve Me* (1953), was widely read in Cuba.

Both Castros were released in a general amnesty on May 15, 1955. Fidel and Raúl Castro then went to Mexico with a small group of Cuban exiles and soon organized another fighting force called the 26th of July Revolutionary Movement. On December 2, 1956, the Castro brothers and some 80 exiles boarded the yacht *Granma* and headed to the Cuban shore. Of the original *Granma* crew, only twelve survived their initial confrontations with Batista's military. The twelve stragglers retreated to the Sierra Maestra mountains and waged continuous guerrilla warfare against the Batista government. From the Sierra Maestra mountains Fidel Castro organized a parallel government, carried out a mini-agrarian reform, established controlled territories with agricultural and manufacturing production, set up a radio station, and even created a small air force.

In the face of one victory after another by the revolutionary forces led by Castro, a defeated Batista fled the country on New Year's Day 1959, the same day that Castro entered Havana.

Castro had led the first successful guerrilla movement in Latin America to defeat a twentieth century military. The U.S. government recognized the new Cuban government on January 7, 1959. In his first major speech on January 8, Castro informed Cubans:

We cannot ever become dictators. . . . We will never turn away from our principles. . . . If I should be an obstacle to peace, from this very moment the people can decide about us and tell us what to do. I am a man who knows when to leave.

Castro assumed the position of premier in February 1959. Since then he has also acquired the titles of president of the Councils of State and of the Ministries of Cuba, first secretary of the Communist Party, and commander-in-chief.

Soon after he assumed power in Cuba, friction arose between Castro and the U.S. government when the new Cuban government began expropriating American-owned properties on the island. In February 1960 Castro made an agreement to buy Russian oil. U.S. oil refiners in Cuba, in consultation with the U.S. government, agreed not to process the oil. As a result the oil companies, and nearly all other American-owned properties in Cuba, were soon expropriated with virtually no compensation. Subsequently the United States cut off Cuba's sugar exports to the United States. Castro was immediately rescued by the Soviets, who bought the Cuban sugar crop years in advance and gave massive assistance to the Cuban police and military. Castro's embrace of this Communist aid led the United States to break diplomatic relations three weeks before the inauguration of President John F. Kennedy.

During the last year of the Eisenhower administration the United States launched a number of covert efforts, all unsuccessful, to dislodge the Castro government. In the first months of the Kennedy administration, on April 17, 1961, a force of over 1,000 Cuban exiles, supported by the American Central Intelligence Agency, made an unsuccessful attempt to invade Cuba at a southern coastal area called the Bay of Pigs. The Kennedy administration assumed that the invasion would inspire the Cuban population to rise up and overthrow Castro.

It was a disastrous miscalculation; the Cuban population supported Castro more firmly than ever.

In October 1962, when the U.S. government discovered the Soviet Union was setting up long-range ballistic missiles in Cuba, President Kennedy instituted a naval blockade of Cuba that lasted until Khrushchev agreed to remove the missiles. After this incident relations between the United States and Cuba remained hostile.

Relations between the Soviet Union and Cuba were also strained. Castro believed that he had been acting as a true soldier of international Communism in accepting the Soviet missiles, which were ill-suited for the actual defense of Cuba.

When Khrushchev agreed to have the missiles withdrawn without consulting the Cubans, Castro was furious. Cuba, he felt, had been betrayed. "It never really crossed my mind that the alternative of withdrawing the missiles was ever conceivable," Castro told his biographer, Tad Szulc. The Soviet leadership, in fact, had become distressed by Castro's recklessness during the missile crisis.

Castro's only solace was a highly guarded and conditional "no invasion pledge" from the Americans. The United States never did, again, mount an invasion threat (except, elliptically, in the first eighteen months of the Reagan administration in reaction to Cuban subversion in Central America and Africa). But U.S. efforts to unseat Castro continued into the late 1960s.

Castro has supported a number of other revolutionary movements in Latin America and Africa. In 1959 his government aided armed expeditions against Panama, the Dominican Republic, and Haiti. During the 1960s and 1970s other countries including Guatemala, Colombia, Venezuela, Peru, and Bolivia faced Cuban-backed guerrilla insurgencies. All of the efforts proved abortive.

Castro claimed to be a committed Marxist-Leninist since 1960 when he began the complete nationalization of industry, confiscation of private property, and collectivized agriculture. Although some of Castro's policies have benefited laborers and peasants, the Cuban economy stagnated from the mid-1980s as Soviet subsidies dwindled. No doubt many of Cuba's economic woes were exacerbated by the loss of some 800,000 middle-class Cubans who fled the country in the early years of Castro's rule, establishing a large, active anti-Castro community in Miami, Florida.

The Cuban government ultimately reconciled with the Soviets. In fact, its dependence on the Soviet Union ran at about $5 billion per year in the last years of the Soviet Union.

The Cuban economy subsequently almost collapsed, and Cuba was forced to seek its peace with whomever would make it—the Pope, the Europeans, and throughout the Americas, with the exception of the United States. But relations between Cuba and the United States seem frozen in time.

Although there were overtures toward normalizing relations with Cuba during the presidencies of Johnson, Nixon, and Carter, no real accommodation has proved possible. One real chance was lost in the Kennedy years. As Castro later revealed to CNN:

It was noon of November 22, 1963, and we were just talking about it when we were informed of the assassination attempt. The delivery of his message [JFK's message indicating a new line toward Cuba] coincided exactly with the moment of his death. This is why I have always maintained the impression that Kennedy had been meditating over the question of relations with Cuba. For us, for Cuba and for relations between the U.S. and Cuba, Kennedy's death was a terrible blow.

During the Reagan, Bush, and Clinton years the prospect of rapprochement receded, in no small part owing to the impact of the sizable and politically influential community of Cuban Americans who view Castro with loathing.

In 1999, when a five-year-old Cuban boy was pulled from the winter sea off the coast of Florida, Castro claimed the child was "kidnapped." The child's mother, who had been fleeing Cuba, died at sea, and his relatives in Florida were anxious to care for him. But the divorced father in Cuba claimed the child as well. The case became a vehicle for Castro to once again mobilize Cuban nationalism against purported American bullying.

A key to his long tenure is his ability with the spoken word. In speeches he partly takes on the twin roles of educator and cheerleader. The famed writer Gabriel García Márquez, a friend of Castro, has described his style as a kind of magic. His style may seem repetitive and excessive, but its power is undeniable. In fact, when Castro was released from prison in 1955 the Batista government allowed him to publish but did not permit him to speak in public.

Castro's personal life is little documented. His marriage ended in divorce in 1954. He is said to have children from that marriage and perhaps more by one of his mistresses, one of whom, along with his sister Juana, sought exile in the United States in the 1990s.

Andrei Andreievich Gromyko (1909–1989)

A Soviet diplomat for over forty-five years, Gromyko was a key liaison to many U.S. presidents. During the Cuban Missile Crisis he earned the enmity of the Kennedy administration as a duplicitous and unreliable agent of his own country's interest and an accurate interpreter of his American negotiating interlocutors. From the 1960s on, the U.S. government frequently reverted to channels other than the ones Gromyko handled in order to deal with the Soviet Union. Gromyko and the department he handled were deemed too inflexible and unimaginative.

Andrei Gromyko was born in 1909 in Belorussia, now Belorus, the son of a peasant. He attended agricultural school in Minsk and became a researcher in agricultural economics at the Soviet Academy of Sciences. At the time the Soviet foreign service was so depleted by the purges of Joseph Stalin that in 1939, after just three years as a researcher in the Foreign Ministry, Gromyko was offered a post as chief of the American division of the People's Commissariat of Foreign Affairs. In the same year, while still learning English, he was assigned to the Soviet Embassy in Washington.

In 1943 Stalin appointed him to be ambassador to the United States. Gromyko helped Stalin in convincing President Franklin Roosevelt to move toward the Soviet position at the Yalta Conference. At the end of World War II he served at the United Nations and then returned to Moscow as a deputy foreign minister and candidate member of the Central Committee, the Soviet second tier of rule. After a stint in Britain as ambassador in the early 1950s, Gromyko returned to Russia as a full member of the Central Committee.

In 1957 Soviet premier Nikita Khrushchev made Gromyko his foreign minister, a post he held until 1985. He was notoriously dour and rigid, reflecting the classic "gray" diplomacy of the Soviet era. Indeed, those who managed to succeed in the Soviet Foreign Ministry were famous for their endurance of epic drudgery, dictatorial administration, and a pervasive atmosphere of internal suspiciousness and backbiting.

On October 18, 1962, as the Cuban Missile Crisis was building, President Kennedy went through with a previously scheduled meeting with Gromyko. Kennedy and his advisors were unsure if Gromyko knew of the missiles in Cuba or if he knew that the Americans knew. If Gromyko was alerted to the missiles, the American side would lose some of its edge in devising a response. Consequently Kennedy could not confront Gromyko directly. But when Gromyko read a statement to Kennedy saying the Soviet

aid to Cuba was "solely for the purpose of contributing to the defense capabilities of Cuba. . . . If it were otherwise, the Soviet government would have
never become involved in rendering such assistance," Kennedy was
amazed. After the meeting Kennedy remarked to an advisor that he wanted
to take the enlarged reconnaissance photographs from his desk and ask
"What do these look like?" Instead, he blandly re-read a statement he had
made on September 4 indicating that the United States would not tolerate
offensive weapons in Cuba. Later that evening a black-tie dinner was held in
Gromyko's honor. Gromyko reported back to Khrushchev that the U.S.
government had no suspicion of Khrushchev's plan to spring the missiles as
a surprise on the Kennedy administration.

Gromyko was not known to have ever strayed from his brief. The instructions to lie to Kennedy came from Khrushchev. Gromyko later explained that
he thought Kennedy already knew about the missiles in Cuba and it was
not necessary for him to embarrass the president in the midst of their two-
part dissimulation. Such an interpretation seems strained, however.

By 1971, Gromyko could boast that on the world scene "no question of
any significance could be decided today without the Soviet Union or in opposition to it." As Soviet military power increased in the 1970s, Gromyko
commonly accompanied Soviet leaders abroad. Finally in 1973, after sixteen years as a candidate member, he gained a full seat on the Politburo, the
governing body of the Soviet Union. Later, Gromyko toured with Soviet
President Mikhail S. Gorbachev.

In 1984 Gromyko nominated Gorbachev for president, saying he "has a
nice smile, but iron teeth." Gromyko's endorsement, viewed as strange at
the time, was his undoing. Within a year Gromyko found himself semi-re-
tired. Named head of the Soviet Communist Party, in reality he was "promoted" to make way for the younger, more vigorous Eduard A. Shevardnadze,
a man much closer to Gorbachev. When Gromyko left power, the flavor of
the classic Soviet-era gray diplomacy largely went with him.

With Foreign Minister Shevardnadze firmly in charge of steering Russia
toward a reconciliation with the West, Gromyko was placed in the merely
honorific position of president of the Soviet legislature. But his time for
honors was over. Soon he was purged from the Politburo and, in April
1989, was removed from the Central Committee as well. He died later
that year. His autobiography (*Memoirs*), published in Russia in 1988 and
in the West in 1990, is as gray as its author.

John Fitzgerald Kennedy (1917–1963)

The thirty-fifth president of the United States and the first one born in the
twentieth century, John F. Kennedy was president at the time of the Cuban

Missile Crisis. His father, Joseph, was as controversial as he was wealthy; and he played a crucial role not only in the upbringing of his famous sons but also in furthering their political careers.

Kennedy was born in 1917, the second of nine children of Joseph P. and Rose Kennedy. As a child, John was challenged by his slight physique. His left side was smaller than his right, and he nearly died from several childhood illnesses. From adolescence on he suffered from "jaundice" (later diagnosed as Addison's disease) as well as colitis and a fragile back.

Kennedy attended Harvard University and in 1940 wrote a thesis entitled "Why England Slept," an argument that democracy may have inherent problems in mobilizing to meet all but immediate threats. The book was promoted by the elder Kennedy, who helped ensure its publishing success.

Despite his weak back, Kennedy enlisted in the U.S. Navy in 1941. In 1943 his small patrol boat, PT109, was rammed by a Japanese destroyer. John Kennedy bravely rescued his crew, swimming one man to safety while holding on to the injured sailor's clothes with his teeth. The effort had ruinous results for Kennedy's back but proved an immense boon to his later political career, for the famed journalist John Hershey was informed of the story by the future president's father. Hershey's story of John Kennedy's heroism was printed in the widely popular *Reader's Digest*; later the story of Kennedy on PT109 became a book and a Hollywood movie.

After World War II Kennedy contemplated entering politics. He faced three political handicaps. The first was his father's reputation as an early advocate of isolationism and his father's dubious associations during Prohibition. Second, and more important, was the problem of Kennedy's health. He had contracted malaria during the war and later became desperately ill from his chronic Addison's disease. Moreover Kennedy's back caused him great suffering, which surgeries did little to improve. His life, said his brother Robert, was marked by constant pain, which he bore with grace and no little help of stimulants, cortisone, and painkillers.

Third, there was the problem of Kennedy's religion. As a Roman Catholic in mid-century America, Kennedy faced suspicion as to his "loyalties." In his 1960 campaign Kennedy countered, "nobody asked my religion when I joined the United States Navy. Nobody asked my brother [Joseph] his religion when he climbed into the cockpit to fly his last mission."

In 1946 Kennedy ran for the U.S. House of Representatives from Boston's eleventh district. He won and served three terms as a fiscally conservative congressman. In 1952, he successfully ran for Senate. Four years later, while recovering from back surgery, Kennedy wrote *Profiles in Courage* (1956) with the assistance of Theodore Sorenson. The book detailed the life and exploits of Americans who had placed the national interest above expediency. Soon the book was a best-seller. And by year's end it won a Pulitzer Prize.

In the Senate, Kennedy mostly aimed at staking out an original position in foreign policy. Although he was earning a reputation as a strong anticommunist, Kennedy was outspoken on the issue of French colonialism in North Africa and Indochina. In a 1958 foreign affairs article he argued that the Eisenhower administration had erred in neglecting nationalism in the former colonial world as well as the latent nationalism simmering in the Soviets' central European Communist bloc.

At the Democratic Party national convention in 1956 Kennedy lobbied furiously for the vice presidential nomination, but despite an electrifying speech his effort failed. Kennedy was defeated but not daunted, and he formally announced ha presidential bid in January 1960.

In his acceptance speech at the Democratic Party national convention in July 1960, Kennedy referred to his vision for America as a "New Frontier." He began his campaign by citing the failings of President Dwight Eisenhower in developing missiles, in sustaining U.S. prestige, in pushing for civil rights, and in neglecting U.S. defense needs. Kennedy pledged he would "get the country moving again."

Although as a senator Kennedy had regarded Castro as heir to Simón Bolívar's mantle of liberation in Latin America, in the 1960 campaign the Democratic Party candidate pilloried Republicans for "blunder, inaction, retreat, and failure" in Cuba. In debates with his Republican opponent, Vice President Richard Nixon, Kennedy appeared more telegenic and hammered Nixon on the issue of Cuba.

Kennedy's ultimate electoral success was hardly resounding. He ultimately won the presidential election by only some 120,000 votes, the closest race in U.S. history. If it had not been for a suspicious vote count in Chicago, he would not have won.

Kennedy's administration was consumed by foreign and defense policy. The new president immediately asked for a 15 percent increase in defense spending just as he discovered from U.S. intelligence sources that the supposed Soviet advantage in long-range missiles was a myth.

Of all the foreign problems facing the United States, none plagued Kennedy more than Cuba. In the early days of his administration, he acceded to the plans of the Central Intelligence Agency for a military invasion of Cuba spearheaded by Cuban exiles. It was, as many scholars have noted, a "perfect failure."

But in domestic politics the Bay of Pigs disaster proved an odd success as Kennedy graciously embraced responsibility and refused to blame others. "Victory has a thousand fathers," he noted, and defeat is an "orphan." But the blame, he said, was his and belonged to nobody else. The public approved of his forthright performance, and Kennedy's popularity soared to 83 percent, a level not seen again until the victory of American forces in the Persian Gulf in 1991.

America's concern with Cuba dominated the correspondence between Kennedy and Soviet premier Nikita Khrushchev. Despite other issues such as those involving Laos, Vietnam, and Berlin, Cuba colored much of the way the administration proceeded in foreign affairs. Seven months after the failed Bay of Pigs invasion the administration fixed on a secret project, code-named Mongoose, to undo Castro. By early October 1962 the covert undertaking had yet to realize a success. Indeed, it was clear the Soviets were making Cuba into an immense base for purposes that could only be realized at American expense. As a result Robert Kennedy, the president's brother and attorney general, took personal charge of the CIA's operation against Cuba.

By now public opinion was beginning to leave the president over the Cuba issue. More than 70 percent of those polled in a sample survey of American "elites" claimed they wanted "more action" on the issue of Communism in Cuba. But administration "action" was propelled primarily by the surreptitious Soviet installation of intermediate and medium range ballistic missiles in Cuba in October 1962. The resolution of the Cuban Missile Crisis that ensued was largely the result of President Kennedy's resourcefulness.

Against the advice of most of his immediate entourage and virtually all of his senior defense advisors, as well as most in Congress, Kennedy pursued a negotiated settlement with Khrushchev. The public result, a Soviet capitulation, was in truth more of a compromise (the U.S. government agreed to remove Jupiter missiles from Turkey in exchange for the Soviet pullout from Cuba); but it did yield Kennedy a hugely favorable rating in public opinion, around 75 percent, and a better position from which to establish a modus vivendi with the Soviet empire.

The first steps were agreements to ban nuclear weapons in outer space, to establish a hot line for efficient communication between Russian and U.S. heads of state, and to sign a test ban treaty. In October 1963 Kennedy was pursuing several initiatives for a détente with Castro. At the same time the CIA, still prodded by Robert Kennedy, was promoting yet another effort to assassinate Castro.

Most of the problems on the Kennedy administration's foreign policy agenda had been mastered in less than three years. Laos was liquidated. Cuba was stabilized. Berlin, for most purposes, was a Soviet defeat. China was marginalized in world politics. The only remaining problem was Vietnam. Kennedy was considering whether to reinforce the 15,000 American troops committed to the defense of South Vietnam against Communism, or to scale back the effort, when he was gunned down by an assassin, Lee Harvey Oswald, on November 22, 1963.

Despite later revelations of peccadilloes and personal failings, Kennedy is in retrospect widely admired and well remembered for numerous achievements and great, unrealized promise. The Kennedy legacy was a substantial tide of idealism, still present in the ranks of the Peace Corps, which he began, and the space problem to which he was highly committed.

His haunting death diminished America, and its circumstances led many Americans to the shore of a bitterness toward public events that the nation yet endures.

Nikita Sergeyevich Khrushchev (1894–1971)

Nikita Khrushchev was the Soviet leader who faced President John F. Kennedy in the Cuban Missile Crisis, the most dangerous and personal contest of the Cold Warn. Born in 1894, the son of a miner, Khrushchev went to work while still a boy. "I worked at a factory owned by Germans, at coal pits owned by Frenchmen, and at a chemical plant owned by Belgians," he recalled. "There I discovered something about capitalists. They are all alike, whatever their nationality."

Soon he represented miners at political meetings. He joined the Red Army in 1919, and during his stint of service his first wife died in 1921. By the end of the 1930s, Khrushchev had come to the attention of Joseph Stalin. Khrushchev was given the assignment of supervising the final Sovietization of Ukrainian agriculture. The result was a huge displacement of the Ukraine's population into collectives. Their crops and animals were given to the state, and millions starved. But Ukrainian peasant and nationalist resistance was pummeled into silence. Then, in 1939, Khrushchev became a member of the Politburo, the chief political committee of the Soviet party.

Khrushchev was transferred to the front in World War II and thereafter was given the brief of agriculture. The results were not especially good. In September 1953, after Stalin's death, Khrushchev admitted the number of cattle in the Soviet Union was lower than it had been in 1916. As first secretary of the Communist Party in the post-Stalin "collective leadership," Khrushchev continued to concentrate on agriculture. His initiative was to exploit the "virgin lands" on the steppes of Kazakhstan and southwestern Siberia. Using 120,000 tractors to plow 32 million acres, he tripled the existing acreage. The problem, blessed by good rains, was an initial success.

Soon Khrushchev bid for supreme leadership. Allied with "hard-liners," he attacked his rivals for "betraying socialism" in considering a settlement with the West. In 1955, in a turn of the tables, Khrushchev made common cause with those in the leadership who wanted an accommodation with the West.

Meeting the other three Western heads of states in a summit conference at Geneva in 1955, Khrushchev impressed the West, especially the British, with his ebullience and apparent openness. He also made unprecedented visits to the developing world. His undeniable energy and his critical position as first secretary of the Communist Party won him a place at the top of the post-Stalin leadership by the start of 1956.

In February 1956, Khrushchev gave a "secret speech" to the 20th Party Congress denouncing Stalin's "cult of personality." The speech was leaked to the West and played back to the Soviet Bloc countries via the Voice of America. "De-Stalinization" won him much initial popularity among the Russian people, but there was substantial bitterness among remaining Stalinist loyalists. Later in 1956 Khrushchev narrowly escaped an assassination attempt when a ship blew up minutes after he disembarked.

An unanticipated fallout of the secret speech was the attempted defection of Hungary from the Warsaw Pact Treaty Organization. But Khrushchev crushed the Hungarian rebellion in November 1956. Another consequence was the growing separation of China from Russia. In October 1957 the Chinese, under Mao Tse Tung, began to criticize Khrushchev personally for his position on Stalin. To Mao, the assault on the "cult of personality" was an attack on his own authority in China. Khrushchev took Mao's concerns seriously and visited Beijing repeatedly in an effort to mollify Mao. Khrushchev's attention to the Far East as the "jewel" of Soviet power was consuming. But the Soviet leader deeply resented Mao's personal attacks. And Mao seemed increasingly reckless, at one point signaling that he would welcome a U.S. invasion; for once American troops were concentrated in the Chinese interior they would be easy targets for Soviet atomic bombs!

Sino-Soviet relations were irreparably breached in 1960. The break between Mao and Khrushchev occurred over the issue of the Soviet Union's improving relations with the United States. In 1959 Khrushchev visited the United States for the first time and behaved as if he were running for office. He lunched with Hollywood stars and visited with Iowa corn farmers, and in a *Life* magazine cover story he was depicted as a good-humored, earthy, family man. Khrushchev delivered an amazing farewell over national television in which he complimented his "American friends" on their "beautiful cities and kind-hearted people."

After meeting President Eisenhower in America, Khrushchev hinted that his prior deadline on settling the nettlesome Berlin issue might be suspended altogether pending an "end to the Cold War." His subsequent meeting with Eisenhower in May 1960, however, was a disaster. After the shoot-down of an American spy plane in the U.S.S.R. two weeks earlier, Khrushchev reverted to the routines of the Cold War.

Khrushchev did come to the United States again, in 1960, to give an in-flammatory address at the United Nations on the prospects of socialism in the third world. His trip was also a much publicized chance to meet with and render his public support to Fidel Castro, who also attended the UN session. Pictures of Castro and Khrushchev embracing bespoke a great deal about the warmth of the burgeoning Soviet-Cuban relations and the return of the Cold War's iciest winds.

As the U.S. presidential campaign got under way John Kennedy was, said Khrushchev, "his candidate" for U.S. president. Khrushchev disliked the Republican candidate, Vice President Richard Nixon, and did every-thing he could to help Kennedy win, even instructing the KGB to engage in "special operations" that might help Kennedy. Khrushchev believed Ken-nedy was a "typical pragmatist" whose election would allow "a possibility of mutually satisfactory settlement . . . on the basis of mutual willingness to avoid nuclear war."

At this time Khrushchev was at the height of confidence. In part it was a result of Soviet breakthroughs in the arms race and space exploration. In February 1961 Khrushchev had news of a successful test of the first ad-vanced intercontinental ballistic missile (ICBM). And in April 1961 he an-nounced the launch of the first person into space, Yuri Gagarin.

At the same time that Gagarin orbited the earth, the unfolding disaster of the failed Bay of Pigs invasion occurred half a world away. Undoubtedly both events buoyed Khrushchev when he met Kennedy in Vienna in June 1961. The meeting proved disastrous in that Khrushchev came away with the feeling that Kennedy was a boy "in short-pants" and "a light-weight."

Thereafter Khrushchev moved quickly to settle the Berlin situation on his terms, having learned that the idea of "something like a Wall" had been floated in Washington, especially among people close to or part of the Ken-nedy administration. When the Communists erected the Berlin Wall in Au-gust 1961, Khrushchev sensed he could be certain of U.S. acquiescence to the division of Berlin. He also felt the Wall resolved the real substance of confrontation.

In 1962, while strolling along the beach of his Black Sea retreat, Khrush-chev began to think about the newest addition to the Communist Bloc—Cuba. He feared the United States might strike at the island. Convinced that

Castro was in a precarious position and that U.S. missiles in Turkey were an affront to Soviet pride, Khrushchev ordered the Soviets to defend Cuba with nuclear missiles.

A former close associate recalled thirty-five years later that Khrushchev "was always anxious about our prestige, he was afraid the Americans would force us to back down somewhere. He'd worked too long with Stalin and well remembered his words, 'When I'm gone, they'll strangle you like a kitten.' " Khrushchev's son gave a similar explanation. "When my father was thinking over the missile crisis," he told students at the University of Kansas in 1995, "he said that if we want to be a great country, then we must protect our allies and show America that we are not a weak country."

Thus Soviet missiles were sent to Cuba camouflaged as agricultural machinery. When U.S. intelligence sources confirmed their presence in Cuba, the Cuban Missile Crisis ensued.

Surprised that the Kennedy administration had discovered the Soviet missiles before he was prepared to announce them, Khrushchev worked around the clock to control the crisis. According to his associates, Khrushchev was distraught and panicked. "The storm's about to break! It's too late to change anything!" he exclaimed.

Afraid that the American policy machinery could not be controlled and that nuclear war would result, he sent a long and emotional letter to the U.S. president stating his acceptance of Kennedy's maximum demands—a withdrawal of the missiles in exchange for a pledge that the United States would not attack Cuba.

But then Khrushchev regrouped and upped the ante, demanding in a subsequent letter that the United States also withdraw its missiles from Turkey. In public Kennedy and Khrushchev agreed to a withdrawal of Soviet missiles from Cuba in exchange for a pledge not to assault Castro with American arms. In private Kennedy acceded to Khrushchev's maximum demands. Khrushchev considered it a victory. He commented in his 1970 memoir *Khrushchev Remembers*:

even the most pressing dispute can be solved by compromise. And a compromise over Cuba was indeed found. . . . The Caribbean crisis was a triumph of Soviet foreign policy and a personal triumph. . . . We achieved, I would say, a spectacular success without having to fire a single shot!

But the Cuban crisis denouement, like the Berlin Wall, was a public relations disaster for Russia. Khrushchev's authority oozed away. At the same time, living conditions in Russia were deteriorating. In June 1962 Khrushchev ordered protesting workers in Novocherkassk to be met by armed special police. Hundreds died in a hail of gunfire. More were executed later.

Even the families of the dead were exiled. Thereafter, Khrushchev's domestic and international authority slipped away.

The humiliation of the Soviet military in the Cuban crisis gave momentum to the anti-Khrushchev cabal. He was deposed and sent into retirement. He died in 1971 after taping hundreds of hours of memoirs that were leaked to the West with the help of the KGB.

After Khrushchev died a Russian sculptor, Ernst Neizvestny, built a monument for his grave. One half of the face is white stone; the other half is black marble. The white side represents Khrushchev's strengths: he was impulsive, smart, warm, and humorous. On the other hand, he was also crude and despotic. And, in the end, his rashness in placing missiles in Cuba cost him his job and his reputation.

John McCone (1902–1991)

John McCone was director of the Central Intelligence Agency at the time of the Cuban Missile Crisis. His constant intuition that Russia was placing missiles in Cuba prodded U.S. intelligence sources to discover the missiles soon after they were uncrated.

McCone was born into a wealthy San Francisco family in January 1902. He was trained as an engineer at the University of California at Berkeley, where he graduated in 1922. He soon rose through the ranks of several steel firms and then managed to make large sums of money in construction, even during the Great Depression.

During World War II his $100,000 investment in the California Shipbuilding Corporation yielded a return of nearly $44 million profit. McCone's financial success at wartime defense business brought hostile scrutiny from Congress, but no illegality was ever demonstrated.

Being a conservative Republican and an ardent convert to Catholicism made McCone something of an outsider in the Roosevelt administration, but he served comfortably as a deputy to Secretary of the Navy James Forrestal in the latter part of World War II and later worked with Secretary of Defense Forrestal in developing the CIA during the Truman administration. McCone also served in the Eisenhower administration as undersecretary of the Air Force (1950–51) and as chairman of the influential Atomic Energy Commission (1958–61). In the latter role he promoted the civilian uses of atomic power and the miniaturization of warheads (which helped make it possible to mount more bombs on missiles and thus vastly increase the nuclear striking power of the U.S. strategic arsenal). Also as a California Institute of Technology trustee during the 1950s, McCone criticized ten

Cal-Tech scientists for supporting Illinois Governor Adlai Stevenson's proposal for a nuclear test ban.

After the failed Bay of Pigs invasion, when CIA director Allen Dulles
was removed, President Kennedy decided that the Republican McCone
would be a politically safe replacement. In fact, Kennedy received abundant
criticism from within and without the administration for appointing such an
avowedly conservative member of the Eisenhower-era national security
community. McCone's vocal policy views had made enemies, but Kennedy
judged McCone would be a capable manager. In fact, McCone became the
president's personal link to retired president Eisenhower and also became a
close personal friend of Robert Kennedy.

Kennedy was attracted to McCone for his reputation as a man of action.
In 1965, Robert Kennedy recalled that "I had a very good personal relationship with John McCone. . . . He liked Ethel very much because, when his
wife died, Ethel went over and stayed with him. So he had a good deal of
feeling for us, and I think he liked the President very much. But he liked one
person more—and that was John McCone." Robert Kennedy's oral history
testimony about McCone was tempered by some bitterness. McCone was
Robert Kennedy's personal candidate to be CIA director in the Kennedy administration after Allen Dulles was discharged in the aftermath of the Bay
of Pigs.

Ultimately Robert Kennedy and McCone broke over interpretation of the
Cuban Missile Crisis. Before, during, and after the crisis, McCone consistently strove to prove that the intelligence community had not erred in dealing with Cuba. He was particularly energetic in leaving a legacy to record
his own foresight in understanding that the Soviets would be making Cuba
into a ballistic missile base. McCone correctly surmised that the initial evidence of a comprehensive surface to air defense system in Cuba presaged
the installation of ballistic missiles. It was a correct inference, some scholars noted. But it was not a logically necessary conclusion, because the Soviets had placed surface to air missiles in at least three other countries in
the late 1950s and early 1960s, and nowhere else had they located ballistic
missiles.

Some members of the Kennedy administration alleged that McCone sab-
otaged the president's efforts to promote a test ban treaty. They charged
McCone with steering CIA expert testimony to the Senate in a fashion that
would prejudice an atmospheric test ban treaty that President Kennedy had
set his sights on from the onset of his administration.

In early 1963, McCone's simmering feud with Robert McNamara broke
into the open. When the hypothetical suggestion was raised by McNamara
before the Cuban Missile Crisis that Castro ought to be removed by assassi-

nation, McCone was indignant (an ironic reaction, considering that his agency had developed at least six such plots during his tenure). Later, when McNamara tried to pressure the CIA to produce an optimistic estimate about the American prospects in Vietnam, McCone gave President Johnson his "personal assessments" indicating that Vietnam was a losing proposition. McCone resigned in 1965 partly because the CIA's intelligence sources in Vietnam were being ignored.

History may view McCone's overall record as mixed. During his tenure at the CIA a war in Laos, kept secret from Congress and the public, intensified. The government of Vietnam under Ngo Dinh Diem was overthrown with CIA assistance, notwithstanding most CIA analysts' serious reservations about Vietnam's future under a military junta. Also, CIA-assisted efforts to overthrow President Sukarno of Indonesia increased during McCone's tenure. Although Sukarno may have fallen from his own mismanagement and misjudgments, the CIA's contribution was important. The cost was catastrophic for the people of Indonesia. Some one million ethnic Chinese were killed in the hostilities that attended to Sukarno's downfall. (Some critics have noted that McCone owned $1 million in stock from Standard Oil of California, which had extensive operations in Indonesia at a time when oil operations were threatened by Sukarno's socialist policies.)

McCone claimed later that he knew nothing about the several attempts on Castro's life that occurred during his tenure as CIA director. However, his successor, Richard Helms, was skeptical: "He was involved in this up to his scuppers just the way everybody else was," said Helms.

Finally, the Warren Commission investigated the assassination of President Kennedy while McCone was CIA director. There is considerable evidence that the CIA obstructed some avenues of inquiry. The cost, of course, has been some 40 years of conspiracy speculation and considerable contribution to the erosion of national trust among Americans in their government.

McCone's post-CIA days were also controversial. He both served as a director of International Telephone and Telegraph (ITT) and remained a consultant to the CIA. At one point McCone testified that these were platforms for him to encourage both ITT and the CIA to work together to impede Chile's president, Salvador Allende, from consolidating power in the early 1970s.

In the mid-1970s, McCone became one of the directors of the Committee on the Present Danger, an important military preparedness lobby of the 1970s and 1980s. He was also director of several major financial service and natural resource companies. After a short retirement John McCone died on February 14, 1991.

Robert Strange McNamara (1916–   )

The U.S. secretary of defense and a principal advisor to President John F. Kennedy during the Cuban Missile Crisis, McNamara was born on June 9, 1916, in San Francisco, California. As a youth he was an Eagle Scout, which he claimed "set his values" ass well as contributed to a life-long passion for the outdoors. McNamara's early memories include attending primary school during the 1920s in a wooden shack.

After graduating from the University of California at Berkeley in 1937, McNamara earned a graduate degree at the Harvard Business School, where he began to teach and gained a reputation as a dazzling lecturer. When war started in Europe, McNamara received two deferments from military service. First, he received an educational deferment because he was teaching at Harvard in an Officer Candidate School program. Second, he gained a deferment because he had a one-year-old child.

Nonetheless in 1942 McNamara left his teaching position and volunteered for the U.S. Army Air Corps. Because of his talents and poor eyesight, and because he was a superb briefer, he was assigned to a series of managerial positions. McNamara's group, called "the whiz kids," was made up of ten gifted officers who worked on problems of applying statistical controls to military operations. The whiz kids developed a system for tracking planes, monitoring troops, and auditing the "train" of military supplies.

After the war, the whiz kids were hired at Ford Motor Company to revitalize automobile design. There, McNamara and his associates were successful in overseeing the introduction of a new system of cost accounting and the introduction of several new models. Most of the new cars were a commercial success. The Edsel was not.

In November 1960, at the age of 44, McNamara became the first person outside the Ford family to assume presidency of the company. However, after just five weeks as Ford's president, he resigned to join the Kennedy administration as secretary of defense.

Even though he attacked a number of Pentagon bastions, most notably the power of the Joint Chiefs of Staff and the belief that there was a missile gap that favored the Soviet Union, McNamara's early reviews were highly favorable. Senator Barry Goldwater described McNamara in 1961 as "one of the best secretaries ever, an IBM machine with legs."

McNamara brought modern business programming and budgeting to the Department of Defense. The results were mixed, at best, in the short run, as some projects that made apparent economic sense turned out to be military failures and inordinately costly. Similarly, business management in the Vietnam theater of war yielded poor results that were veiled by McNamara's energetic quest for positive statistical affirmation of the war's "progress."

McNamara was also at the center of a drive to alter U.S. military strategy. He wanted to move away from the "massive retaliation" of the Eisenhower years to a "flexible response," emphasizing counterinsurgency techniques and other "conventional" uses of military power.

Adopting the views of the strategist Bernard Brodie, McNamara concluded that the Soviets would eventually catch up with the United States in the arms race and that rough parity was the best that could be achieved in the nuclear age. Each side would look enough be capable of obliterating the other in a retaliatory strike, even after a sneak attack. At that point, any attempt by either side to achieve an illusory superiority would only destabilize the balance of power and tempt one or the other into launching a first strike. Whether the Soviets ever shared this doctrine of "mutual assured deterrence" is unclear.

During the Cuban Missile Crisis, McNamara strove mightily to keep control of American forces with some success, but less than he believed at the time. He also concurred with President Kennedy that (1) the political importance of the Soviet missiles in Cuba was more important than their strategic value, and (2) a conventional strike on Soviet forces in Cuba would leave the United States no better off and, in fact, more at risk than if the United States attempted to find a negotiated settlement.

McNamara also supported the deepening military involvement of the United States in Vietnam. On visits to South Vietnam in 1962, 1964, and 1966, the secretary publicly expressed optimism that the National Liberation Front (the Viet Cong) and its North Vietnamese allies would soon abandon their attempt to overthrow the U.S.-backed regime in Saigon, South Vietnam, even though by the end of 1965 he was privately convinced that the United States could not secure a military victory at an acceptable price. Regardless of his doubts, McNamara became a leading spokesman for the day-to-day operations of the war and acted as President Lyndon B. Johnson's principal deputy in the war's prosecution. At the same time, his wife and three children joined the ranks of protesters against the war in Vietnam.

Subsequently McNamara himself began to openly question the wisdom of continuing the U.S. military campaign, and in early 1967 he initiated a full-scale investigation of the American commitment to Vietnam (later published as *The Pentagon Papers*). Later in 1967 he told a congressional inquiry that he was opposed to the continued U.S. bombing of North Vietnam.

By then, McNamara had lost his access to Lyndon Johnson and much of the confidence of the foreign policy community. In the summer of 1967, McNamara's tempering on the use of force in Vietnam, as well as his hauteur toward those who did not agree with him or whom he did not regard as his intellectual equals, drove the Joint Chiefs of Staff to conspire a counter-attack. They planned to call a news conference and resign en masse. It would have been the most important civil-military crisis of the Cold War and was only avoided because the Chairman of the Joint Chiefs got cold feet at the last moment.

McNamara was clearly torn. After he began having sudden fits of crying in meetings, President Johnson became worried about his mental health. LBJ spoke with McNamara's wife in August 1967 and others that, "We just can't afford another Forrestal." (James Forrestal, the first secretary of the then new defense department in the Truman years, committed suicide.) McNamara was eased out of government in February 1968 and spent the next thirteen years as head of the World Bank.

In his new position McNamara showed considerable sensitivity to the needs of third world nations and advanced many developing countries a series of large loans for development projects. Although infrastructure development projects may have been useful, many of the controls that McNamara had instituted previously at Ford and the Pentagon were not applied by the World Bank. In part, this was at the heart of a third world banking crisis in the early 1980s.

McNamara retired from the World Bank in 1981 but remained active in such areas as world hunger, East-West relations, and arms control. In 1995 McNamara published a memoir, *In Retrospect: The Tragedy and Lessons of Vietnam*, in which he described his mistaken assumptions and misjudgments that contributed to the Vietnam debacle. In 1999 he issued an updated argument, entitled *Argument without End*, in which he conceded more points made by American opponents of the war.

Dean David Rusk (1909–1994)

Secretary of state during the Cuban Missile Crisis, Rusk played a central role as the quiet and long-unappreciated advisor to President Kennedy.

Born on February 9, 1909, Dean Rusk was one of five children of a red-clay farmer, postman, minister, and sometime schoolteacher in Cherokee County, Georgia. Years later Rusk recalled that he walked to school, like other poor children of the South, shoeless. He worked his way to a Bachelor of Arts degree from Davidson College in North Carolina and, at graduation, won a Rhodes scholarship to Oxford University in England.

Rusk's professional career started in international law, which he taught at Mills College in California after he returned from England. His academic career lasted for over a decade until his growing academic reputation was interrupted by World War II. Rusk volunteered to serve as an infantry officer in the China-Burma theater. Rising from lieutenant to colonel, he found himself a staff aide to Army Chief of Staff General George Marshall at the war's end.

Entering the State Department, Rusk was assigned to oversee the early days of the UN as America's first assistant secretary for United Nations affairs. He rose to deputy undersecretary of state, the third highest position in the department, but took a nominal demotion to work as assistant secretary of state for Far Eastern affairs at the time of the Korean War. He soon became identified as the war's fierce defender in the face of growing criticism over the war's stalemate at the 38th parallel.

In 1951 Rusk left government service and became president of the Rockefeller Foundation, one of America's largest charitable trusts at the time. In 1960 President-elect John F. Kennedy asked Dean Acheson and others to recommend a new secretary of state. Acheson, former secretary of state under President Harry Truman, placed Dean Rusk's name near the top of the list. As the journalist David Halberstam said (uncharitably but accurately), he was everyone's number two choice for the position.

Rusk campaigned for the job. In the Spring 1960 issue of the establishment's flagship publication, *Foreign Affairs*, he placed a subtle self-promotion for his candidacy for the job of secretary of state. His article seemed to suit the inclinations of both presidential candidates in that it called for the president to take more of the burden of decision than had been the custom during the Eisenhower administration.

President Kennedy preferred Senator William Fulbright. But Fulbright had signed a declaration opposing desegregation, which Kennedy found unacceptable. Rusk, however, had written a personal letter to the president-elect a few weeks after the election, beginning with his own declaration: "As a Georgia-born citizen who believes that the Supreme Court decision on integration was long overdue. . . ."

Rusk rose to the top of the list. Only McGeorge Bundy actively opposed the appointment. Bundy thought Rusk's controlled, deferential, courtly manner was evidence of a "second rate intellect."

When President Kennedy offered Rusk the job, the Rockefeller family arranged a financial package to enable their man to go to Washington. And Rusk accepted without ever having met the president.

But he did not fit easily into the company of the president or his most intimate advisors. Kennedy always addressed the secretary by his title. Sometime early in the Kennedy presidency, according to journalist Richard Reeves, Kennedy asked Rusk to arrange for a vacant Rockefeller Foundation villa to be made available for a tryst. Shocked, Rusk refused.

Rusk said that although he was opposed to the Bay of Pigs operation in 1961, he "deeply regretted" not expressing that opposition more forcefully to Kennedy. "My opposition was not known even within the State Department," he wrote. But documents recently published in the State Department's *Foreign Relations of the United States* series show that Rusk, in meetings with Kennedy present, was continually skeptical of an invasion of Cuba.

Rusk feared that the plan would seriously damage U.S. relations with other Latin American nations. He successfully argued to Kennedy that full air support of the ill-fated exile invading force would provoke an anti-American firestorm within the Western Hemisphere, among U.S. allies, and at the United Nations.

Rusk's role in the Cuban Missile Crisis was widely misunderstood for twenty years. His detractors, mostly Harvard-bred "New Frontiersmen," had the first say. Rusk was deemed colorless, detached, too busy, or too agitated by the looming prospect of Armageddon to stomach discussions with the self-styled luminati that populated the Kennedy national security team.

But it was Rusk's feeling that he owed Kennedy his personal advice, and he did not care to share his counsel with others. "It was never my practice to dictate memoranda of conversations," Rusk told one historian.

I did not keep an office diary. . . . My view was that a President was entitled to have a completely private conversation with his Secretary of State. . . . I did not always tell my colleagues [about] . . . these instructions derived directly from the President.

Most memoirs of the early Kennedy administration portrayed Rusk unkindly. Even his virtues were somehow labeled flaws. For instance, he was termed "gentle, gracious Rusk" by one of Kennedy's closest political confidants, Theodore Sorenson, but also as "too amiable." When asked to respond to "White House initiatives," he was "too eager to disapprove charges of State Department softness by accepting Defense Department toughness." And Rusk bore with "too much composure . . . criticism . . . aimed at the frequent sterility of the State Department bureaucracy." Rusk was also criticized as being "inscrutable . . . [and] [c]ompulsively colorless [and] Buddha like." However, even his nastiest critics allowed that Rusk was "splendid" in negotiations.

Kennedy's advisors did not understand Rusk's self-control and discretion. Most of the Kennedy entourage, even Attorney General Robert Kennedy, could hardly contain their disdain. Rusk's son, Richard, noted in their book *As I Saw It* (1990) that his father took pride in being an enigma. But the quiet virtues of General [and later, Secretary of State] George Marshall had gone out of fashion in Washington.

Rusk felt he had the ear of the president and bore in silence the scorn of those "gossips" who later committed their opinions of him to paper—a practice he thought was an abuse of a public trust.

At a retrospective conference on the Cuban Missile Crisis in 1987, Rusk, perhaps agitated by the presence of so many who had been so vicious and so wrong, revealed evidence that his role was central in resolving the Cuban Missile Crisis. It turns out not only that it was Rusk who orchestrated the diplomatic support for the Cuban blockade that was an essential element of legitimizing American power, but it was also Rusk who worked out the modalities for settling the crisis, as Kennedy had wanted from the first, by means of negotiation. Rusk, among all the close Kennedy advisors, seems best vindicated by history.

The great exception to Rusk's remarkable record of achievement is Vietnam. His son, Richard, long estranged from his father over the war in Vietnam, termed his father "an architect of a war that killed 58,000 Americans and nearly a million Vietnamese" in *As I Saw It*. The elder Rusk reluctantly cooperated with his son to write a memoir. The explanation for Vietnam, said Rusk in *As I Saw It*, was plain.

For me, the issue at stake in Vietnam was a treaty commitment to South Vietnam. The integrity of [an] American commitment . . . involves the life or death of [a] nation. . . . If those opposing us think the word of the United States is not worth very much . . . we will face dangers we've never dreamed of.

Rusk saw the insurgency in Vietnam as an extension of Chinese Communist aggression. No amount of protest by the younger officers at the State Department that there was a profound difference between Vietnamese nationalism and Chinese nationalism could phase the secretary. To Rusk, it made no difference what the source or instrument of disorder was; aggression had to be contained.

Later, Rusk conceded that he "underestimated the tenacity of the North Vietnamese [and] I overestimated the patience of the American people." Hence, before hostilities broke out in the Persian Gulf War of the early 1990s, he favored isolating Iraq rather than taking up arms against Saddam Hussein: "We learned a long time ago the American people are very impatient about war." Later, when arms were chosen by President Bush and backed by the Congress, Rusk characteristically moved to support the effort without reservation.

Rusk opposed racism all his life. When his daughter, Peggy, married an African-American officer, *Time* magazine ran a picture of the wedding on its cover. To *Time* and middle Americans, it might have been controversial. To Rusk, it was not.

When he left the seventh floor of the State Department he, like Marshall, took only his appointment calendar and headed for home. Rusk had been attacked in the Georgia State Legislature and by Governor Lester Maddox for years as an agent of race mixing. But Georgia was home. And he became comfortable in Athens, where he once again taught law as he had forty years earlier. In time he was revered at the University of Georgia as a teacher and exemplar.

Rusk's courtly style disguised great verbal dexterity and precision. During the Cuban Missile Crisis he noted to McGeorge Bundy that the United States and Russia had been "eyeball to eyeball, and I think the other fellow just blinked." The symbiosis between force and diplomacy was summarized by Rusk with evocative pitch: "The eagle (in the Great Seal of the United States) has two claws, one holding the arrows of war, the other the palms of peace."

Rusk died in Georgia at the age of 85. The once-young officers who had most disagreed with him about Vietnam gave some of the most moving eulogies.

Adlai Ewing Stevenson (1900–1965)

Stevenson was the figure who in some ways could have been critical to the settlement of the Cuban Missile Crisis as U.S. ambassador to the United Nations, yet he emerged from the crisis with his reputation tarnished by none other than President Kennedy himself.

Stevenson was born on February 5, 1900, in Los Angeles and raised in Bloomington, Illinois. The grandson of President Grover Cleveland and the son of an Illinois congressman, Stevenson grew up in a household of substantial means. He graduated from Princeton University in 1922 and then attended Harvard Law School for two years. His marks at Harvard were not good so he left early and went to Cincinnati, where he worked as a newspaper reporter. He subsequently returned to Illinois and resumed his legal studies at Northwestern University, from which he graduated in 1926. Stevenson then practiced law in Chicago, but with no real enthusiasm.

His major interest was government. He was an early member of Franklin Roosevelt's New Deal, joining the Agricultural Adjustment Administration in 1933. The next year he became chief counsel for the newly created Federal Alcohol Control Administration, which was to help oversee the repeal of Prohibition.

Leaving Washington in 1935, Stevenson returned to Chicago, practiced law, and raised his civic profile by becoming active in the Chicago Council on Foreign Relations. As president of the Chicago Council, Stevenson confronted the overwhelming isolationism of the day with increasingly polished forensic gifts. In June 1940 he took over a small but increasingly influential group of citizens that argued for vigorous assistance to England, then standing alone against Nazi attacks.

In 1941 Stevenson returned to Washington as senior aide to Secretary of the Navy Frank Knox. In late 1943 and early 1944 Stevenson headed a mission to Italy to determine what assistance the new Foreign Economic Administration might provide as soon as the Nazis were expelled and Italy joined the Allies. The nest year Stevenson joined the State Department and helped work on the founding of a successor organization to the failed League of Nations. In 1946 and 1947 Stevenson served as a delegate to the fledgling United Nations.

In 1948 Stevenson was elected governor of Illinois. During his tenure he opposed several legislative measures that were, he said, "more dangerous to ourselves than to our foes." When, in 1951, several black families purchased homes in a suburb of Chicago, they were greeted by a mob of white rioters. Stevenson was one of the first governors to use the National Guard to quell such disturbances.

Stevenson accepted a draft by the Democratic Party to be the candidate for president in 1952. During the campaign Stevenson's considerable abilities on the public stump were buttressed by some of the best speechwriters ever assembled in public life: Arthur Schlesinger, John Kenneth Galbraith, John Bartlow Martin, and Archibald MacLeish. But well-reasoned speeches, in which Stevenson's own hand was evident, were no match for Dwight Eisenhower's popularity and a Republican Party more than normally anxious to accede to power after years of being trounced by President Roosevelt's New Deal and then by President Truman's Fair Deal.

It was a hard campaign for Stevenson. FBI director J. Edgar Hoover, fearing Stevenson was soft on Communism and a dangerous liberal, instructed some of his agents to talk publicly about how Adlai Stevenson was a closet homosexual. Such rumors were curious given Hoover's own sexual secrets, but they were very hurtful nonetheless. The larger reason that Stevenson lost, however, was that the Democrats had controlled the White House for twenty years and the Republican Eisenhower seemed a fresh voice, promising to end the war in Korea and deal forcefully with Communism.

Stevenson made another run for the presidency in 1956. At the Democratic Party national convention in Chicago, Senator John Kennedy actively sought the vice presidential nomination. Kennedy believed he had reached a deal with Stevenson that guaranteed him a place on the ticket. But at the last moment Stevenson, under pressure from Democratic Party stalwarts, announced—when Kennedy was within thirty votes of nomination—that the vice presidential nomination was going to be thrown open to the convention delegates. Kennedy lost to Estes Kefauver.

John Kennedy's sense of betrayal was buttressed by the loathing of his brother, Robert Kennedy, who had worked on the Stevenson campaign for six weeks. To Robert Kennedy, Stevenson was out of touch with people and obsessed with Richard Nixon, Eisenhower's vice president. When he was not trying to lay Nixon low, Stevenson seemed to work against himself. In the South, he talked of civil rights. In coal mining towns, he talked about foreign policy. To Democratic ward healers, he would say that Democrats should sometimes vote split tickets. Robert Kennedy was so disenthralled that he voted for Eisenhower.

During his 1956 presidential campaign, a woman called out to Adlai E. Stevenson, "Senator, you have the vote of every thinking person!" Stevenson called back, "That's not enough, madam, we need a majority!"

Stevenson's loss in 1956 was overwhelming—there were 548 votes for Eisenhower and only 73 for Stevenson in the electoral college. Strangely, in 1960 Stevenson allowed his name to be placed in nomination a third time but the Democratic convention chose John F. Kennedy by a huge majority.

Stevenson hoped to be secretary of state in the Kennedy administration. During the 1960 convention Kennedy asked Stevenson to exchange his delegates—Stevenson still had a considerable following—in return for the position of secretary of state. But Stevenson considered Kennedy's suggestion tawdry, a sentiment that caused Robert Kennedy, John Kennedy's campaign manager, to develop a special antipathy toward Stevenson. Knowing they needed to find a suitable position for Stevenson, President-elect Kennedy offered him the position of ambassador to the United Nations. When Stevenson refused to comment on the offer, believing it was a bit "beneath his dignity," Kennedy was furious. Symbolic of the President's mood, after Stevenson accepted the offer, was the conspicuous absence of a limousine for Stevenson to ride in from the Capitol Hill swearing-in to the White House. Stevenson was the only Cabinet member left out in the cold to fend for himself.

During the Cuban Missile Crisis in 1962, Soviet ambassador Valerian Zorin hedged on answering Stevenson's questions regarding the presence of Russian missiles in Cuba. In a now-famous retort Stevenson exclaimed, "I am prepared to wait until hell freezes over!" When Zorin did not answer, Stevenson proceeded to show U.S. reconnaissance photographs of the Russian missile bases in Cuba to a worldwide audience watching the UN proceedings on television.

However, neither the president nor the attorney general seemed to think much of Stevenson during the Cuban crisis. On Wednesday, October 17, Stevenson wrote the president:

We must be prepared for the wide-spread reaction that if we have missiles in Turkey and other places surrounding the Soviet Union, surely they have a right to one in Cuba. If we attack Cuba, an ally of the USSR, isn't an attack on NATO bases equally justified?

Robert Kennedy read the memo in an ExCom meeting and turned to Theodore Sorenson, saying, "Tell me which side he is on."

Because Stevenson forcefully urged concessions that the president might well have considered, but not in front of his principal advisors, a foreign policy expert of unimpeachable Cold War credentials, John McCloy, was sent to the UN during the crisis with the brief of "stiffening" Stevenson. Although Stevenson, through the UN secretary general, was helpful in offering the kind of diplomatic alternatives for settling the crisis that the president privately preferred, later President Kennedy set out to discredit him. He told two prominent reporters that it was Stevenson who was arguing for cowardly concessions. Stevenson was being punished for sins going back to the Democratic Party convention of 1956.

After defending the Johnson administration's invasion of the Dominican Republic in 1965, Stevenson had decided to retire so that he could "sit in the shade with a glass of wine . . . and watch the people dance." He had little time. He was still ambassador to the UN when he succumbed to a fatal heart attack on July 14, 1965, at the age of 65. He died in a flutter of classified papers that dropped from his brief case when he died within eye-sight of the American embassy.

Primary Documents of the
Cuban Missile Crisis

Document 1
THE INSPECTOR GENERAL'S SURVEY OF THE
CUBAN OPERATION

The Bay of Pigs invasion was a central element of the Cuban Missile
Crisis. President Kennedy believed his resolve had been impeached by
the decision not to rescue the beleaguered invasion force of Cuban exiles as they were gunned down on the beach. Kennedy and Khrushchev
exchanged barbs about the fiasco in the lead-up to the missile crisis and
even during the crisis itself, when Khrushchev cited the U.S. attempt at
the Bay of Pigs as the warrant for placing nuclear weapons in Cuba.
The Bay of Pigs disaster put the Kennedy administration on the defensive with the Russians from the onset; Kennedy's greatest worry was
that the failure to provide assistance to the exiles as they were being
gunned down was a sign of timidity on the part of the United States that
would embolden the Russians.

The following excerpts are from "The Inspector General's Survey of the
Cuban Operation," the Central Intelligence Agency's internal inquiry into
the Bay of Pigs invasion in 1961. The report was released under the Freedom of Information Act to the National Security Archive, a nonprofit group
that collects and publishes declassified government reports. The CIA's Historical Review Program released this survey as "sanitized" in 1997.

31. The agency committed . . . extremely serious mistakes in planning:

a. Failure to subject the project especially in its latter frenzied stages, to a cold and objective appraisal. . . .

b. Failure to advise the president, at an appropriate time, that success had become dubious and to recommend that the operation be therefore canceled and that the problem of unseating Castro be restudied.

c. Failure to recognize that the project had become overt and that the military effort had become too large to be handled by the agency alone.

32. Timely . . . scrutiny of the operation in the months before the invasion . . . would have demonstrated to agency officials that the clandestine paramilitary operations had almost totally failed, that there was no controlled and responsive underground movement ready to rally to the invasion force. . . .

33. It would also have raised the question of why the United States should contemplate pitting 1,500 soldiers, however well trained and armed, against an enemy vastly superior in number and armament on a terrain which offered nothing but vague hope of significant local support . . .

37. Cancellation would have been embarrassing. The brigade . . . would have spread their disappointment far and wide. Because of multiple security leaks in this huge operation . . . the agency's embarrassment would have been public.

38. However, cancellation would have averted failure, which brought even more embarrassment, carried death and misery to hundreds, destroyed millions of dollars worth of U.S. property, and seriously damaged U.S. prestige . . .

40. . . . [W]e can confidently assert that the agency had no intelligence evidence that Cubans in significant numbers could or would join the invaders or that there was any kind of an effective and cohesive resistance movement under anybody's control, let alone the agency's. . . .

41. The choice was between retreat without honor and a gamble between ignominious defeat and dubious victory. The agency chose to gamble, at rapidly decreasing odds.

42. The project had lost its covert nature by November 1960. As it continued to grow, operational security became more and more diluted. For more than three months before the invasion the American press was reporting, often with some accuracy, on the recruiting and training of Cubans. . . . Plausible denial was a pathetic illusion.

Document 2
PRESIDENT KENNEDY REPORTS TO THE AMERICAN PEOPLE

The Berlin crisis and the missile crisis in Cuba were both linked to the Kennedy administration's firm belief that the credibility of the United

States, as well as the balance of power, were at risk at this point during the Cold War. Both crises saw American military forces respond in ways that troubled responsible officials, especially the president. Both were settled by unacknowledged American initiatives. Finally, both crises ended as public relations disasters for the Russians.

The preparation of the American people for a season of confrontation began with President Kennedy's speech on July 25, 1961, when he asked for a tripling of the draft and a call-up of the military reserves. The president wanted to convey to the Russians (1) the appearance that he was not the callow youth that Khrushchev suspected, and (2) a determination that America fully expected to retain its rights inherited from the resolution of World War II.

The Berlin crisis was effectively settled by the construction of the Berlin Wall, a solution that the Russian leader was willing to accept both publicly and privately via emissaries of the Kennedy administration. It was to be a model for the solution of the Cuban Missile Crisis. That is, the Kennedy administration would threaten and prepare for war while at the same time privately proffering abundant hints at a much more moderate solution. Underscoring what the administration conceived as an acceptable solution was this address to the nation wherein the president emphasized repeatedly U.S. rights in West Berlin. A close reading of the speech makes it clear that the Soviets were offered a free hand in the Eastern zone as long as they permitted Allied access to it and allowed West Germany to remain a part of the German Federal Republic.

Good Evening.

Seven weeks ago tonight I returned from Europe to report on my meeting with Premier Khrushchev. . . . In Berlin, as you recall, he intends to bring to an end, through a stroke of the pen, first our legal rights to be in West Berlin and secondly our ability to make good on our commitment to the 2 million free people in that city. That we cannot permit. . . .

The immediate threat to free men is in West Berlin. But that isolated outpost is not an isolated problem. The threat is worldwide. . . . We face a challenge in Berlin, but there is also a challenge in Southeast Asia, where the borders are less guarded, the enemy harder to find, and the dangers of communism less apparent to those who have so little. . . .

. . . The NATO shield was long ago extended to cover West Berlin. . . . For West Berlin . . . is more than a showcase of liberty, a symbol, an island of freedom in a communist sea. It is even more than a link with the free world, a beacon of hope. . . .

I hear it said that West Berlin is militarily untenable. And so was Bastogne. And so, in fact, was Stalingrad. Any dangerous spot is tenable if men—brave men—will make it so. . . . We must meet our oft-stated pledge to the free peoples of West Berlin—and maintain our rights and their safety, even in the face of force. . . .

So long as the communists insist that they are preparing to end by themselves unilaterally our rights in West Berlin and our commitments to its people, we must be prepared to defend those rights. . . . We will at all times be ready to talk, if talk will help. . . .

The supplementary defense buildups that I asked from the Congress in March and May . . . included . . . the strengthening of our missile power and for putting 50 percent of our B-52 and B-47 bombers on a ground alert. . . . These measures must be speeded up. . . .

But even more importantly, we need the capability of placing in any critical area at the appropriate time a force . . . to meet all levels of . . . pressure with whatever levels of force are required. We intend to have a wider choice than humiliation or all-out nuclear action.

. . . Everything essential to the security of freedom must be done; and if that should require more men, or more taxes, or more controls, or other new powers, I shall not hesitate to ask them. . . .

Accordingly, I am now taking the following steps:

1. I am tomorrow requesting [of] the Congress . . . an additional $3,247,000,000 of appropriations for the armed forces.

2. . . . I am requesting an increase in the Army's total authorized strength from 875,000 to approximately 1 million men.

3. I am requesting an increase of 29,000 and 63,000 men respectively in the active duty strength of the Navy and the Air Force.

4. . . . I am ordering that our draft calls be doubled and tripled in the coming months. . . .

5. Many ships and planes once headed for retirement are to be retained or reactivated. . . .

6. Finally, some $1.8 billion—about half of the total sum—is needed for the procurement of non-nuclear weapons, ammunition, and equipment. . . .

. . . I am well aware of . . . the burden of these requests. Studies or careers will be interrupted; husbands and sons will be called away; incomes in some cases will be reduced. But these are burdens which must be borne if freedom is to be defended. . . .

We have another sober responsibility. To recognize the possibilities of nuclear war. . . . In May, I pledged a new start on Civil Defense. . . . Tomorrow, I am requesting of the Congress new funds . . . to identify . . . space in existing structures . . . that could be used for fallout shelters . . . to stock those shelters with . . . [the] minimum essentials for survival; to increase their capacity; to improve our air-raid warning and fallout detection systems, including a new household warning system which is now under development; and to take other measures . . . to save millions of lives . . . [i]n the event of an attack. . . .

. . . This is an increase in the defense budget of $6 billion since January, and has resulted in official estimates of a budget deficit of over $5 billion. . . .

I realize that no public revenue measure is welcomed. . . . But I am certain that every American wants to pay his fair share, and not leave the burden of defending freedom entirely to those who bear arms. . . .

. . . Our peacetime military posture is traditionally defensive; but our diplomatic posture need not be. . . .

. . . [W]e shall always be prepared to discuss international problems with any and all nations. . . . If they have proposals—not demands—we shall hear them. If they seek genuine understanding—not concessions of our rights—we shall meet with them. We have previously indicated our readiness to remove any actual irritants in West Berlin, but the freedom of that city is not negotiable.

. . . We recognize the Soviet Union's historical concern about their security . . . after a series of ravaging invasions, and we believe arrangements can be worked out which will help to meet those concerns, and make it possible for both security and freedom to exist in this troubled area.

. . . The world is not deceived by the communist attempt to label Berlin as a hotbed of war. There is peace in Berlin today. The source of world trouble and tension is Moscow, not Berlin. And if war begins, it will have begun in Moscow and not Berlin.

. . . The solemn vow each of us gave to West Berlin in time of peace will not be broken in time of danger. If we do not meet our commitments to Berlin, where will we later stand? If we are not true to our word there, all that we have achieved in collective security, which relies on these words, will mean nothing. . . .

Today, the endangered frontier of freedom runs through divided Berlin. . . . The Soviet government alone can convert Berlin's frontier of peace into a pretext for war. . . .

With your help, and the help of other free men, this crisis can be surmounted. . . .

In meeting my responsibilities in these coming months as president, I need your good will, and your support—and above all, your prayers.

Thank you, and good night.

Source: "Radio and Television Report to the American People on the Berlin Crisis, July 25, 1961 in *Public Papers of the President, John F. Kennedy* (Washington, DC: U.S. Government Printing Office, 1962), 535ff.

Document 3
MEMO FROM THE CIA

The following memo from a former CIA official, Sheffield Edwards, was prepared at the request of Attorney General Robert Kennedy in the spring of 1962 while Kennedy was considering how to dislodge Castro. It reveals that the CIA arranged for an intermediary to approach senior members of a Chicago organized crime "syndicate" with the request to murder Fidel Castro. The intermediary was Robert Maheu, a private investigator (and later a close aide to the eccentric billionaire Howard Hughes). He contacted John Rosselli and Sam Giancana, who had connections in Miami and Havana. (Not noted in the memo is that Sam Giancana had a close personal relationship with at least one of the former mistresses of the president.)

Later, Giancana and Rosselli were murdered before they might have been called to testify in front of the Senate committee that investigated these matters in 1975.

It is hard to believe that Robert Kennedy and the president were insulated from the facts of these approaches to the Mafia, although there is no record of such an apprehension on the part of either Kennedy. Indeed, there is some contrary evidence: no White House had ever been more vigorous in seeking prosecutions of organized crime than was the Kennedy administration.

Washington, May 14, 1962

Memorandum for the Record

This memorandum for the record is prepared at the request of the Attorney General of the United States following a complete oral briefing of him relative to a sensitive CIA operation conducted during the period approximately August 1960 to May 1961. [A FRUS editorial note states: " . . . The body of the report . . . was based largely upon interviews with CIA officials. . . . The Inspector General's report on these attempts to assassinate Castro was supplied in 1975 to the Senate Select Committee to Study Governmental Operations with Respect to Intelligence Activities. . . . "] In August 1960 the undersigned was approached by Mr. Richard Bissell, then Deputy Director for Plans of CIA, to explore the possibility of mounting this sensitive operation against Fidel Castro. It was thought that certain gambling interests which had formerly been active in Cuba might be willing and able to assist and further, might have both intelligence assets in Cuba and communications between Miami, Florida, and Cuba.

Accordingly, Mr. Robert Maheu, a private investigator of the firm of Maheu and King, was approached by the undersigned and asked to establish contact with a member or members of the gambling syndicate to explore their capabilities. Mr. Maheu was known to have accounts with several prominent businessmen and organizations in the United States. Maheu was to make his approach to the syndicate as appearing to represent big business organizations which wished to protect their interests in Cuba.

Mr. Maheu accordingly met and established contact with one John Rosselli of Los Angeles. Mr. Rosselli showed interest in the possibility and indicated he had some contacts in Miami that he might use. Maheu reported that John Rosselli said he was not interested in any remuneration but would seek to establish capabilities in Cuba to perform the desired project.

Towards the end of September Mr. Maheu and Mr. Rosselli proceeded to Miami, where, as reported, Maheu was introduced to Sam Giancana of Chicago. Sam Giancana arranged for Maheu and Rosselli to meet with a "courier" who was going back and forth to Havana. From information received back by the courier the proposed operation appeared to be feasible and it was decided to obtain an official Agency approval in this regard.

A figure of one hundred fifty thousand dollars was set by the Agency as a payment to be made on completion of the operation and to be paid only to the principal or principals who would conduct the operation in Cuba.

Maheu reported that Rosselli and Giancana emphatically stated that they wished no part of any payment. The undersigned then briefed the proper senior officials of this Agency on the proposal. Knowledge of this project during its life was kept to a total of six persons and never became a part of the project current at the time for the invasion of Cuba, and there were no memoranda on the project nor were there other written documents or agreements. The project was duly orally approved by the said senior officials of the Agency.

Sheffield Edwards

Source: Foreign Relations of the United States, 1961–1963, Volume X, Cuba, 1961–1962, Louis J. Smith, ed. (Washington, DC: U.S. Government Printing Office, 1997), Doc. 37.

Document 4
MEMO FROM McGEORGE BUNDY

The context of this document is the growing sense that Cuba was rapidly becoming a well-armed outpost of Soviet power and perhaps even a missile base, as CIA director John McCone feared. McCone was pressing the White House to approve more vigorous operations against Cuba and more active reconnaissance. Both were approved, as was another intelligence study that all but dismissed the possibility that the Soviets would place ballistic missiles in Cuba.

The president and his closest advisors did not believe the Russians would install ballistic missiles in Cuba. However, lest the Russians be tempted to do so, the Kennedy administration strove to approach the Turks in an effort to remove obsolete U.S. Jupiter missiles before they were made fodder for a swap. The Turks balked. And the State Department did not address the issue again until the height of the missile crisis six weeks later.

National Security Action Memorandum No. 181
Washington, August 23, 1962
NSAM 181, Cuba
(A). Top Secret; Sensitive.

TO: Secretary of State
Secretary of Defense
Attorney General
Acting Director, CIA
General Taylor

The President has directed that the following actions and studies be undertaken in the light of evidence of new bloc activity in Cuba.

1. What action can be taken to get Jupiter missiles out of Turkey? . . .

2. What information should be made available in the U.S. and abroad with respect to these new bloc activities in Cuba? . . .

3. There should be an organized effort to bring home to governments of our NATO allies in particular the meaning of this new evidence of Castro's subservience to the Soviets, and the urgency of action on their part to limit their economic cooperation with Cuba. . . .

4. The line of activity projected for Operation Mongoose Plan B plus should be developed with all possible speed. . . .

5. An analysis should be prepared of the probable military, political, and psychological impact of the establishment in Cuba of either surface-to-air missiles or surface-to-surface missiles. . . .

6. A study should be made of the advantages and disadvantages of making a statement that the U.S. would not tolerate . . . military forces . . . which might launch a nuclear attack from Cuba against the U.S. . . .

7. A study should be made of . . . military alternatives . . . to eliminate any installations in Cuba capable of launching nuclear attack on the U.S. . . .

8. A study should be made . . . of action to liberate Cuba by blockade or invasion or other action beyond Mongoose B plus. . . .

. . . The President emphasizes again the sensitive character of these instructions.

McGeorge Bundy

Source: Foreign Relations of the United States, 1961–1963, Volume X, Cuba, 1961–1962, Louis J. Smith, ed. (Washington, DC: U.S. Government Printing Office, 1997), Doc. 386.

Document 5
TELEGRAM FROM FOREIGN MINISTER GROMYKO TO CHAIRMAN KHRUSHCHEV

The following is Gromyko's report of October 18, 1962. It was sent directly to Khrushchev. Recently it was recovered from the Russian archives by Japanese television, NHK, and now is part of the collection of the National Security Archive of George Washington University. The translation is by Mark H. Doctoroff.

On October 18, 1962, four days after U.S. reconnaissance planes began to take pictures of Soviet missiles in Cuba, President Kennedy met with Soviet foreign minister Andrei Gromyko. Even under prodding, Gromyko refused to say anything about the Soviet missiles in Cuba; and Kennedy, not wanting the Soviets to suspect American military preparations, also said nothing. Gromyko reported back to the Kremlin that the Soviet plan to install missiles was intact and that the Americans were in no mood for a confrontation. It was a good indication of just how out of touch Soviet diplomacy had become. For just as the Soviet foreign minister penned these remarks, the U.S. government was mobilizing every resource to respond to the imposition of Soviet missiles in Cuba.

CABLE TELEGRAM FROM SOVIET FOREIGN MINISTER
A. A. GROMYKO TO THE CC CPSU, OCTOBER 19, 1962

TOP SECRET Making Copies Prohibited; Copy No. 1 CIPHERED TELEGRAM to the CC CPSU

Everything which we know about the position of the USA government on the Cuban question allows us to conclude that the overall situation is completely satisfactory. This is confirmed by official announcements of American officials, including Kennedy, in his discussion with us on October 18, and all information which reaches us via unofficial channels and from representatives of other countries.

There is reason to believe that the USA is not preparing an intervention in Cuba and has put its money on obstructing Cuba's economic relations with the USSR . . . so as to destroy its economy . . . and in this way . . . prompting an uprising against the regime. This is based on a belief that the Soviet Union will not over a long period be able to provide Cuba with everything it needs.

The main reason for this American position is that the Administration and the overall American ruling circles are amazed by the Soviet Union's courage in assisting Cuba. . . .

... Newspapers bleat about the approaching crisis vis-à-vis West Berlin. ... The goal ... is to divert somewhat public attention from the Cuba issue. All this is not without the participation of the White House. ...

The wide publication of the results of an election survey conducted ... showing that the vast majority of Americans are against an American intervention in Cuba serves this same goal. ...

Also deserving of attention is the fact that Congress has now "gone on recess." This suggests that the pressure on Kennedy from the extreme groups in Congress will be less during the recess. ...

[T]aking into account the undeniable objective facts ... and also the assurances given to us that the USA has no plans for intervention in Cuba (which undeniably commits them in many respects), it is possible to say that ... a USA military adventure against Cuba is almost impossible to imagine.

A. Gromyko

Document 6
AUDIOTAPES OF PRESIDENT KENNEDY'S ASSESSMENT OF THE SITUATION

Recently the John F. Kennedy Library at Harvard University released audiotapes of the ExCom meetings. They can be accessed at the Library's home page on the World Wide Web and heard via the Internet. They are also available on C-Span's Web pages. Through these deliberations, President Kennedy is revealed as a quintessential realist—perhaps the most succinct, clear-eyed, and prudent of all the voices caught in these recordings.

CUBAN MISSILE CRISIS: JFK's Thoughts on Situation (4:00) Tape 31.2—October 19—9:45 A.M.—Cabinet Room

Speaker: John F. Kennedy (JFK), President of the United States

JFK: Let me just say a little first about what the problem is from my point of view. First, I think we ought to think of why the Russians did this. Well, actually, it was a rather dangerous, but rather useful play of theirs. If we do nothing, they have a missile base there with all the pressure that brings to bear on the United States, and damage to our prestige. If we attack Cuba with the missiles—or Cuba in any way—it gives them a clear line to take Berlin. ...

Now, that's what makes our problem so difficult. If we go in and take them out in a quick air strike, we neutralize the chance of danger to the United States of these missiles being used. ... One the other hand, ... there's bound to be a reply from the Soviet Union—there always is—of their just going in and taking Berlin by force at some point, which leaves me only one alternative, which is to fire nuclear weapons, which is a hell of an alternative. . . .

. . . So we've got to do something. Now the question really is, what are we going to do about this thing?

CUBAN MISSILE CRISIS CLIP #4: Military Advice to JFK (3:03), Tape 31.2—October 19—9:45 A.M.—Cabinet Room

Speakers: General Maxwell Taylor, Chairman of the Joint Chiefs of Staff; John F. Kennedy (JFK), President of the United States; General Curtis LeMay, Air Force Chief of Staff

Taylor: Well, . . . I think we'd all be unanimous in saying that really our strength in Berlin—our strength anyplace in the world—is the credibility of our response. . . .

JFK: That's right. That's right. So that's why we've got to respond. Now the question is, what type of response.

LeMay: Well . . . I'd emphasize a little strongly perhaps that we don't have any choice except direct military action. If we do this blockade that's proposed and political action, the first thing that's going to happen is your missiles are going to disappear into the woods, particularly your mobile ones. Now we can't find them, regardless of what we do, and then we're going to take some damage if we try to do anything later on.

JFK: But there may—can't there be some in the undercover now . . . ?

LeMay: There's the possibility . . . [but] [i]f they were going to hide any of them, you'd think they'd have hidden them all. . . . Now as for the Berlin situation, I don't share your view that if we knock off Cuba, they're going to knock off Berlin. . . .

JFK: What do you think their reply would be?

LeMay: I don't think they're going to make any reply. If we tell them that the Berlin situation is just like it's always been: If they make a move, we're going to fight. . . . This blockade and political action, I see leading into war. . . . This is almost as bad as the appeasement of Munich, because if this blockade comes along, the MIGs are going to fly, the IL-28s are going to fly . . . and we're just going to gradually drift into war . . . with missiles staring us in the face. . . . So we just drift into war under conditions that we don't like. So I just don't see any other solution except direct military intervention—right now.

Document 7
DISCUSSIONS IN THE OVAL OFFICE

The *Foreign Relations of the United States* series contains the records of a meeting in the Oval Office the day before the missile crisis was announced to the American people but one week after Kennedy administration advisors began considering options. The Joint Chiefs of Staff had pressed for an attack on Cuba. But there was a profound military problem. Although perhaps "90 percent" of the Soviet missiles in Cuba might be destroyed, of the remaining 10 percent there might be four that could be launched to devastating effect on any large city within the continental United States. Robert Kennedy, perhaps the closest advisor to the president, argued that a surprise attack would be too much like the Japanese attack on Pearl Harbor—a morally dubious effort that would go against American traditions. The younger Kennedy's argument carried the day with Secretary of Defense Robert McNamara and CIA director John McCone.

Washington, October 21, 1962

1. . . . The Secretary of Defense stated that following the start of an air attack, the initial units of the landing force could invade Cuba within 7 days. The movement of troops in preparation for such an invasion will start at the time of the President's speech. . . .

General Sweeney outlined the following plan of air attack, the object of which would be the destruction of the known Cuban missile capability. . . . [A] total of approximately 250 sorties would be flown.

General Sweeney stated that he was certain the air strike would be "successful"; however, even under optimum conditions, it was not likely that all of the known missiles would be destroyed. . . . General Taylor, General Sweeney, and the Secretary of Defense all strongly emphasized that . . . initial air strike must be followed by strikes on subsequent days and that these in turn would lead inevitably to an invasion. . . . General Sweeney strongly recommended that any air strike include attacks on the MIG aircraft and, in addition, the IL-28s. To accomplish the destruction of these aircraft, the total number of sorties of such an air strike should be increased to 500.

The President agreed that if an air strike is ordered, it should probably include in its objective the destruction of the MIG aircraft and the IL-28s. . . . He asked the Attorney General and Mr. McCone for their opinions:

a. The Attorney General stated he was opposed to such a strike because:

1. "It would be a Pearl Harbor type of attack."

2. It would lead to unpredictable military responses by the Soviet Union which could be so serious as to lead to general nuclear war.

He stated we should start with the initiation of the blockade and there-after "play for the breaks." . . . Mr. McCone agreed with the Attorney General. . . .

Source: Foreign Relations of the United States, 1961–1963, Volume XI, Cuban Missile Crisis and Aftermath, Edward C. Keefer et al., eds. (Washington, DC: U.S. Government Print-ing Office, 1996), Doc. 36, "Notes on Meeting with President Kennedy."

Document 8
PRESIDENT KENNEDY'S ADDRESS TO THE NATION, OCTOBER 22, 1962

At 7:00 P.M. on October 22, 1962, President Kennedy informed the na-tion and the world that the Soviets had installed missiles in Cuba. Im-portant for his plan was the backing of the Organization of American States. Hence he noted early in the speech that the threat was hemi-spheric. Kennedy also noted that the Soviet introduction of missiles was alarming because it was "secret" and "in an area well known to have a special and historical relationship to the United States."

The Soviet missiles in Cuba, said Kennedy, were a "violation of So-viet assurances" and therefore constituted a "deliberately provocative and unjustified change in the status quo."

What was at stake, Kennedy also stated privately, was not so much the balance of power by the *appearance* of the balance of power. Not only are appearances important in themselves in international politics, but they are a significant element of international leadership; thus the missiles would have to be removed from Cuba.

Washington, D.C., October 22, 1962

Good evening, my fellow citizens:

This Government, as promised, has maintained the closest surveillance of the Soviet military buildup on the island of Cuba. Within the past week, unmistakable evidence has established the fact that a series of offensive missile sites is now in preparation on that imprisoned island. The purpose of these bases can be none other than to provide a nuclear strike capability against the Western Hemisphere.

Upon receiving the first preliminary hard information of this nature last Tuesday morning at 9:00 A.M., I directed that our surveillance be stepped up. . . .

[T]hese new missile sites . . . include medium range ballistic missiles, ca-pable of carrying a nuclear warhead for a distance of more than 1,000 nauti-cal miles. Each of these missiles, in short, is capable of striking Washington, D.C., the Panama Canal, Cape Canaveral, Mexico City, or any other city in the southeastern part of the United States, in Central America, or in the Caribbean area.

Additional sites not yet completed appear to be designed for [missiles] . . . traveling more than twice as far and thus capable of striking most major cities in the Western Hemisphere, ranging as far north as Hudson Bay, Canada, and as far south as Lima, Peru. In addition, jet bombers, capable of carrying nuclear weapons, are now being uncrated and assembled. . . .

This urgent transformation of Cuba into an important strategic base . . . constitutes an explicit threat to the peace and security of all the Americas, in flagrant and deliberate defiance of the Rio Pact of 1947, the traditions of this Nation and hemisphere, the joint resolution of the 87th Congress, the Charter of the United Nations, and my own public warnings to the Soviets on September 4 and 13. This action also contradicts the repeated assurances of Soviet spokesmen, both publicly and privately delivered. . . .

The size of this undertaking makes clear that it has been planned for some months. Yet only last month . . . the Soviet Government publicly stated on September 11 that, and I quote, "the armaments and military equipment sent to Cuba are designed exclusively for defensive purposes," that, and I quote the Soviet Government, "there is no need for the Soviet Government to shift its weapons . . . for a retaliatory blow to any other country, for instance Cuba," and that, and I quote their government, "the Soviet Union has so powerful rockets to carry these nuclear warheads that there is no need to search for sites for them beyond the boundaries of the Soviet Union." That statement was false.

Only last Thursday, as evidence of this rapid offensive buildup was already in my hand, Soviet Foreign Minister Gromyko told me in my office that he was instructed to make it clear once again, as he said his government had already done, that Soviet assistance to Cuba, and I quote, "pursued solely the purpose of contributing to the defense capabilities of Cuba, . . . and if it were otherwise," Mr. Gromyko went on, "the Soviet Government would never become involved in rendering such assistance." That statement also was false.

Neither the United States of America nor the world community of nations can tolerate deliberate deception and offensive threats on the part of any nation, large or small. We no longer live in a world where only the actual firing of weapons represents a sufficient challenge to a nation's security to constitute maximum peril. Nuclear weapons are so destructive and ballistic missiles are so swift, that any substantially increased possibility of their use or any sudden change in their deployment may well be regarded as a definite threat to peace.

For many years, both the Soviet Union and the United States, recognizing this fact, have deployed strategic nuclear weapons with great care, never upsetting the precarious status quo. . . . Our own strategic missiles have never been transferred to the territory of any other nation under a cloak of secrecy and deception. . . . Nevertheless, American citizens have become adjusted to living daily on the bull's-eye of Soviet missiles located inside the U.S.S.R. or in submarines.

In that sense, missiles in Cuba add to an already clear and present danger, although it should be noted the nations of Latin America have never previously been subjected to a potential nuclear threat.

But this secret, swift, and extraordinary buildup of Communist missiles in an area well known to have a special and historical relationship to the United States and the nations of the Western Hemisphere, in violation of Soviet assurances, and in defiance of American and hemispheric policy—this sudden, clandestine decision to station strategic weapons for the first time outside of Soviet soil is a deliberately provocative and unjustified change in the status quo which cannot be accepted by this country, if our courage and our commitments are ever to be trusted again. . . .

The 1930s taught us a clear lesson: aggressive conduct, if allowed to go unchecked, ultimately leads to war. This nation is opposed to war. We are also true to our word. Our unswerving objective, therefore, must be to prevent the use of these missiles against this or any other country, and to secure their withdrawal or elimination from the Western Hemisphere.

Our policy has been one of patience and restraint. . . . But now further action is required—and it is under way; and these actions may only be the beginning. We will not prematurely or unnecessarily risk the costs of worldwide nuclear war in which even the fruits of victory would be ashes in our mouth—but neither will we shrink from that risk. . . .

Acting, therefore, in the defense of our own security and of the entire Western Hemisphere, and under the authority entrusted to me by the Constitution as endorsed by the Resolution of the Congress, I have directed that the following initial steps be taken immediately:

First: To halt this offensive buildup, a strict quarantine on all offensive military equipment under shipment to Cuba is being initiated. All ships of any kind bound for Cuba from whatever nation or part will, if found to contain cargoes of offensive weapons, be turned back. . . . We are not at this time, however, denying the necessities of life as the Soviets attempted to do in their Berlin blockade of 1948.

Second: I have directed the continued and increased close surveillance of Cuba and its military buildup. . . . Should these offensive military preparations continue, thus increasing the threat to the hemisphere, further action will be justified. . . .

Third: If shall be the policy of this Nation to regard any nuclear missile launched from Cuba against any nation in the Western Hemisphere as an attack by the Soviet Union on the United States, requiring a full retaliatory response upon the Soviet Union.

Fourth: As a necessary military precaution, I have reinforced our base at Guantánamo, evacuated today the dependents of our personnel there, and ordered additional military units to be on a standby alert basis.

Fifth: We are calling tonight for an immediate meeting of . . . the Organization of American States, to consider this threat . . . and to invoke Articles 6 and 8 of the Rio Treaty in support of all necessary action. . . . Our other allies around the world have also been alerted.

Sixth: Under the Charter of the United Nations, we are asking tonight that an emergency meeting of the Security Council be convoked without delay. . . .

Seventh and finally: I call upon Chairman Khrushchev to halt and eliminate this clandestine, reckless, and provocative threat to world peace and to stable relations between our two nations. I call upon him further to abandon this course of world domination, and to join in an historic effort to end the perilous arms race and to transform the history of man. He has an opportunity now to move the world back from the abyss of destruction—by returning to his government's own words that it had no need to station missiles outside its own territory. . . .

This Nation is prepared to present its case against the Soviet threat to peace, and our own proposals for a peaceful world, at any time and in any forum. . . .

But it is difficult to settle or even discuss these problems in an atmosphere of intimidation. That is why this latest Soviet threat . . . must and will be met with determination. Any hostile move . . . including in particular the brave people of West Berlin will be met by whatever action is needed.

Finally, I want to say a few words to the captive people of Cuba, to whom this speech is being directly carried by special radio facilities. I speak to you as a friend. . . . I have watched . . . with deep sorrow how your nationalist revolution was betrayed. . . . Now your leaders are no longer Cuban leaders inspired by Cuban ideals. They are puppets and agents of an international conspiracy which has turned Cuba . . . into the first Latin American country to become a target for nuclear war. . . .

. . . Many times in the past, the Cuban people have risen to throw out tyrants who destroyed their liberty. And I have no doubt that most Cubans today look forward to the time when they will be truly free—free from foreign domination. . . . And then shall Cuba be welcomed back to the society of free nations and to the associations of this hemisphere.

My fellow citizens: let no one doubt that this is a difficult and dangerous effort on which we have set out. No one can foresee precisely what course it will take or what costs or casualties will be incurred. Many months of sacrifice and self-discipline lie ahead, months in which both our patience and our will will be tested. . . . But the greatest danger of all would be to do nothing.

The path we have chosen for the present is full of hazards . . . but it is the one most consistent with our character and courage as a nation and our commitments. . . .

Our goal is not the victory of might, but the vindication of right—not peace at the expense of freedom, but both peace and freedom, here in this hemisphere, and, we hope, around the world. God willing, that goal will be achieved.

Thank you and good night.

"Radio and Television Address to the Nation on the Cuban Missile Crisis, October 22, 1962" in *Public Papers of the President, John F. Kennedy* (Washington, DC: U.S. Government Printing Office, 1963).

Document 9
AMBASSADOR DOBRYNIN TALKS TO ROBERT KENNEDY

Anatoly Dobrynin became Soviet ambassador to the United States in March 1962. Avuncular and charming, he soon gained a reputation as a new kind of Soviet diplomat in that he was flexible, authoritative, and trustworthy. However, his reputation almost vanished as soon as it was gained when he unwittingly relayed the Kremlin's false assurances that Moscow had not placed missiles in Cuba. Because, as Dobrynin later recalled to CNN, it "wasn't always possible to contact the president," the president's brother Robert "talked . . . on behalf of the president. Of course, it was a hush-hush. . . . It was double diplomacy in a way, because I officially dealt with the State Department, but at the same time I dealt with Robert." The memo of this conversation, written by Robert Kennedy, reveals the administration's domestic and international concerns. It is different in tone, but not in substance, from the president's speech to the nation on October 22, 1962.

Washington, D.C., October 24, 1962

I met with Ambassador Dobrynin last evening on the third floor of the Russian Embassy and as you suggested made the following points:

1. . . . I said that I wanted to give him some background on the decision of the United States Government and wanted him to know that the duplicity of the Russians had been a major contributing factor. . . . I said based on that statement which I had related to the President plus independent intelligence information at that time, the President had gone to the American people and assured them that the weapons being furnished by the Communist to Cuba were defensive and that it was not necessary for the United States to blockade or take any military action. I pointed out that this assurance of Dobrynin to me had been confirmed by the TASS statement and then finally, in substance, by Gromyko when he visited the President on Thursday.

2. I said that based on these assurances the President had taken a different and far less belligerent position than people like Senators Keating and Capehart, and he had assured the American people that there was nothing to be concerned about. I pointed out, in addition, that the President felt he had a very helpful personal relationship with Mr. Khrushchev. Obviously, they did not agree on many issues, but he did feel that there was a mutual trust and confidence between them on which he could rely.

As an example of this statement I related the time that Mr. Khrushchev requested the President to withdraw the troops from Thailand and that step was taken within twenty-four hours. I said that with the background of this relationship, plus the specific assurances that had been given to us, and then the statement of Dobrynin from Khrushchev to Ted Sorensen and to me that no incident would occur before the American elections were completed, we felt the action by Khrushchev and the Russians at this time was hypocritical, misleading, and false. I said this should be clearly understood by them as it was by us.

Dobrynin's only answer was that he had told me no missiles were in Cuba but that Khrushchev had also given similar assurances through TASS and as far as he (Dobrynin) knew, there were still no missiles in Cuba.

Dobrynin in the course of the conversation made several other points. The one he stressed was why the President did not tell Gromyko the facts on Thursday. . . .

I answered this by making two points: Number one, there wasn't anything the President could tell Gromyko that Gromyko didn't know already. . . . I said in addition the President was so shocked at Gromyko's presentation . . . that he felt that any effort to have an intelligent and honest conversation would not be profitable.

Dobrynin went on to say that from his conversations with Gromyko he doesn't believe Gromyko thought there were any missiles in Cuba. He said he was going to contact his government to find out about this matter.

I expressed surprise that after all that had appeared in the papers, and the President's speech, that he had not had a communication on that question already.

Dobrynin seemed extremely concerned. When I left I asked him if ships were going to go through to Cuba. He replied that was their instructions last month and he assumed they had the same instructions at the present time. . . . I left around 10:15 P.M.. . . .

Source: Foreign Relations of the United States, 1961–1963, Volume XI, Cuban Missile Crisis and Aftermath, Edward C. Keefer et al., eds. (Washington, DC: U.S. Government Printing Office, 1996), Doc. 53, "Memorandum from Attorney General Kennedy to President Kennedy."

Document 10
PRESIDENT KENNEDY RESPONDS TO CHAIRMAN KHRUSHCHEV

Khrushchev's reaction to President Kennedy's October 22 speech was one of incredulity. He seemed to think that the president had suddenly fallen under the influence of military warmongers. "Who asked you to do this?" he asked. But Khrushchev nonetheless tried to play out his hand. Calling the American blockade piratical, he claimed he had no intention of heeding it. The consequence of challenging Soviet or bloc ships, he indicated, could well be war. President Kennedy's response indicated that the United States was concerned that Khrushchev believed the Americans were "amazed" at Soviet power. Kennedy's reply is a firm clarification of his position.

Washington, D.C., October 25, 1962, 1:59 A.M.

Dear Mr. Chairman:

I have received your letter of October 24, and I regret very much that you still do not appear to understand what it is that has moved us in this matter. The sequence of events is clear. In August there were reports of important shipments of military equipment and technicians from the Soviet Union to Cuba.

In early September I indicated very plainly that the United States would regard any shipment of offensive weapons as presenting the gravest issues. After that time, this Government received the most explicit assurance from your Government and its representatives, both publicly and privately, that no offensive weapons were being sent to Cuba.

If you will review the statement issued by TASS in September, you will see how clearly this assurance was given. In reliance of these solemn assurances I urged restraint upon those in this country who were urging action in this matter at that time. And then I learned beyond doubt what you have not denied—namely, that all these public assurances were false and that your military people had set out recently to establish a set of missile bases in Cuba.

I ask you to recognize clearly, Mr. Chairman, that it was not I who issued the first challenge in this case, and that in the light of this record these activities in Cuba required the responses I have announced. I repeat my regret that these events should cause a deterioration in our relations. I hope that your Government will take the necessary action to permit a restoration of the earlier situation.

Sincerely yours,
John F. Kennedy

Source: Foreign Relations of the United States, 1961–1963, Volume XI, Cuban Missile Crisis and Aftermath, Edward C. Keefer et al., eds. (Washington, DC: U.S. Government Printing Office, 1996), Doc. 52.

Document 11
REPORT FROM THE TURKISH AMBASSADOR
TO NATO

The report from the Turkish ambassador to NATO was indicative of the Turkish position throughout the crisis. The Turks were not especially enthusiastic about ballistic missiles being stationed on their territory; but once the missiles had been approved, they did bring status for the Turks within the NATO alliance. If, under pressure to resolve the Cuban Missile Crisis via an arrangement with the Soviets, the United States were to remove Turkey's nuclear guarantee, the Turks would not only be humiliated but the American commitment to Turkey would be called into question.

In the following report, Ambassador Thomas Finletter indicates that if the Turks were consulted, perhaps they would work out with the United States a way by which the missiles could be removed. The various modalities of providing medium range ballistic missiles to European NATO partners—whether via Polaris subs as Finletter indicates or, later, in discussions of the Reagan years over Pershing missiles—were to plague NATO until the end of the Cold War, when all such missiles were withdrawn and destroyed.

Paris, October 25, 1962, 9:00 P.M.

. . . Eyes only for Secretary.

1. Turkish [ambassador] here has consistently made it clear that Turks set great store in Jupiters placed in Turkey. He makes very clear that Turkey re-

gards these Jupiters as symbol of Alliance's determination to use atomic weapons against Russian attack on Turkey. . . . Fact that Jupiters are obsolescent and vulnerable does not apparently affect present Turkish thinking. . . .

2. For above reason any arrangement of kind suggested [Referenced telegram] which would not have received prior complete support by [Government of Turkey] would, it seems to us, be most damaging. . . . I think it should be an arrangement freely arrived at by them. . . .

6. . . . As all know, these weapons were put in Europe as result of heads of government decision in 1957 in response to boastful Soviet MRBM threat to Europe. . . .

7. Re question of removal Jupiters accompanied by stationing of Polaris submarines in area, doubt whether mere deployment Polaris would be attractive to Turks. . . .

Finletter

Source: Foreign Relations of the United States, 1961–1963, Volume XI, Cuban Missile Crisis and Aftermath, Edward C. Keefer et al., eds. (Washington, DC: U.S. Government Printing Office, 1996), Doc. 75.

Document 12
LETTER FROM CHAIRMAN KHRUSHCHEV TO PRESIDENT KENNEDY, OCTOBER 26, 1962

The following document is a remarkably lengthy, rambling letter penned by the Soviet chairman himself. It offers an exchange of the Soviet missile withdrawal for a non-invasion pledge on the part of the U.S. government. This would have settled the crisis if it had been confirmed. But as Khrushchev's subsequent message (Document 13) shows, the offer was amended in a formal message the next day.

Telegram from the Embassy in the Soviet Union to the Department of Moscow, October 26, 1962, 7:00 P.M.

Dear Mr. President:

I have received your letter of October 25. From your letter, I got the feeling that you have some understanding of the situation which has developed. . . . I value this.

. . . We, Communists, are against all wars. . . . We have always regarded war as a calamity, and not as a game. . . . Our goals are clear, and the means to attain them is labor. . . .

. . . I see, Mr. President, that you too are not devoid of a sense of anxiety . . . of what war entails. What would a war give you? . . .

We must not succumb to intoxication and petty passions. . . . These are all transient things, but if indeed war should break out, then it would not be in

our power to contain or stop it, for such is the logic of war. I have partici-
pated in two wars and know that war ends when it has rolled through cities
and villages, everywhere sowing death and destruction.

In the name of the Soviet Government and the Soviet people, I assure you
that your arguments regarding offensive weapons on Cuba are groundless. .
. . You are a military man and, I hope, will understand me. Let us take for example a simple cannon. What sort of means is this: offensive or defensive? . . .

. . . All the means located there, and I assure you of this, have a defensive
character, are on Cuba solely for the purpose of defense. . . .

But, Mr. President, do you really seriously think that Cuba can attack the
United States and that even we together with Cuba can advance upon you
from the territory of Cuba? . . . [W]e are normal people . . . that . . . correctly
understand and correctly evaluate the situation. Consequently, how can we
permit the incorrect actions which you ascribe to us? Only lunatics or sui-
cides, who themselves want to perish and to destroy the whole world before
they die, could do this. We, however, want to live and do not at all want to destroy your country. . . .

You have now proclaimed piratical measures, which were employed in
the Middle Ages, when ships proceeding in international waters were attacked, and you have called this "a quarantine" around Cuba. Our vessels,
apparently, will soon enter the zone which your Navy is patrolling. I assure
that these vessels, now bound for Cuba, are carrying the most innocent
peaceful cargoes. . . . The weapons which were necessary for the defense of
Cuba are already there. . . . And in what direction are events now developing? If you stop the vessels, then, as you yourself know, that would be pi-
racy. If we started to that with regard to your ships, then you would also be as
indignant as we. . . . To what would all this lead?

Let us normalize relations. We have received an appeal from the Acting
Secretary General of the UN, U Thant, with his proposals. . . . His proposals
come to this, that our side should not transport armaments of any kind to
Cuba during a certain period of time, while negotiations are being conducted—and we are ready to enter such negotiations—and the other side
should not undertake any sort of piratical actions against vessels engaged in
navigation on the high seas. I consider these proposals reasonable.

. . . You have asked what happened, what evoked the delivery of weapons
to Cuba? . . . I will tell you frankly, Mr. President. . . . We were very grieved . . .
that . . . an attack on Cuba was committed, as a result of which many Cubans
perished. You yourself told me then that this had been a mistake. . . .

Why have we proceeded to assist Cuba with military and economic aid?
The answer is: we have proceeded to do so only for reasons of humanitari-
anism. . . . But . . . [i]t is also not a secret to anyone that the threat of armed at-

tack, aggression, has constantly hung, and continues to hang over Cuba. It was only this which impelled us to respond to the request of the Cuban Government to furnish it aid. . . .

If assurances were given by the President . . . that the USA itself would not participate in an attack on Cuba and would restrain others from actions of this sort, if you would recall your fleet, this would immediately change everything. . . . Then, . . . the question of armaments would disappear. . . . Then, too, the question of the destruction, not only of the armaments which you call offensive, but of all other armaments as well, would look different.

. . . Let us therefore show statesmanlike wisdom. I propose: we, for our part, will declare that our ships, bound for Cuba, are not carrying any armaments. You would declare that the United States will not invade Cuba with its forces and will not support any sort of forces which might intend to carry out an invasion of Cuba. Then the necessity for the presence of our military specialists in Cuba would disappear.

Mr. President, I appeal to you to weigh well what the aggressive, piratical actions, which you have declared. . . . If, however, you have not lost your self-control and sensibly conceive what this might lead to, then, Mr. President, we and you ought not now to pull on the ends of the rope in which you have tied the knot of war, because the more the two of us pull, the tighter that knot will be tied. And a moment may come when that knot will be tied so tight that even he who tied it will not have the strength to untie it. . . .

Consequently, if there is no intention to tighten that knot and thereby to doom the world to the catastrophe of thermonuclear war, then let us not only relax the forces pulling on the ends of the rope, let us take measures to untie that knot. We are ready for this. . . . There, Mr. President, are my thoughts . . . dictated by a sincere desire to relieve the situation, to remove the threat of war.

Respectfully yours,
N. Khrushchev

Source: Foreign Relations of the United States, 1961–1963, Volume XI, Cuban Missile Crisis and Aftermath, Edward C. Keefer et al., eds. (Washington, DC: U.S. Government Printing Office, 1996), Doc. 84.

Document 13
KHRUSHCHEV DEMANDS THE UNITED STATES WITHDRAW ITS MISSILES FROM TURKEY

The second message from Chairman Khrushchev to President Kennedy arrived on October 27, 1962. It was also released by the Russian news agency, TASS. The letter was a dramatic about-face from Khrushchev's October 26 letter. More formal and more careful, it was also more worrisome; indeed, some members of the ExCom feared that it indicated the Kremlin was in the midst of a power struggle. In truth, according to later comments by the Soviet leader's aides, Khrushchev was in a kind of "sellers remorse," a feeling he had settled the crisis too cheaply. Thus he decided to add the demand that the United States withdraw its missiles from Turkey.

Moscow, October 27, 1962

Dear Mr. President,

. . . I understand your concern for the security of the United States, Mr. President, because this is the primary duty of a President. But we too are disturbed about these same questions. . . .

. . . You wish to ensure the security of your country, and this is understandable. But Cuba, too, wants the same thing; all countries want to maintain their security.

But how are we, the Soviet Union, our Government, to assess your actions which are expressed in the fact that you have surrounded the Soviet Union with military bases; surrounded our allies with military bases; placed military bases literally around our country; and stationed your missile armaments there?

. . . You are disturbed over Cuba. You say that this disturbs you because it is 90 miles by sea from the coast of the United States of America.

But Turkey adjoins us; our sentries patrol back and forth and see each other. Do you consider, then, that you have the right to demand security for your own country and the removal of the weapons you call offensive, but do not accord the same right to us?

You have placed destructive missile weapons, which you call offensive, in Turkey, literally next to us. How then can recognition of our equal military capabilities be reconciled with such unequal relations between our great states? This is irreconcilable.

. . . I therefore make this proposal: We are willing to remove from Cuba the means which you regard as offensive. We are willing to carry this out and to make this pledge in the United Nations. Your representatives will make a declaration to the effect that the United States, for its part, considering the uneasiness and anxiety of the Soviet State, will remove its analogous means from Turkey. . . .

. . . We, in making this pledge, in order to give satisfaction and hope of the peoples of Cuba and Turkey and to strengthen their confidence in their security, will make a statement within the framework of the Security Council to the effect that the Soviet Government gives a solemn promise to respect the inviolability of the borders and sovereignty of Turkey, not to interfere in its internal affairs, not to invade Turkey, not to make available our territory as a bridgehead for such an invasion. . . . The United States Government will make a similar statement within the framework of the Security Council regarding Cuba. . . .

These means are situated in Cuba at the request of the Cuban Government and are only for defense purposes. Therefore, if there is no invasion of Cuba, or attack on the Soviet Union or any of our other allies, then of course these means are not and will not be a threat to anyone.

. . . These are my proposals, Mr. President.

Respectfully yours,
N. Khrushchev

Source: *Foreign Relations of the United States, 1961–1963, Volume XI, Cuban Missile Crisis and Aftermath*, Edward C. Keefer et al., eds. (Washington, DC: U.S. Government Printing Office, 1996), Doc. 91.

Document 14
THE EXCOM MEETING, OCTOBER 27, 1962

The morning ExCom meeting of October 27, 1962, was extremely tense. The United States was preparing to have a Soviet ship boarded. Khrushchev had agreed to recall the missiles in exchange for a U.S. pledge not to invade Cuba and then, inexplicably, upped the ante. The ExCom meeting notes are particularly revealing in that the pressure to board a Soviet ship was increasing and, withal, the odds of war were increasing as well. Moreover, the notes reveal the president working the group toward the argument that obsolete missiles in Turkey might be a good trade for missiles in Cuba that would vastly increase the Russians' nuclear striking power.

Washington, D.C., October 27, 1962, 10:00 A.M.

Director McCone highlighted the intelligence information contained in the first two pages of the attached CIA Cuba Crisis Memorandum.

Secretary McNamara reported on the positions of Soviet Bloc ships moving toward Cuba. He said we do not know yet whether any such ships will enter the interception area. He recommended that we be prepared to board the *Groznyy*. . . . If she refuses to stop, we would stop her by force and sink her. . . .

The discussion then turned to the question of U.S. missiles in Turkey.

Mr. Nitze said it would be an anathema to the Turks to pull the missiles out. He feared the next Soviet step would be a demand for the denuclearization of the entire NATO area. . . .

The President commented that the statement was a very tough position and varied considerably from the tone of Khrushchev's personal letter to the President received last night. . . .

. . . The President recalled that he had asked that consideration be given to the withdrawal of U.S. missiles from Turkey some days previously. . . . The President commented that the Russians had made the Turkish missile withdrawal proposal in the most difficult possible way. Now that their proposal is public, we have no chance to talk privately to the Turks about the missiles. . . .

He suggested that we talk to the Turks about the missiles, pointing out to them the great peril facing them during the next week. . . .

. . . The President returned to a discussion of where we now find ourselves, i.e., we now have Soviet public proposals and Khrushchev's private proposals. What we must seek is an immediate cessation of the work on offensive missiles in Cuba. Once this work stopped we could talk to the Russians. . . .

The President noted that it appeared to him that the Russians were making various proposals so fast, one after the other, that they were creating a kind of shield behind which work on the missile sites in Cuba continued. He said we had a perfectly defensible position, i.e., work on the missile sites must stop.

. . . Mr. Bundy suggested that we tell Khrushchev privately that the position in their public statement was impossible for us, but that the position Khrushchev took in his private letter was different and we were studying these proposals. In the meantime, however, time is running out.

. . . The President recalled that over a year ago we wanted to get the Jupiter missiles out of Turkey because they had become obsolete and of little military value.

If the missiles in Cuba added 50% to Soviet nuclear capability, then to trade these missiles for those in Turkey would be of great military value.

But we are now in the position of risking war in Cuba and in Berlin over missiles in Turkey which are of little military value.

From the political point of view, it would be hard to get support on an airstrike against Cuba because many would think that we would make a good trade if we offered to take the missiles out of Turkey in the event the Russians would agree to remove the missiles from Cuba. We are in a bad position if we appear to be attacking Cuba for the purpose of keeping useless missiles in Turkey.

We cannot propose to withdraw the missiles from Turkey, but the Turks could offer to do so.

The Turks must be informed of the great danger in which they will live during the next week and we have to face up to the possibility of some kind of a trade over missiles.

The President left the meeting. . . . The discussion continued in the President's absence.

. . . [T]he Attorney General repeated his view that we should keep the focus on the missile bases. He preferred to let the Soviet tankers through the quarantine line in order to avoid a confrontation with the Soviets over one of their ships.

He said if we attack a Soviet tanker, the balloon would go up. He urged that we buy time now in order to launch an air attack Monday or Tuesday. Secretary McNamara expressed his view that before we attack Cuba we must notify the Cubans.

Source: Foreign Relations of the United States, 1961–1963, Volume XI, Cuban Missile Crisis and Aftermath, Edward C. Keefer et al., eds. (Washington, DC: U.S. Government Printing Office, 1996), Doc. 90.

Document 15
TELEGRAM FROM THE DEPARTMENT OF STATE TO THE EMBASSY IN THE SOVIET UNION, OCTOBER 27, 1962

Following the suggestions of McGeorge Bundy and Robert Kennedy, President Kennedy accepted Khrushchev's initial offer of October 26 and said nothing about the letter of October 27.

Washington, D.C., October 27, 1962, 8:05 P.M.

Dear Mr. Chairman

I have read your letter of October 26 with great care. . . . The first thing that needs to be done . . . is for work to cease on offensive missile bases in Cuba and for all weapons systems in Cuba capable of offensive use to be rendered inoperable, under effective United Nations arrangements. . . .

As I read your letter, the key elements of your proposals—which seem generally acceptable as I understand them—are as follows:

1. You would agree to remove these weapons systems from Cuba under appropriate United Nations observation and supervision; and undertake, with suitable safeguards, to halt the further introduction of such weapons systems into Cuba.

2. We, on our part, would agree—upon the establishment of adequate arrangements through the United Nations to ensure the carrying out and continuation of these commitments—(a) to remove promptly the quarantine

measures now in effect and (b) to give assurances against an invasion of Cuba and I am confident that other nations of the Western Hemisphere would be prepared to do likewise.

... The effect of such a settlement on easing world tensions would enable us to work toward a more general arrangement regarding "other armaments," as proposed in your second letter which you made public. . . . For this reason I hope we can quickly agree along the lines outlined in this letter and in your letter of October 26.

John F. Kennedy

Source: Foreign Relations of the United States, 1961–1963, Volume XI, Cuban Missile Crisis and Aftermath, Edward C. Keefer et al., eds. (Washington, DC: U.S. Government Printing Office, 1996), Doc. 95.

Document 16
ROBERT KENNEDY MEETS WITH AMBASSADOR
DOBRYNIN, OCTOBER 27, 1962

Questions about Robert Kennedy's original account in his posthumously published book, *Thirteen Days* (1969), were common. Later, Theodore Sorensen acknowledged that as an unaccredited editor of the manuscript he had deleted "explicit" references to the arrangement Robert Kennedy and Soviet ambassador Anatoly Dobrynin reached on the evening of October 27, 1962, regarding the removal of U.S. Jupiter missiles from Turkey. It was a trade known to perhaps nine officers of the U.S. government. "There was no leak," McGeorge Bundy recalled in *Danger and Survival* (1988). "As far as I know, none of the nine of us told anyone else what had happened. We denied in every forum that there was any deal, and in the narrowest sense what we said was usually true" (p. 434). The problem with the denials was a badly skewed understanding of the role diplomacy and compromise played in the resolution of the crisis, and a series of misplaced assumptions about the ability of U.S. force to dictate events.

The following is a memo from Robert Kennedy to his brother, describing the meeting that crackles with tension and mutual threats. In the end, the terms of an explicit trade were hammered out with the caveat that the Soviets would not make it public.

MEMORANDUM FOR DEAN RUSK ON MEETING WITH
ANATOLY F. DOBRYNIN ON 27 OCTOBER 1962

TOP SECRET Office of the Attorney General
Washington, D.C., October 30, 1962
Memorandum for the Secretary of State from the Attorney General

At the request of Secretary Rusk, I telephoned Ambassador Dobrynin at approximately 7:15 P.M. on Saturday, October 27th. I asked him if he would come to the Justice Department at a quarter of eight.

We met in my office. I told him first that we understood that the work was continuing on the Soviet missile bases in Cuba. Further, I explained to him that in the last two hours we had found that our planes flying over Cuba had been fired upon and that one of our U-2's had been shot down and the pilot killed. I said these men were flying unarmed planes.

I told him that this was an extremely serious turn in events. We would have to make certain decisions within the next 12 or possible 24 hours. There was very little time left. If the Cubans were shooting at our planes, then we were going to shoot back. . . .

He raised the point that . . . we were violating Cuban air space. I replied that if we had not been violating Cuban air space then we would still be believing what he and Khrushchev had said—that there were no long-range missiles in Cuba. In any case I said that this matter was far more serious than the air space over Cuba and involved peoples all over the world.

I said that he had better understand the situation and he had better communicate that understanding to Mr. Khrushchev. Mr. Khrushchev and he had misled us. The Soviet Union had secretly established missile bases in Cuba while at the same time proclaiming, privately and publicly, that this would never be done. I said those missile bases had to go and they had to go right away. We had to have a commitment by at least tomorrow that those bases would be removed. This was not an ultimatum, I said, but just a statement of fact. He should understand that if they did not remove those bases then we would remove them. His country might take retaliatory action but he should understand that before this was over, while there might be dead Americans there would also be dead Russians.

He asked me then what offer we were making. I said a letter had just been transmitted to the Soviet Embassy which stated in substance that the missile bases should be dismantled and all offensive weapons should be removed from Cuba [see Document 15 of this volume]. In return, if Cuba and Castro and the Communists ended their subversive activities in other Central and Latin American countries, we would agree to keep peace in the Caribbean and not permit an invasion from American soil.

He then asked me about Khrushchev's other proposal dealing with the removal of the missiles from Turkey. I replied that there could be no quid pro quo—no deal of this kind could be made. This was a matter that had to be considered by NATO and that it was up to NATO to make the decision. I said it was completely impossible for NATO to take such a step under the present threatening position of the Soviet Union. [The following sentence at the end of this paragraph was crossed out: "If some time elapsed—and per your instructions, I mentioned four or five months—I said I was sure that these matters could be resolved satisfactory."]

Per your instructions I repeated that there could be no deal of any kind and that any steps toward easing tensions in other parts of the world largely depended on the Soviet Union and Mr. Khrushchev taking action in Cuba and taking it immediately.

I repeated to him that this matter could not wait and that he had better contact Mr. Khrushchev and have a commitment from him by the next day to withdraw the missile bases under United Nations supervision for otherwise, I said, there would be drastic consequences.

Source: Foreign Relations of the United States, 1961–1963, Volume XI, Cuban Missile Crisis and Aftermath, Edward C. Keefer et al., eds. (Washington, DC: U.S. Government Printing Office, 1996), Doc. 96.

Document 17
THE SOVIET UNION ACCEPTS PRESIDENT KENNEDY'S TERMS, OCTOBER 28, 1962

On October 28, 1962, Chairman Khrushchev sent a message to President Kennedy in which the Soviet Union publicly accepted Kennedy's terms. To make sure there was no misunderstanding or delay, it was broadcast on Moscow radio. With Khrushchev's acceptance, the Cuban Missile Crisis was effectively over.

Moscow, October 28, 1962

Dear Mr. President:

I have received your message of October 27. I express my satisfaction and thank you for the sense of proportion you have displayed and for realization of the responsibility which now devolves on you for the preservation of the peace of the world.

I regard with great understanding your concern and the concern of the United States people in connection with the fact that the weapons you describe as offensive are formidable weapons indeed. Both you and we understand what kind of weapons these are.

In order to eliminate as rapidly as possible the conflict which endangers the cause of peace, to give an assurance to all people who crave peace, and to reassure the American people, who, I am certain, also want peace, as do the people of the Soviet Union, the Soviet Government, in addition to earlier instructions on the discontinuation of further work on weapons construction sites, has given a new order to dismantle the arms which you described as offensive, and to crate and return them to the Soviet Union.

Mr. President, I should like to repeat what I had already written to you in my earlier messages—that the Soviet Government has given economic assistance to the Republic of Cuba, as well as arms, because Cuba and the Cuban people were constantly under the continuous threat of an invasion of Cuba.

A piratic vessel had shelled Havana. They say that this shelling was done by irresponsible Cuban émigrés. Perhaps so, however, the question is from where did they shoot. It is a fact that these Cubans have no territory, they are fugitives from their country, and they have no means to conduct military operations. . . .

Mr. President, I should like to say clearly once more that we could not remain indifferent to this. The Soviet Government decided to render assistance to Cuba with the means of defense against aggression—only with means for defense purposes. We have supplied the defense means which you describe as offensive means. We have supplied them to prevent an attack on Cuba—to prevent rash acts.

I regard with respect and trust the statement you made in your message of October 27, 1962, that there would be no attack, no invasion of Cuba, and not only on the part of the United States, but also on the part of other nations of the Western Hemisphere, as you said in your same message. Then the motives which induced us to render assistance of such a kind to Cuba disappear.

It is for this reason that we instructed our officers—these means as I had already informed you earlier are in the hands of the Soviet officers—to take appropriate measures to discontinue construction of the aforementioned facilities, to dismantle them, and to return them to the Soviet Union. As I had informed you in the letter of October 27, we are prepared to reach agreement to enable United Nations Representatives to verify the dismantling of these means.

Thus in view of the assurances you have given and our instructions on dismantling, there is every condition for eliminating the present conflict. . . .

In conclusion, I should like to say something about a détente between NATO and the Warsaw Treaty countries that you have mentioned. We have spoken about this long since and are prepared to continue to exchange views on this question with you and to find a reasonable solution.

We should like to continue the exchange of views on the prohibition of atomic and thermonuclear weapons, general disarmament, and other problems relating to the relaxation of international tension.

Although I trust your statement, Mr. President, there are irresponsible people who would like to invade Cuba now and thus touch off a war. If we do take practical steps and proclaim the dismantling and evacuation of the means in question from Cuba, in so doing we, at the same time, want the Cuban people to be certain that we are with them and are not absolving ourselves of responsibility for rendering assistance to the Cuban people.

. . . I should like to remind you, Mr. President, that military reconnaissance planes have violated the borders of the Soviet Union. In connection with this there have been conflicts between us and notes exchanged. In 1960 we shot down your U-2 plane. . . .

But during your term of office as President another violation of our border has occurred, by an American U-2 plane in the Sakhalin area. We wrote you about that violation on 30 August. At that time you replied that violation had occurred as a result of poor weather, and gave assurances that this would not be repeated. We trusted your assurances, because the weather was indeed poor in that area at that time. . . .

A still more dangerous case occurred in 28 October, when one of your reconnaissance planes intruded over Soviet borders in the Chukotka Peninsula area in the north and flew over our territory. The question is, Mr. President: How should we regard this? What is this: A provocation? . . . Is it not a fact that an intruding American plane could be easily taken for a nuclear bomber, which might push us to a fateful step?

. . . [T]hrough my officers in Cuba, I have reports that American planes are making flights over Cuba.

. . . Mr. President, it is no secret that we have our people in Cuba. Under such a treaty with the Cuban Government we have sent there officers, instructors, mostly plain people: specialists, agronomists, zoo technicians, irrigators, land reclamation specialists, plain workers, tractor drivers, and others. We are concerned about them.

I should like you to consider, Mr. President, that violation of Cuban airspace by American planes could also lead to dangerous consequences. . . .

We must be careful now and refrain from any steps which would not be useful to the defense of the states involved in the conflict. . . . Therefore, we must display sanity. . . . We value peace perhaps even more than other peoples because we went through a terrible war with Hitler. But our people will not falter in the face of any test. Our people trust their Government, and we assure our people and world public opinion that the Soviet Government will not allow itself to be provoked. . . . But we are confident that reason will triumph. . . .

In connection with the current negotiations between [United Nations] Acting Secretary General U Thant and representatives of the Soviet Union, the United States, and the Republic of Cuba, the Soviet Government has sent First Deputy Foreign Minister V. V. Kuznetsov to New York to help

U Thant in his noble efforts aimed at eliminating the present dangerous situation.

Respectfully yours,

N. Khrushchev

Source: *Foreign Relations of the United States, 1961–1963, Volume XI, Cuban Missile Crisis and Aftermath*, Edward C. Keefer et al., eds. (Washington, DC: U.S. Government Printing Office, 1996), Doc. 102.

Document 18
PRESIDENT KENNEDY PROMOTES PEACE

President Kennedy accepted Chairman Khrushchev's broadcast message of October 28 even before the official text reached him. In his acceptance, Kennedy pledged to "devote urgent attention to the problem of disarmament," with "prioirity to questions relating to the proliferation of nuclear weapons, on earth and in outer space, and to the great effort for a nuclear test ban."

The biggest step in seeking a modus vivendi with the Soviets came the next year in a graduation speech that Kennedy delivered at American University on June 10, 1963. The speech put forward a fundamentally new emphasis on the peaceful and the positive in U.S. relations with the Soviets. The American press largely underplayed the speech, and various congressional Republicans called it a "soft line that can accomplish nothing."

But the Russians, as well as America's European partners, realized the speech marked a real departure. After fifteen years of almost uninterrupted jamming, the Soviets jammed only one paragraph of the speech when it was relayed overseas in Russian by the Voice of America. No part of the speech was jammed on rebroadcast. In subsequent months, the Russians stopped jamming all Western broadcasts. The door to détente was opening.

... It is with great pride that I participate in this ceremony. ... "There are few earthly things more beautiful than a university," wrote John Masefield, in his tribute to English universities. ... He admired the splendid beauty of the university, he said, because it was "a place where those who hate ignorance may strive to know, where those who perceive truth may strive to make others see."

I have, therefore, ...[come to] this place to discuss a topic on which ignorance too often abounds ... yet it is the most important topic on earth: world peace.

What kind of peace do I mean? What kind of peace do we seek? Not a Pax Americana enforced on the world by American weapons of war. Not the peace of the grave or the security of the slave. I am talking about genuine peace, the kind of peace that makes life on earth worth living, the kind that enables men and nations to grow and to hope and to build a better life for their children—not merely peace for Americans but peace for all men and women, not merely peace in our time but peace for all time.

I speak of peace because of the new face of war. Total war makes no sense in an age when great powers can maintain large and relatively invulnerable nuclear forces and refuse to surrender without resort to those forces. It makes no sense in an age when a single nuclear weapon contains almost ten times the explosive force delivered by all of the allied air forces in the Second World War. It makes no sense in a n age when the deadly poisons produced by a nuclear exchange would be carried by wind and water and soil and seed to the far corners of the globe and to generations yet unborn.

. . . I speak of peace, therefore, as the necessary rational end of rational men. I realize that the pursuit of peace is not as dramatic as the pursuit of war—and frequently the words of the pursuer fall on deaf ears. But we have no more urgent task.

Some say that it is useless to speak of world peace or world law or world disarmament—and that it will be useless until the leaders of the Soviet Union adopt a more enlightened attitude. I hope they do. I believe we can help them do it. But I also believe that we must reexamine our own attitude—as individuals and as a Nation—for our attitude is as essential as theirs. . . .

First: Let us examine our attitude toward peace itself. Too many of us think it is impossible. Too many think it unreal. But that is a dangerous, defeatist belief. It leads to the conclusion that war is inevitable . . . that we are all gripped by forces we cannot control.

We need not accept that view. Our problems are manmade—therefore, they can be solved by man. . . . No problem of human destiny is beyond human beings. . . .

I am not referring to the absolute, infinite concept of universal peace and good will of which some fantasies and fanatics dream. . . . Let us focus instead on a more practical . . . peace—based . . . on a series of concrete actions and effective agreements which are in the interest of all concerned.

. . . Genuine peace must be the product of many nations, the sum of many acts. It must be dynamic, not static, changing to meet the challenge of each new generation. For peace is a process—a way of solving problems.

With such a peace, there will still be quarrels and conflicting interests, as there are within families and nations. World peace, like community peace, does not require that each man love his neighbor—it requires only that they live together in mutual tolerance, submitting their disputes to a just and peaceful settlement. And history teaches us that enmities between nations, as between individuals, do not last forever. However fixed our likes and dislikes may seem, the tide of time and events will often bring surprising changes in the relations between nations and neighbors.

So let us persevere. Peace need not be impracticable, and war need not be inevitable. . . .

Second: Let us reexamine our attitude toward the Soviet Union. It is discouraging to think that their leaders may actually believe what their propagandists write. It is discouraging to read a recent authoritative Soviet text on *Military Strategy* and find, on page after page, wholly baseless and incredible claims—such as the allegation that

American imperialist circles are preparing to unleash different types of wars . . . [and that] the political aims of the American imperialists are to enslave economically and politically the European and other capitalist countries . . . [and] to achieve world domination . . . by means of aggressive wars.

Truly, as it was written long ago: "The wicked flee when no man pursueth." Yet it is sad to read these Soviet statements—to realize the extent of the gulf between us. But it is also a warning—a warning to the American people not to fall into the same trap as the Soviets. . . .

No government or social system is so evil that its people must be considered as lacking in virtue. . . .

Among the many traits the peoples of our two countries have in common, none is stronger than our mutual abhorrence of war. Almost unique, among the major world powers, we have never been at war with each other. And no nation in the history of battle ever suffered more than the Soviet Union suffered in the course of the Second World War. At least 20 million lost their lives. Countless millions of homes and farms were burned or sacked. A third of the nation's territory, including nearly two thirds of its industrial base, was turned into a wasteland—a loss equivalent to the devastation of this country east of Chicago.

Today, should total war ever break out again—no matter how—our two countries would become the primary targets. It is an ironic but accurate fact that the two strongest powers are the two in the most danger of devastation. All we have built, all we have worked for, would be destroyed in the first twenty-four hours. . . .

. . . We are both caught up in a vicious and dangerous cycle in which suspicion on one side breeds suspicion on the other, and new weapons beget counterweapons.

In short, both the United States and its allies, and the Soviet Union and its allies, have a mutually deep interest in a just and genuine peace and in halting the arms race.

Agreements to this end are in the interests of the Soviet Union as well as ours—and even the most hostile nations can be relied upon to accept and keep those treaty obligations, and only those treaty obligations, which are in their own interest.

So, let us not be blind to our differences—but let us also direct attention to our common interests and to the means by which those differences can be resolved. And if we cannot end now our differences at least we can help make the world safe for diversity. For, in the final analysis, our most basic common link is that we all inhabit this small planet. We all breathe the same air. We all cherish our children's future. And we are all mortal.

Third: Let us reexamine our attitude toward the cold war, remembering that we are not engaged in a debate, seeking to pile up debating points. We are not here distributing blame or pointing the finger of judgment. We must deal with the world as it is, and not as it might have been had the history of the last eighteen years been different.

We must, therefore, persevere in the search for peace in the hope that constructive changes within the Communist bloc might bring within reach solutions which now seem beyond us. We must conduct our affairs in such a way that it becomes in the Communists' interest to agree on a genuine peace.

. . . For we can seek a relaxation of tensions without relaxing our guard. And, for our part, we do not need to use threats to prove that we are resolute. We do not need to jam foreign broadcasts out of fear our faith will be eroded. We are unwilling to impose our system on any unwilling people—but we are willing and able to engage in peaceful competition with any people on earth.

Meanwhile, we seek to strengthen the United Nations, to help solve its financial problems, to make it a more effective instrument for peace, to develop it into a genuine world security system—a system capable of resolving disputes on the basis of law, of insuring the security of the large and the small, and of creating conditions under which arms can finally be abolished.

At the same time we seek to keep peace inside the non-Communist world, where many nations, all of them our friends, are divided over issues which weaken Western unity, which invite Communist intervention, or which threaten to erupt into war. . . . We have also tried to set an example for others—by seeking to adjust small but significant differences with our own closest neighbors in Mexico and in Canada.

Speaking of other nations, I wish to make one point clear. We are bound to many nations by alliances. Those alliances exist because our concern and theirs substantially overlap. . . . The United States will make no deal with the Soviet Union at the expense of other nations and other peoples, not merely because they are our partners but also because their interests and ours converge.

Our interests converge, however, not only in defending the frontiers of freedom but in pursing the paths of peace. . . . The Communist drive to impose their political and economic system on others is the primary cause of world tension today. For there can be no doubt that if all nations could refrain from interfering in the self-determination of others, the peace would be much more assured.

This will require a new effort to achieve world law—a new context for world discussions. It will require increased understanding between the Soviets and ourselves. And increased understanding will require increased contact and communication.

One step in this direction is the proposed arrangement for a direct line between Moscow and Washington, to avoid on each side the dangerous delays, misunderstandings, and misreadings of the other's actions which might occur at a time of crisis.

We have also been talking in Geneva about other first-step measures of arms control, designed to limit the intensity of the arms race and to reduce the risks of accidental war.

Our primary long-range interest in Geneva, however, is general and complete disarmament—designed to take place by stages, permitting parallel political developments to build the new institutions of peace which would take the place of arms.

The pursuit of disarmament has been an effort of this Government since the 1920s. It has been urgently sought by the past three administrations. And however dim the prospects may be today, we intend to continue this effort—to continue it in order that all countries, including our own, can better grasp what the problems and possibilities of disarmament are.

The one major area of these negotiations where the end is in sight, yet where a fresh start is badly needed, is in a treaty to outlaw nuclear tests. The conclusion of such a treaty, so near and yet so far, would check the spiraling arms race in one of its most dangerous areas. It would place the nuclear powers in a position to deal more effectively with one of the greatest hazards which man faces in 1963, the further spread of nuclear arms. It would increase our security—it would decrease the prospects of war. . . .

I am taking this opportunity, therefore, to announce two important decisions in this regard.

First: Chairman Khrushchev, Prime Minister Macmillan, and I have agreed that high-level discussions will shortly begin in Moscow, looking toward early agreement on a comprehensive test ban treaty. Our hopes must be tempered with the caution of history—but with our hopes go the hopes of all mankind.

Second: To make clear our good faith and solemn convictions on the matter, I now declare that the United States does not propose to conduct nuclear tests in the atmosphere so long as other states do not do so. We will not be the first to resume. Such a declaration is no substitute for a formal binding treaty, but I hope it will help us achieve one. Nor would such a treaty be a substitute for disarmament, but I hope it will help us achieve it.

Finally, my fellow Americans, let us examine our attitude toward peace and freedom here at home. The quality and spirit of our own society must justify and support our efforts abroad. We must show it in the dedication of our own lives—as many of you who are graduating today will have a unique opportunity to do, by serving without pay in the Peace Corps abroad or in the proposed National Service Corps here at home.

But wherever we are, we must all, in our daily lives, live up to the age-old faith that peace and freedom walk together. In too many of our cities today, the peace is not secure because freedom is incomplete.

It is the responsibility of the executive branch at all levels of government—local, State, and National—to provide and protect that freedom for all of our citizens by all means within their authority. It is the responsibility of the legislative branch at all levels, wherever that authority is not now adequate, to make it adequate. And it is the responsibility of all citizens in all sections of this country to respect the rights of all others and to respect the law of the land.

All this is not unrelated to world peace. "When a man's ways please the Lord," the Scriptures tell us, "he maketh even his enemies to be at peace with him." And is not peace, in the last analysis, basically a matter of human rights—the right to live out our lives without fear of devastation, the right to breathe air as nature provided it, the right of future generations to a healthy existence?

While we proceed to safeguard our national interests, let us also safeguard human interests. And the elimination of war and arms is clearly in the interest of both.

No treaty, however much it may be to the advantage of all, however tightly it may be worded, can provide absolute security against the risk of deception and evasion. But it can—if it is sufficiently effective in its enforcement and if it is sufficiently in the interests of its signers—offer far more security and far fewer risks that an unabated, uncontrolled, unpredictable arms race.

The United States, as the world knows, will never start a war. We do not want a war. We do not now expect a war. This generation of Americans has already had enough—more than enough—of war and hate and oppression. We shall be prepared if others wish it. We shall be alert to try to stop it. But we shall also do our part to build a world of peace where the weak are safe and the strong are just. We are not helpless before that task or hopeless of its success. Confident and unafraid, we labor on—not toward a strategy of annihilation but toward a strategy of peace.

Source: "Commencement Address at American University," *Public Papers of the Presidents, John F. Kennedy* (Washington, DC: U.S. Government Printing Office, 1964), pp. 459–64.

Annotated Bibliography

GENERAL WORKS AND HISTORIOGRAPHY

Abel, Elie. *The Missile Crisis*. Philadelphia: Lippincott; New York: Bantam Books, 1966. A good reporter's summary of events told without the benefits of many materials released twenty years later.

Aguilar, Luis, ed. *Operation Zapata: The "Ultrasensitive" Report and Testimony of the Board of Inquiry on the Bay of Pigs*. Frederick, MD: University Publications of America, 1981. A good look at the declassified version of the Board of Inquiry on the Bay of Pigs incident after-action inquest report.

Allison, Graham T., ed. *The Secret Cuban Missile Crisis Documents: Central Intelligence Agency*. New York: Brassey's, 1994. Documents that were declassified in 1992.

Allison, Graham T. *Essence of Decision: Explaining the Cuban Missile Crisis*. Boston: Little, Brown, 1971.

Allison, Graham T., and Philip Zelikow. *Essence of Decision: Explaining the Cuban Missile Crisis*, 2nd ed. New York: Longman, 1999. These books are among the most important in four generations of scholarship on the Cuban Missile Crisis, although they emphasize the organizational rather than the historical context of the decisions made during the crisis.

Allyn, Bruce J., James G. Blight, and David A. Welch., eds. *Back to the Brink: Proceedings of the Moscow Conference on the Cuban Missile Crisis, January 27–28, 1989*. Lanham, MD: University Press of America, 1992. Starting in 1987, Allyn, Blight, and Welch helped organize decision-makers from the United States, the former Soviet Union, and Cuba who

were critical players in the Cuban Missile Crisis to discuss the crisis
from a historical perspective.

Ayers, Bradley E. *The War That Never Was: An Insider's Account of CIA Operations against Cuba.* Indianapolis: Bobbs-Merrill, 1976. Ayers was a U.S.
Army officer assigned to the CIA to train guerrillas as part of the U.S. effort to unseat Castro and oust Communism from Cuba. Ayers' book was
one of the first looks by a CIA operative to be published.

Bechloss, Michael R. *The Crisis Years: Kennedy and Khrushchev, 1960–1963.*
New York: HarperCollins, 1991. A well-crafted and engaging account
of behind-the-scenes maneuvers, containing fine portraits of the principal players—KGB agents, heads of state, and advisors to Kennedy and
Khrushchev.

Bernstein, Barton J. "Commentary: Reconsidering Khrushchev's Gambit—Defending the Soviet Union and Cuba." *Diplomatic History* 14, no. 2
(1990): 231–39. Bernstein, a leading historian of the Cold War, suggests
how close the crisis was to getting out of control. He also examines the
political element of the crisis and the central issue of the Jupiter missiles.

Bird, Kai. *The Color of Truth: McGeorge Bundy and William Bundy, Brothers in
Arms.* New York: Simon & Schuster, 1998. A revealing portrait. Chap-
ters 1 and 2 are especially good on McGeorge Bundy's role in the Cuban
Missile Crisis and the Bay of Pigs incident.

Blight, James G. *The Shattered Crystal Ball: Fear and Learning in the Cuban
Missile Crisis.* Lanham, MD: Rowman and Littlefield, 1992.

Blight, James, G., and David A. Welch, eds. *Intellligence and the Cuban Missile
Crisis.* London: Frank Cass, 1998.

Blight, James G., and David A. Welch. *On the Brink: Americans and Soviets Reexamine the Cuban Missile Crisis.* New York: Hill & Wang, 1989. (2nd
ed.: New York: Noonday, 1990.)

Blight, James G., Bruce J. Allyn, and David A. Welch. *Cuba on the Brink: Castro, the Missile Crisis, and the Soviet Collapse.* New York: Pantheon,
1993.

Blight, James G., David Lewis, and David A. Welch, eds. *Cuba between the Su-
perpowers: The Antigua Conference on the Cuban Missile Crisis.* Provi-
dence, RI: Center for Foreign Policy Development, Thomas J. Watson
Jr. Institute for International Studies, Brown University, 1991.

James Blight and his colleagues at Brown and Harvard have created a remarkably
extensive record of the Cuban Missile Crisis. These analyses are about
as clear as anything in Cold War history.

Brenner, Philip. "Cuba and the Missile Crisis." *Journal of Latin American Studies*
22, no. 1 (February 1990): 115–42. No American scholar has so consistently or ably been able to relate the Cuban position to Americans as has
Brenner.

Brugioni, Dino, A. *Eyeball to Eyeball: The Inside Story of the Cuban Missile Crisis.* New York: Random House, 1991. A senior photo interpreter at the

National Photographic Intelligence Center, Brugioni was the first to "see" and "understand" what the United States was facing during the Cuban Missile Crisis.

Bundy, McGeorge. *Danger and Survival: Choices about the Bomb in the First Fifty Years.* New York: Random House, 1988. In this work, Bundy gave the first confirmation that secret trade involving the Jupiter missiles in Turkey was involved in the settlement of the Cuban Missile Crisis.

Chang, Laurence, and Peter Kornbluh, eds. *The Cuban Missile Crisis, 1962: A National Security Archive Documents Reader.* New York: New Press, 1992. A crucial collection of declassified documents.

Chayes, Abram. *The Cuban Missile Crisis.* New York: Oxford University Press, 1974. Chayes, the State Department's senior legal advisor, had the unenviable task of justifying the blockade of Cuba during the missile crisis. Blockades, illegal in international law, were given a legal patina by the remarkable efforts of the State Department and the evident proportionality, efficacy, and necessity of the American response to the appearance of radical redefinition of the balance of power.

Criss, Nur Bilge. "Strategic Nuclear Missiles in Turkey: The Jupiter Affair, 1959–1963," *Journal of Strategic Studies* 20, no. 3 (1997). An insightful account of the Turkish position on trading the NATO medium range missiles stationed on the Urko-Russian frontier.

Dobrynin, Anatoly. *In Confidence: Moscow's Ambassador to America's Six Cold War Presidents.* New York: Times Books, 1995. Dobrynin was instrumental as the go-between who carried the messages that settled the crisis. Some of his recollections of Robert Kennedy give a different flavor to the state of play between Washington and Moscow.

Escalante, Fabian. *CIA Targets Fidel: Secret 1967 CIA Inspector General's Report on Plots to Assassinate Fidel Castro by the United States Central Intelligence Agency.* New York: Ocean Press, 1996. This rendering of the long-secret and disturbing history of the plots against Castro is essential, along with a reading of the 1975 reports of the Senate Committee on Intelligence.

Foreign Relations of the United States, "Cuba," Vol. X, 1961–1962 (Louis J. Smith, ed.). Washington, DC: U.S. Government Printing Office, 1997.

Foreign Relations of the United States, "Cuban Missile Crisis and Aftermath," Vol. XI, 1961–1963 (Edward C. Keefer et al., eds.). Washington, DC: U.S. Government Printing Office, 1997. These two works constitute an indispensable collection of primary documents relating to the crisis from the standpoint of U.S. policy.

Fursenko, Alexander, and Timothy J. Naftali. *One Hell of a Gamble: Khrushchev, Castro, Kennedy and the Cuban Missile Crisis, 1958–1964.* New York: Norton, 1997. Fursenko and Naftali have produced some of the soundest and most intriguing work on the crisis to date. They are particularly good on issues of perception and misperception.

Garthoff, Raymond. L. *Reflections on the Cuban Missile Crisis*. Washington, DC: Brookings Institution, 1987. Rev. ed., 1989. Raymond Garthoff is a linguist, intelligence analyst, former ambassador, and historian; his book is especially good at assessing what U.S. intelligence knew and when during the crisis.

Gribkov, Anatoli I., and William Y. Smith. *Operation ANADYR*. Chicago: Edition Q, 1994. A comparison of the views of two senior military officers in Russia and in the United States. The book is an especially good review of the Soviet buildup from a logistical standpoint.

Halberstam, David. *The Best and the Brightest*, 2nd ed. New York: Bantam, 1988. For a sense of the men who advised Presidents Kennedy and Johnson, this first assessment remains the best.

Hersh, Seymour M. *The Dark Side of Camelot*. New York: Back Bay Books, 1998. An interesting although somewhat tendentious account arguing that President Kennedy's activities went beyond minor abuses of power and personal indulgences and threatened national security in that Kennedy could not deliver his full attention to his office. The account is belied by the White House tapes.

Hershberg, James G. "Anatomy of a Controversy: Anatoly Dobrynin's Meeting with Robert F. Kennedy, Saturday, 27 October 1962." *Cold War International History Project Bulletin*, no. 5 (Spring 1995): 75, 77–80.

———. "Before the Missiles of October: Did Kennedy Plan a Military Strike against Cuba?" *Diplomatic History* 14, no. 2 (Spring 1990): 163–98.

———. "More on Bobby [Attorney General Robert F. Kennedy] and the Cuban Missile Crisis." *Cold War International History Project Bulletin no. 8–9* (Winter 1996–97): 274, 344–47.

———. "More New Evidence on the Cuban Missile Crisis: More Documents from the Russian Archives." *Cold War International History Project, Bulletin 8–9 (Winter 1996–97): 270–338.* James Hershberg's work on the Cuban Missile Crisis and the Cold War is pivotal. As head of the Smithsonian Institution's Cold War History Project, Hershberg and his associates unearthed vast quantities of unique and essential documents. Along with the work cooperatively housed at the National Security Archive of George Washington University, this material is essential and unique.

Higgins, Trumbull. *The Perfect Failure: Kennedy, Eisenhower, and the CIA at the Bay of Pigs*. New York: Norton, 1987. This work was the best documented look at the Bay of Pigs incident until the release of the CIA inspector general's report in 1997. Higgins' book remains extremely useful.

Hilsman, Roger. *The Cuban Missile Crisis: The Struggle over Policy*. Westport, CT: Praeger, 1996.

Johnson, Haynes B., et al. *The Bay of Pigs: The Leaders' Story of Brigade 2506.* New York: Norton, 1964. A good look at the human face of the Bay of Pigs invasion.

Kennedy, Robert F. *Thirteen Days: A Memoir of the Cuban Missile Crisis.* New York: Norton, 1969. The important, first, although incomplete and misleading narrative that told the tale of the ExCom meetings until revelations in the mid-1980s regarding the extent to which there were explicit arrangements with Russia to trade U.S. missiles in Turkey for Soviet missiles in Cuba.

Khrushchev, Nikita S. *Khrushchev Remembers* (Strobe Talbot, trans.). Boston: Little, Brown, 1970.

———. *Khrushchev Remembers: The Last Testament* (Strobe Talbot, trans.). Boston: Little, Brown, 1974. These fascinating memoirs were taped during Khrushchev's retirement. They are very well edited and, on Cuban Soviet relations, are vindicated by the great wave of documentation released decades later.

Kornbluh, Peter. *Bay of Pigs Declassified: The Secret CIA Report on the Invasion of Cuba (National Security Archive Documents).* New York: New Press, 1998. An explosive government report that is particularly hard on American CIA leadership.

Lebow, Richard Ned, and Janet Gross Stein. *We All Lost the Cold War.* Princeton, NJ: Princeton University Press, 1994. Lebow's 1994 book adds to the record some interviews and documents unearthed in Moscow at a time when Russia was very forthcoming with archives and records. The interpretation of Russian motivation, the most generous in all the literature, relies heavily on inferences from various theories of learning, perception, and behavioral psychology.

May, Ernest R., and Philip D. Zelikow. *The Kennedy Tapes: Inside the White House during the Cuban Missile Crisis.* Cambridge, MA: Harvard University Press, 1997. Essential for day-to-day detail regarding the crisis. In nearly every meeting, President Kennedy emerges as the most clear eyed and level headed of all the players.

McAuliffe, Mary S., ed. *CIA Documents on the Cuban Missile Crisis, 1962.* Washington, DC: Central Intelligence Agency, 1992. CIA director John McCone took meticulous notes on his participation in the crisis; they constitute one of history's great "I told you so's." (Also available commercially from Brassey's; see Allison entry.)

McNamara, Robert S., James G. Blight, and Robert K. Brigham. *Argument without End: In Search of Answers to the Vietnam Tragedy.* New York: Public Affairs Press, 1999. McNamara makes connections between Vietnam and the Cuban Missile Crisis.

Nash, Philip. *The Other Missiles of October: Eisenhower, Kennedy, and the Jupiters, 1957–1963.* Chapel Hill: University of North Carolina Press, 1997. The only complete study of the struggle to place Jupiter missiles in

Turkey and Italy and then to secure their eventual withdrawal in exchange for the removal of Soviet missiles from Cuba. A first-rate account.

Nathan, James A., ed. *The Cuban Missile Crisis Revisited*. New York: St. Martin's Press, 1992. A re-evaluation of the materials gathered by the National Security Archive by senior academics who have long studied the
Cuban Missile Crisis.

Paterson, Thomas G. "Commentary: The Defense-of-Cuba Theme and the Missile Crisis." *Diplomatic History* 14, no. 2 (1990): 249–56.

———. "The Historian as Detective: Senator Kenneth Keating, the Missiles in
Cuba, and His Mysterious Sources." *Diplomatic History* 11, no. 1 (Winter 1987): 67–70.

Paterson, Thomas G., and William J. Brophy. "October Missiles and November
Elections: The Cuban Missile Crisis and American Politics, 1962."
Journal of American History 73, no. 1 (June 1986). Paterson is the dean
of living American diplomatic historians. Everything he writes about the
Cuban Missile Crisis is essential reading.

Quirk, Robert E. *Fidel Castro*. New York: W. W. Norton, 1993. This review of
Castro's early years is as revealing and complete as it is engaging.

Rusk, Dean (as told to Richard Rusk). *As I Saw It*. New York: W. W. Norton, 1990.
Rusk is no more forthcoming in this book with his son than ever before in
private or public. But he is a good, accurate, and sensitive story-teller.

Schlesinger, Arthur M., Jr. *A Thousand Days: John F. Kennedy in the White
House*. New York: Fawcett Crest, 1967.

———. *Robert Kennedy and His Times*. New York: Ballantine, 1978. Schlesinger's books on the Kennedys are uncritical in their enthusiasm for the
subject matter, save conspicuously and unfairly harsh on Dean Rusk.

Scott, L. V. *MacMillan, Kennedy and the Cuban Missile Crisis: Political, Military
and Intelligence Aspects (Contemporary History in Context)*. New York:
St. Martin's Press, 1999. This is the first and very solid full-length treat-
ment of the substantial British contribution to the Cuban Missile Crisis.

Szulc, Tad. *Fidel: A Critical Portrait*. New York: Avon Books, 1985. A finely
crafted portrait, this book is one of the best and most even-handed looks
at Castro.

Thompson, Robert Smith. *The Missiles of October: The Declassified Story of
John F. Kennedy and the Cuban Missile Crisis*. Old Tappan, NJ: Simon
& Schuster, 1992. The narrative is engaging, but the inferences and
some of the data are suspect.

Walker, Martin. *The Cold War. A New History*. New York: Henry Holt, 1994. A
good, short, balanced journalistic overview of the context of the Cuban
Missile Crisis.

Welch, David A. "Intelligence Assessment in the Cuban Missile Crisis." *Queen's
Quarterly* 100, no. 2 (Summer 1993): 421–37.

Welch, David A., and James G. Blight. "The Eleventh Hour of the Cuban Missile Crisis: An Introduction to the ExCom Transcripts." *International Security* 12, no. 3 (Winter 1987–88): 5–29.

Welch, David A., James G. Blight, and Bruce J. Allyn. "Essence of Revision: Moscow, Havana, and the Cuban Missile Crisis." In *The Use of Force: Military Power and International Politics*, 4th ed., eds. Robert J. Art and Kenneth N. Waltz. Lanham, MD: University Press of America, 1993. Welch, Blight, and others from Harvard and Brown are remarkably persevering in gathering people and materials on the Cuban Missile Crisis and allowing both types of sources to speak clearly.

Wohlstetter, Albert, and Roberta Wohlstetter. *Controlling the Risks in Cuba: Adelphi Papers*. London: Institute for Strategic Studies, 1965.

Wohlstetter, Roberta. *Cuba and Pearl Harbor: Hindsight and Foresight*. Santa Monica, CA: Rand, 1965. Both monographs are extremely good conventional readings of the strategic dimension of the Cuban Missile Crisis. The analogy between Cuba and Pearl Harbor is heuristic and holds up well.

INTERNET RESOURCES

CNN and BBC produced a 24-hour documentary on the Cold War in 1998. The Web site has valuable interviews, documents, and transcripts of the 50-minute videos as well as some material not included in the films that aired. The work on the Cuban Missile Crisis was the tenth in this series. See: *http://cnn.com/SPECIALS/cold.war/episodes/10/*

For transcripts of ExCom meetings in streaming audio, see: *http://www.hpol.org//jfk/cuban/* and *http://www.state.gov/www/about_state/history/frusX/index.html*

The Cold War History Project, a joint effort of George Washington University and the National Security Archive, has especially good documents on the Cuban Missile Crisis. See: *http://cwihp.si.edu/pdf.htm*

C-SPAN Online provides RealAudio clips and transcripts from tapes that President Kennedy secretly recorded in the White House, RealAudio newsreels from 1962, an image gallery of the major players and surveillance photos, and RealAudio archives. See: *http://www.c-span.org/guide/society/cuba/*

The Department of State's definitive volumes relating to the Cuban Missile Crisis are available online: *Foreign Relations of the United States, "Cuba," Vol. X, 1961–1963*; and *Foreign Relations of the United States, "Cuban Missile Crisis and Aftermath," Vol. XI, 1961–1963*. See: *http://www.state.gov/www/about_state/history/frusX/index.htm*

Documents Relating to American Foreign Policy: The Cuban Missile Crisis is a site maintained by Mount Holyoke College. The collection includes documents, links, and other historical materials concerning the Cuban Missile Crisis. See: *http://www.mtholyoke.edu/acad/intrel/cuba.htm*

"14 Days in October: The Cuban Missile" posted by ThinkQuest. Documents, photos, dossiers, briefings, and audio are available in a well-constructed and useful setting. See: *http://library.advanced.org/ 11046/briefing/*

Mississippi State University has site with a number of useful links, especially to the speeches of Fidel Castro. See: *http://www.msstate.edu/Archives/History/cuba/*

Yale University School of Law has a massive collection of documents, commentaries, and links. See: *http://www.yale.edu/lawweb/avalon/diplomacy/forrel/cuba/cubamenu.htm*

VIDEOS

CNN Perspectives Presents the Cold War: Cuba, 1959–1962. Vol. 4, The Cold War, CNN, 1998. Film No. 10. ISBN 0-7806-2390-8.

The Cuban Missile Crisis. Public Broadcasting Television, 1992. A thirty-year retrospective in the Frontline series.

The Cuban Missile Crisis: 30 Years Later, NBC, 1992. A two-hour documentary with some important interviews of the participants.

Nightline. Hosted by Cokie Roberts, produced and directed by ABC, WXOW, La Crosse, December 20, 1994. This program contains tapes of the meeting that President Kennedy had with Senate leaders on October 22, 1962. Most senators seemed to strongly favor an invasion of Cuba and felt that Kennedy was wrong in ordering a blockade.

One Minute to Midnight, NBC, 1992. Produced by Alexandra Gleysteen, directed by Sid Feders, narrated by Maria Shriver. The film aired in 1992 after the fall of the Soviet Union; there are interviews with Robert McNamara, Dean Rusk, Theodore Sorenson, Pierre Salinger, Sergei Khrushchev, and Fidel Castro, among others.

War and Peace in the Nuclear Age: A History of the Cold War. Vol. 6, The Cuban Missile Crisis. PBS, 1998. The film on the Cuban Missile Crisis is part of a series developed in cooperation with a book written by McGeorge Bundy. The Cuban Missile Crisis segment is the most compelling.

OTHER

The best collection of materials relevant to the Cuban Missile Crisis is held at National Security Archive, The Gelman Library, George Washington University, 2130 H Street NW, Suite 701, Washington, DC 20037. Phone: 202-994-7000; fax: 202-994-7005. Internet: nsarchiv@gwis2.Circ.gwu.edu

Index

About the Author

JAMES A. NATHAN is a former Foreign Service Officer. He has taught at the University of Delaware, Johns Hopkins University, SAIS, the Naval War College and the Army War College. He is the author or coauthor of six books and some 70 articles on international affairs. Presently he is the Khaled Ben Sultan Eminent Scholar at Auburn University at Montgomery, Alabama.